Babies and Beasts

Babies and Beasts

The Argument from Marginal Cases

Daniel A. Dombrowski

University of Illinois Press
Urbana and Chicago

Manufactured in the United States of America
1 2 3 4 5 C P 6 5 4 3 2

This book is printed on acid-free paper.

Library of Congress Cataloging-in-Publication Data
Dombrowski, Daniel A.
Babies and beasts : the argument from marginal cases / Daniel A. Dombrowski.
p. cm.
Includes bibliographical references and index.
ISBN 0-252-02342-0 (alk. paper). —
ISBN 0-252-06638-3 (pbk. : alk. paper)
ISBN 978-0-252-02342-2 (alk. paper). —
ISBN 978-0-252-06638-2 (pbk. : alk. paper)
1. Animal rights—Philosophy. I. Title.
HV4708.D65 1997
179'.3—dc21
96-51232
CIP

Contents

Introduction

For the past twenty years many professional philosophers have used an argument to question the traditional dogma that not only are human beings the sole moral agents, but they are also—all of them—the sole moral patients, or better, the sole moral beneficiaries. Although the argument goes by several names, the most common label for it is "the argument from marginal cases" (hereafter AMC; the name was coined by one of the argument's detractors, Jan Narveson). The argument has created a great deal of controversy, as I will show; some find even the label "marginal cases" to be objectionable. Here is an initial statement of the argument, in a version developed by one of the argument's opponents, Lawrence Becker:[1]

1. It is undeniable that many species other than our own have "interests"—at least in the minimal sense that they feel and try to avoid pain, and feel and seek various sorts of pleasure and satisfaction.
2. It is equally undeniable that human infants and some of the profoundly retarded have interests in *only* the sense that members of these other species have them—and not in the sense that normal adult humans have them. That is, human infants and some of the profoundly retarded (i.e., the marginal cases of humanity) lack the normal adult qualities of purposiveness, self-consciousness, memory, imagination, and anticipation to the same extent that some other species of animals lack those qualities.
3. Thus, in terms of the morally relevant characteristic of having interests, some humans must be equated with members of other species rather than with normal adult human beings.
4. Yet predominant moral judgments about conduct toward these humans are dramatically different from judgments about conduct toward the comparable animals. It is customary to raise the animals for food, to subject them to lethal scientific experiments, to treat them as chattels, and so

forth. It is not customary—indeed it is abhorrent to most people even to consider—the same practices for human infants and the retarded.

5. But absent a finding of some morally relevant characteristic (other than having interests) that distinguishes these humans and animals, we must conclude that the predominant moral judgments about them are inconsistent. To be consistent, and to that extent rational, we must either treat the humans the same way we now treat the animals, or treat the animals the same way we now treat the humans.
6. And there does not seem to be a morally relevant characteristic that distinguishes all humans from all other animals. Sentience, rationality, personhood, and so forth all fail. The relevant theological doctrines are correctly regarded as unverifiable and hence unacceptable as a basis for a philosophical morality. The assertion that the difference lies in the *potential* to develop interests analogous to those of normal adult humans is also correctly dismissed. After all, it is easily shown that some humans—whom we nonetheless refuse to treat as animals—lack the relevant potential. In short, the standard candidates for a morally relevant differentiating characteristic can be rejected.
7. The conclusion is, therefore, that we cannot give a reasoned justification for the differences in ordinary conduct toward some humans as against some animals.

This argument has understandably spawned a debate about whether animals, like human beings, have rights. Nevertheless, even those who, having accepted the AMC, think that animals therefore deserve more respect than they have traditionally received still disagree regarding how much the argument proves. Does it show that animals have inalienable or nearly inalienable rights, *or* does it show that they have, from a utilitarian perspective, "rights"? (The cautionary quotation marks are necessary because utilitarians are willing to override rights if doing so leads to the greater good.) The animal rights debate between Peter Singer and Tom Regan in part consists in their different modes of appropriating this argument for themselves. It should not be assumed, however, that all philosophers who are animal rightists adopt this argument. Some, such as Steve Sapontzis and Mary Anne Warren, think that animals are moral beneficiaries, but not because of the AMC, which they criticize. Stephen R. L. Clark is an animal rightist who defends the argument but resists the label given to it in this book because he finds it obnoxious to think of the severely retarded, say, as marginal humans.

Further, it should not be assumed that all philosophers who are opposed to animal rights are opposed to the argument. R. G. Frey, for example, treats the argument positively, but at places he seems to choose the former of the two disjuncts in step 5. Some humans, he thinks, may be treated as we now treat animals. (Evelyn Pluhar argues that this amounts to throwing out the baby with the nonhuman bathwater.) That is, some animal rightists defend the AMC, and some do not; some who are opposed to animal rights defend the AMC, and some do not. To complicate the issue even more, once comparative judgments are made with respect to the moral beneficiary status of marginal humans and animals, it may turn out, as James Rachels alleges, that if it is commendable under certain circumstances to put animals out of their misery, then the AMC may show it to be commendable to euthanize human beings in misery. Unlike Frey, however, Rachels defends not only euthanasia but also animal rights.

The purpose of this book is quite simply to sort out and evaluate the various uses and abuses of this Protean argument. Philosophers who have either explicitly or implicitly offered reasons in favor of the AMC include the following, in alphabetical order: Stephen R. L. Clark, William Davis, Nicholas Everitt, Joel Feinberg, Charles Hartshorne, Dale Jamieson, Kai Nielson, Evelyn Pluhar, James Rachels, Tom Regan, Bernard Rollin, Peter Singer, and T. L. S. Sprigge. Those who have argued against it, whether explicitly or implicitly, include the following, again in alphabetical order: Lawrence Becker, John Benson, Ruth Cigman, Philip Devine, Cora Diamond, L. P. Francis, H. J. McCloskey, Jan Narveson, Robert Nozick, Roger Paden, Holmes Rolston, Richard Rorty, Steve Sapontzis, and Richard Watson.

My stance regarding the argument will become clear as the book proceeds, but I can state at the outset that I support the argument both with respect to the reasons it supplies in favor of animal rights and with respect to the reasons it supplies in favor of euthanasia; hence my view is closer to Rachels's than to that of any of the other thinkers treated in this book. Nonetheless, my stance rests much more than Rachels's does on a view of human temporal relations as asymmetrical; more simply, I view human life as a *process*—specifically, a process that has implications for the AMC. (And I do not share Rachels's agnosticism, a view that figures at least tangentially in his defense of euthanasia.) Nonetheless, I will try to report all views fairly and clearly in the effort—for the first time, I think—to examine systematically an argument that has generated perhaps more light and heat than any other argument in moral philosophy over the last twenty years. Both one of the most important opponents to animal rights

(R. G. Frey) and one of the most important defenders of them (Dale Jamieson) agree that the AMC has been the most noteworthy argument put forward in defense of animals.

The book is divided into six chapters. Chapter 1 is an attempt to introduce some of the implications of the argument as developed by Singer and Regan, both of whom defend the argument. These thinkers use the argument in quite different ways, however, such that they not only criticize each other but also provide different foci for the argument's detractors. That is, some of the argument's critics attack Singer's utilitarian version and some attack Regan's version. This chapter is intended not so much to resolve the issue of the argument's soundness as to indicate how complex the argument is and to get on the table many of the considerations of concern throughout the book.

I should note at the outset that throughout the book I quote philosophers who refer to marginal cases as *morons, idiots, imbeciles,* and so on, but I will not use these terms in the development of my own view, for the distracting epithet nature of these terms cannot be eliminated. Whereas these terms were once technical designations (idiots were those with the mental age up to two years old, imbeciles had mental ages from three to seven, and morons had IQs between fifty and seventy-five and mental ages between eight and twelve), they eventually became epithets hurled on the playground and the street. Hence it is somewhat unfortunate that defenders and critics of the AMC have continued to use these terms. I will also use terms such as *coma* and *vegetative state* interchangeably, even though in some medical circles the former term is reserved for a short-term state in which patients are unconscious with their eyes closed, and the latter term is reserved for a long-term state in which patients are unconscious but perhaps with their eyes open.

I should also note that the AMC is strengthened by translating it in terms of several different ethical theories, like strands that mutually reinforce each other in a cable. Hence I will not attempt to defend a version of the argument that relies exclusively on one theory, on one chain of reasoning. This is worth noting because some thinkers hold that the ethical theories of Singer and Regan are too coarse to capture certain important moral differences between human beings and animals. It is unlikely that if there are such differences, they would not be noticed by defenders of *any* of the available theories, such as utilitarianism, deontology, contract theory, virtue ethics, or egoism. Hence I examine the AMC from the perspective provided by each of these theories. Finally, I should note that when I refer to animals in the book, I mean, for the sake of convenience, "nonhuman animals." Obviously human beings are also animals.

In chapter 2 I consider the positions of four major critics of the argument—H. J. McCloskey, Jan Narveson, John Rawls, and Richard Watson—all of whom base their opposition on some version of the thesis that only a being capable of reciprocal relations with free, rational beings can have rights. Rawls only implicitly deals with the argument, but all four of these thinkers have generated responses from defenders of the AMC such as Joel Feinberg, Dale Jamieson, James Rachels, Evelyn Pluhar, and Tom Regan. I hope that this chapter shows both the complexity of the reciprocity objection and the persuasiveness of the rejoinders made by the AMC's defenders.

In chapter 3 I move to perhaps the most significant critic of the AMC, R. G. Frey, whose challenge to the argument has influenced both opponents to animal rights and defenders of such rights. I show that Frey is to some extent like his fellow utilitarian Singer and to some extent quite unlike him. The most significant critic of Frey treated in this chapter is Stephen R. L. Clark, whose defense of partial affections and of the AMC puts the latter in a perspective not seen by Singer or Regan, who are committed impartialists. The distinction between what is morally permissible in extremis and what is morally permissible in normal circumstances looms large in this chapter.

In chapter 4 I consider the positions of two of the most recent critics of the AMC, Michael Leahy and Peter Carruthers, along with those of several other critics. I argue that neither Leahy nor Carruthers offers telling criticisms of the argument and that Carruthers in particular (along with Peter Harrison) is unsuccessful in attempting to revive the Cartesian view that animals either do not experience pain at all or do not experience it in a conscious way. Evelyn Pluhar is again treated favorably as an antidote to Harrison and Carruthers.

In addition to the recent works of Leahy, Carruthers, and Harrison treated in chapter 4, other studies published in the 1990s that I treat in this book include those by Ted Benton, Stephen R. L. Clark, Gary Comstock, Philip Devine, Nicholas Everitt, Charles Fink, Susan Finsen, Gary Francione, Edward Hettinger, Tom Huffman, Edward Johnson, Lawrence Johnson, Tibor Machan, Colin McGinn, Roger Paden, Karl Popper, Evelyn Pluhar, James Rachels, Rosemary Rodd, Bernard Rollin, Lilly-Marlene Russow, Richard Ryder, Steve Sapontzis, Richard Sorabji, Kathy Squadrito, Sarah Stebbins, Keith Tester,

Mary Anne Warren, Richard Watson, and several authors who have worked with Peter Singer on the great ape project. The AMC is very much alive and well.

In chapter 5 I examine the efforts of Peter Singer and several others to gain equal rights for chimpanzees, gorillas, orangutans, and the other great apes. Specifically, in it I try to show how these efforts affect the AMC. I also examine the close connection alleged by some defenders of both the great apes and the AMC that opposition to rights for the great apes and to the AMC is often based, explicitly or implicitly, on the belief that animals are, for lack of a better word, "slaves." That is, defense of rights for the great apes and defense of the AMC are integrally connected to the effort to oppose the view of animals as slaves or as increments of capital.

In the final chapter of the book I highlight James Rachels's recent response to Robert Nozick's criticisms of the AMC. This response has implications not only for the AMC but also for the issue of euthanasia. I also consider other authors who amplify the debate between Nozick and Rachels (or better, the debate Rachels has with Nozick), most notably concerning Rachels's defense of moral individualism (the AMC).

I end the book with a summary and an explicit statement of my own view of the AMC, which relies heavily on the idea that temporal relations are asymmetrical.

Before moving to the Singer-Regan debate, it is worthwhile to note that the argument from marginal cases is not a recent one; rather, it played a significant role in the ancient debate over vegetarianism and the moral status of animals, a debate that I examine in detail in *The Philosophy of Vegetarianism* and explore metaphysically in *Hartshorne and the Metaphysics of Animal Rights.*[2] For example, consider a passage in Porphyry's *De abstinentia,* a book-length letter to a Firmus Castricius, a former vegetarian and fellow student of Plotinus who had fallen away from vegetarianism. Porphyry intends his arguments to bring Firmus back within the fold. The relevant text can be found at III.19:

> To compare plants, however, with animals, is doing violence to the order of things. For the latter are naturally sensitive [*aisthanesthai*], and adapted to feel pain, to be terrified and hurt [*kai algein kai phobesthai*]. But the former are entirely destitute of sensation, and in consequence of this, nothing foreign, or evil [*kakon*], or hurtful [*blabe*], or injurious [*adikia*], can befall them. For sensation is the principle of all alliance [*kai gar oikei-*

> *oseos pases kai allotrioseos arche to aisthanesthai*]. . . . And is it not absurd [*alogon*], since we see that many of our own species [*anthropon*] live from sense alone [*aisthesei monon*], but do not possess intellect [*noun*] and reason [*logon*] . . . but that no justice is shown from us to the ox that ploughs, the dog that is fed with us, and the animals that nourish us with their milk, and adorn our bodies with their wool? Is not such an opinion most irrational and absurd?[3]

Indeed it is. Zeno and the Stoics held such an opinion, but the continued popularity of meat eating and experimentation on animals indicates that the defenders of the AMC still have their work cut out for them.

The Singer-Regan Debate

In this chapter I introduce some of the implications of the argument as developed by Peter Singer and Tom Regan, both of whom defend it. Throughout the book I argue that Regan's version of the AMC is stronger than Singer's.

Singer's View

In the 1970s Peter Singer argued in a provocative way for the AMC. Presupposed by his use of the AMC is a distinction between language, which may be necessary for abstract thought, and states such as pain, which are more primitive "and have nothing to do with language."[1] If one refuses to attribute pain states to anything lacking a language, the consequences are rather severe. Human infants and young children, as well as most animals, would have to be denied the ability to experience pain. It is true that most parents understand the responses of their young children better than they do those of other animals, but this does not imply any linguistic phenomena; rather, it seems to be due to our greater contact with young children and hence our greater knowledge of them.

Of course, normal adult human beings have additional mental capacities that will in certain circumstances lead them to suffer more than animals would in the same circumstances, the additional suffering perhaps largely being due to our superior ability to use language. For example, if it were reported that normal adult humans were being kidnapped at random from parks for the purpose of lethal scientific experiments, adults strolling in parks might tend to develop a nervous twitch; indeed, they might be terrorized by the prospect of what might happen to them. This terror would be additional to the pain of the experiments themselves. Animals may well be spared the anticipatory dread of being kidnapped.

Some might immediately jump to the conclusion that we have before us a justification of animal experimentation, but Singer is even quicker to note that this argument, to the effect that animals can be experimented on with equanimity because they do not have anticipatory dread of being experimented on, applies as well to infants (or better, to orphaned infants, so as to avoid dread on the parents' part) and the severely retarded. Neither infants nor retarded humans would know what was going to happen to them, and hence they are in the same moral category here as animals. If they are in the same moral category as animals, we have to ask ourselves whether we are also prepared to justify experiments on infants and retarded people. (As I will show, Singer rejects the barefaced and morally indefensible preference for members of our own species just because they are members of our own species.) There are many matters concerning which the superior mental and linguistic powers of adult humans make a difference, yet these differences do not all point to greater suffering on the part of human beings. Sometimes animals suffer more because of their limited language and understanding; for example, we can sometimes ameliorate the anxiety of normal adult humans by telling them that they are experiencing only temporary suffering. If we capture a wild animal, however, we cannot convince it that we are not threatening its life. The wild animal in this instance cannot distinguish an attempt to confine and an attempt to kill.[2]

The AMC in some way or other is at odds with the view of all human life, and only human life, as sanctified. An infant can be born with massive and irreparable brain damage, such that it can never be any more than a "human vegetable," unable to talk, recognize other people, act independently of others, or develop a sense of self-awareness; according to Singer, it makes sense to wonder whether it deserves moral respect if a healthy nonhuman animal does not. Chimpanzees, dogs, pigs, and members of other species surpass the brain-damaged infant with respect to the previously mentioned characteristics, such as self-awareness. What distinguishes this infant from the animal is only that the former is a member of the species *Homo sapiens,* and it is exactly this kind of arbitrary difference that racists, sexists, or speciesists use in attempting to justify their respective sorts of discrimination. To avoid speciesism, on Singer's account, we must allow that beings who are similar in morally relevant respects have a similar right to life. We can still hold that it is worse to kill a normal adult human, who can plan for the future and have meaningful relations with others, than it is to kill a mouse, which does not have these characteristics. But this does not in itself justify killing the mouse. Whatever criteria we choose for moral beneficiary status will not follow precisely the boundary of our own species. If a chimpanzee, dog, or pig has a greater degree of self-awareness and capacity for meaningful relations with others than does a severely retarded infant or a person in an advanced state of senility, then these animals have a right to life as good as, or better than, that of such retarded or senile humans.[3]

Singer is well aware that the AMC can cut both ways. One can take the argument as showing that the severely retarded and hopelessly senile have no right to life and may be killed for quite trivial reasons, as we now kill animals. He opts (correctly, I think) for a middle position that avoids speciesism but does not (1) make the lives of the retarded and the senile as cheap as the lives of pigs and dogs now are or (2) make the lives of pigs and dogs so sacrosanct that we would not be willing to put them out of hopeless misery. His goal is to bring nonhuman animals within our sphere of moral concern and to cease treating their lives as expendable for trivial purposes. However, the fact that a being is a member of our species does not in itself make it always wrong to kill that being, for if a human being has no prospect of a meaningful life, the most humane course may well be euthanasia. That is, a rejection of speciesism does not necessarily mean that all lives are of equal worth. Self-awareness, hopes for the future, meaningful relations with others, and so on are not relevant to the question of whether we should inflict gratuitous pain on a being, but they are relevant to other questions, including the question of whether a being's life should be taken. The life of a self-aware being capable of abstract thought and complex language is more valuable than the life of a being without these capacities. If we had to make a decision to save the life of a normal human being or an intellectually disabled human being, we would probably save the normal human being. On the other hand, if we had to choose between preventing pain in an intellectually disabled human being (or in an animal) or in a normal human being—say, if we had enough painkiller for only one of them—the issue would not be so clear.[4]

In a way, pain is an evil that is unaffected by other characteristics of the being who feels it, whereas the value of a life *is* affected by these other characteristics. To take the life of a being who hopes and works for some future goal is to deprive that being of the fulfillment of these efforts, whereas to take the life of a being that is below the level needed to understand that it is a being with a future cannot involve this sort of loss. Once again, if we had to decide whether to save a human being or an animal, we should normally choose to save the human, but there may well be special cases where the reverse would hold true. The issue here is not so much when it is wrong to kill an animal painlessly as it is whether we should give to the lives of sentient animals the same respect as we give to the lives of those humans at a similar mental level. Singer's own vegetarianism, say, is decidedly not based on a Jain-like, absolute prohibition on killing. Human beings for the most part are not equal; if we seek some morally relevant characteristic that all of them possess, it would have to be

> a kind of lowest common denominator, pitched so low that no human being lacks it. The catch is that any such characteristic that is possessed by all human beings will not be possessed only by human beings. For example, all human beings, but not only human beings, are capable of feeling pain; and while only human beings are capable of solving complex mathematical problems, not all humans can do this. So it turns out that in the only sense in which we can truly say, as an assertion of fact, that all humans are equal, at least some members of other species are also "equal"—equal, that is, to some humans.[5]

An example of a view that Singer opposes is provided by Richard Wasserstrom, whom Singer thinks is either devious or myopic. Wasserstrom thinks that denying people relief from acute physical pain prevents them from living full and satisfying lives and that the enjoyment of a full and satisfying life differentiates humans from nonhumans.[6] If we ask of speciesists such as Wasserstrom, however, why it should be that all human beings—including infants, the retarded, psychopaths, and so on—have some dignity that no elephant, pig, or chimpanzee can ever achieve, we are not likely to get a convincing answer. To say that all and only human beings have "intrinsic dignity" will not help much, for this phrase in turn would have to be defined in terms of some other morally relevant capacities or characteristics that all and only human beings have. As Singer puts the point, fine phrases such as "intrinsic dignity" are the last resource of those who have run out of arguments.[7]

Infants have the potential to become self-aware and intelligent, and hence Singer is willing to concentrate his case regarding the AMC on permanently and profoundly retarded human beings or on those who are equal to or below the level of many animals regarding these characteristics. Philosophers who have set out to find a characteristic that would distinguish all human beings from animals rarely opt for abandoning the retarded; to do so would be to admit that human beings have the right to perform painful experiments on the retarded and to rear and kill them for food. The easiest way out of this difficulty has been to ignore it. For example, John Rawls asks in *A Theory of Justice* why we owe justice to human beings but not to animals, but he brushes the question aside, assuming that some sort of defining characteristic of human beings, and only human beings, as moral beneficiaries can be found. In contrast, Singer rightly contends that it is impossible to cling to equality of human beings without suggesting a radical revision in the status of nonhumans. I will show why defenders of the AMC are bothered by the claim that the criteria for moral beneficiary status refer to what is normal for the human species. At the very least the speciesist has to be precise here regarding what is normal for human beings and then to explain why the moral status of abnormal human beings ought to be superior to that of animals or much more like that of normal human beings than like that of animals, especially regarding killing.[8]

It seems to be Singer's desire to assert that animals have rights without having to enter into disputes about the word *rights.* (Nonetheless, he does assume, along with most utilitarians, that any being with interests has a right to have its interests considered equally—equal treatment is another matter.) This desire eventually gets him into trouble. The fact that animals come within the scope of the utilitarian principle of equal consideration of interests entails that they have at least one right—namely, the right to equal consideration. This is not so much a right as it is the foundation for having rights, however, as in the right not to have gratuitous pain inflicted on one. Singer hopes to prevent the notion of rights from being so constricted that it refers only to what rational agents would agree to as part of a social contract. If rights are essentially contractual, Singer worries, not only nonhuman animals but also human infants and young children, as well as the mentally defective, do not have them. Those who put forward this version of rights are forced to retreat to the view that moral rights are only one kind of constraint on our conduct, and not necessarily the most important one. Because of these sorts of difficulties, Singer does not think that it is worth the effort to defend rights; his point seems to be that if we deny rights to nonhuman animals, we do little more than place animals in the same moral category as human infants.[9]

If self-consciousness, autonomy, or some similar characteristic is used to establish a gulf between humans and nonhumans, it should be emphasized that mentally defective humans are to be placed on the other side of the gulf. The AMC is forceful, Singer thinks, because most of us are horrified at the idea of using mentally defective humans in painful experiments or fattening them for dinner. Nonetheless, Singer considers three objections to the argument. Some might object that mental defectives should be treated *as if* they were autonomous and rational in that they belong to a species whose members normally possess these characteristics. This amounts to a refusal to consider the actual qualities of the individual in question, such that, if the same procedure were used regarding members of our race or sex, we would need to treat blacks or females not as individuals but only according to the average scores on IQ tests for their race or sex, whatever explanation of that average might be. How can one account for the fact that we should treat blacks and women as individuals but treat animals and mentally defective human beings only as members of some species or other? We cannot consistently insist that beings be treated as individuals in one case but as members of a group in the other, as Singer correctly argues.[10]

The second objection that Singer considers is that, although mental defectives may not possess higher capacities than other animals do, we nonetheless have special relations to them. The danger in eliminating partial affections is allegedly that we may remove the source of all affections. It is a fact that some people have a closer relationship with a seriously retarded human than with any animal, but the question is whether our moral obligations to a being *should* be made to depend on our feelings in this manner. Some human beings (notoriously) have a closer relationship with their cat than with their neighbors. Would those who tie morality to affections accept that these people would be justified in saving their cats from a fire before they saved their neighbors? Note that even those who would be willing to answer this question in the affirmative might not want to go along with racists who argue that because white people have more natural relationships and greater affection toward other whites (or blacks toward other blacks), it is permissible for whites to give preference to interests of other whites over those of blacks (or blacks to give preference to the interests of other blacks over those of whites). Although ethics does not demand of us that we eliminate personal relations and partial affections, it does demand that when we assess the claims of those affected by our actions, we do so independently of these affections.[11]

The third objection alleges that the AMC rests on a slippery slope. If we are looking for a clear line to divide those beings we can eat and on which we can experiment from those that are not amenable to experimentation or being eaten, species membership provides a nice, sharp divide. However, levels of self-consciousness, autonomy, or sentience do not provide a sharp division. Once we allow that a severely retarded human being has no higher moral status than does an animal, we have started on a downward slope, the next level of which is to deny rights to social misfits, and so on, until we reach the absolute nadir: a totalitarian government that disposes of anyone it does not like, justifying this by classifying people as mental defectives. Singer alertly responds to this criticism by saying, in effect, that moral concern is not a pie of a fixed size, such that showing respect to animals leaves nothing for human beings. Rather, his use of the AMC either makes no difference to our treatment of humans or might even improve it, say, by bringing about a more humane view of human beings who are in permanent, miserable pain. In any event, even if species membership does provide an easy demarcation, this does not necessarily mean that such a criterion can be defended against its detractors.[12]

To aim at elevating the status of animals does not entail the denigration of any humans. For example, Singer in no way implies that mentally defective human beings should be force-fed food colorings until half of them die, even if such testing would give us more accurate information than that obtained by such tests on dogs or rabbits. It is excessively pessimistic to think that the best way to interpret the AMC is in terms of a denigration of defective human beings rather than as an elevation of the moral status of animals. Singer's elevation of the moral status of animals includes the claim that some nonhuman animals are persons, if we define "person" as a being who is to some extent self-conscious and rational. On this definition some members of our own species are not persons and some members of other species are persons; according to Singer, no objective assessment can give greater value to the lives of members of our species who are not persons than to the lives of members of other species who are. It does make sense, however, to see the value of persons as superior to that of nonpersons, as when Singer suggests that killing a chimpanzee (who is a person) is worse than killing a gravely defective human (who is not a person).[13]

There is no single answer to the question, "Is it wrong to take the life of an animal?" Some animals give us strong evidence of some sort of self-awareness and of being distinct entities with a past and a future. When this is so, the case against killing is strong, as strong as the case against killing permanently defective human beings at a similar mental level. Singer has in mind here direct reasons against killing rather than the effects on relatives of defective human beings being killed, effects that constitute indirect reasons that sometimes are to the defective human being's advantage, as I will show. The strong case against killing that Singer has in mind applies to those animals with well-developed mental faculties: apes, whales, dolphins, monkeys, dogs, cats, pigs, seals, and bears. This is not an exhaustive list, as Singer admits, but later I will show how Frey calls Singer to task for including only one sort of animal often found on restaurant menus. Singer no doubt would retort that almost all these animals are routinely used for scientific (or oil, sport, or fur) purposes, and hence his strong case against killing , if sound, would have a significant practical effect. The case against killing is weaker when we consider animals without well-developed mental faculties, for these beings are not aware of themselves as distinct beings with a future; these beings are nonetheless morally considerable to the extent that they are sentient.[14]

That is, according to Singer, it is not directly wrong to kill an animal with an undeveloped mental life. If we are not dealing with beings that are aware of themselves as distinct entities, the wrongness of killing amounts to the reduction of pleasure it involves. If the life taken would not have been on balance a pleasurable one, no direct wrong is done. Even if the life taken would have been a pleasurable one, no direct wrong is done if the animal with an undeveloped mental life is killed painlessly and is replaced by another animal with an equally pleasant life. Animals that are not mentally developed are, on utilitarian grounds, interchangeable with each other in a way that mentally developed animals are not. For example, it is morally permissible to raise chickens in such a way that they have pleasant lives; to kill them painlessly, with their deaths brought about in such a way that they do not cause suffering to other animals; and to replace them with animals that would not otherwise have lived. I will argue against Singer's view as the book proceeds. His reasoning does not legitimate what goes on at modern factory farms, however, nor does it legitimate the killing of wild animals, in that the shooting of a duck is not painless and does not lead to its replacement by another.[15]

Singer's distinction between developed and undeveloped mental lives should not distract us from his overall point: on any fair comparison of morally relevant characteristics such as self-consciousness, autonomy, or sentiency, animals—whether pigs, calves, or chickens—come out well ahead of some human beings and ahead of all fetuses, especially those in the early stages of pregnancy before sentiency develops. Nonetheless, he thinks that even late-term abortion is hard to condemn if we are willing to slaughter more developed forms of life for the taste of their flesh. Normal adult human beings have capacities that retarded humans, animals, and fetuses lack, but to defend existing attitudes toward animals, we are required to find some basis for attributing rights that applies to all human beings but not to other animals. If the AMC is sound, no such basis exists. Once again, to rest content with what generally is the case for human beings is to beg the question as to why human beings universally deserve moral respect.[16]

One of the most frequent criticisms of Singer is that he employs the concept of rights when it is convenient for him to do so and retreats from this concept when it is attacked. This is a cogent criticism. Singer's own way of putting the point is to say that disputes about rights are often merely about words rather than substantive issues. If animals come within the scope of equal consideration of interests, they have at least one right: the right to equal consideration. More precisely, equal consideration of interests provides a foundation for having rights, instead of being a right in itself. One of the rights that can be easily derived from equal consideration of interests is the right not to have gratuitous pain inflicted on one. Nevertheless, Singer disagrees with a narrower, contractual view of rights wherein not only animals but also human children and the mentally defective strictly speaking have no rights. Defenders of the contractualist view do not say that we can do as we wish with animals, children, or mental defectives, in that moral rights are only one kind of constraint on our conduct, and not necessarily the most important one, as I will show. This denigration of rights by contractualists is not necessarily bothersome to Singer, however, because of his strong attachment to the AMC. In a sense, the denial of (strong) rights to animals does no more than place them in the same moral category as infants or mental defectives.[17]

By no means is Singer a moral absolutist, unless the classical utilitarian view that he adopts—regarding minimizing pain and maximizing pleasure—is seen as a moral absolute. Not even the principle of equality is an absolute for Singer, in that equality for him merely refers to equality of consideration, to the claim that the interests of every being affected by an action "are to be taken into account and given the same weight as the like interests of any other being." This minimal version of equality serves to dispel the widespread misconception that utilitarians value everything in terms of utility for human beings. But the precise character of Singer's critique of anthropocentrism is also often misunderstood: it is not wrong to eat (mentally undeveloped) animals that have had a pleasant life, were humanely killed, and have been replaced by other animals that are receptacles for pleasurable experiences. Nonetheless, if we are prepared to take the life of another sentient being merely to satisfy our taste for a particular type of food, then we are likely to do things that are morally objectionable. The pleasures of taste, as opposed to the pleasure of alleviating the pain of hunger, are relatively trivial.[18]

One indication that Singer is not an absolutist is his willingness to euthanize animals, but only in ways that we would analogously euthanize human beings. For example, we should euthanize animals with terminal illnesses only in those situations where we would be willing to do the same for human beings with terminal illnesses, and we should euthanize stray dogs only if we are also willing to euthanize some of the homeless. Human beings are valuable, but not because they are members of our species. Furthermore, it may be true that most human beings possess certain morally relevant characteristics not possessed by animals, but this in itself does not establish the boundary for moral beneficiary status precisely along species lines. That is, it is also true (undeniably so, according to Singer) that there are some animals that are superior in mental capacities to some biological humans, for example, a chimpanzee that can solve problems beyond the capacity of a three-year-old human. As I already noted, Singer attributes mentally developed status to baboons, dogs, dolphins, pigs, and others. They are capable not only of sentiency but also of conceiving of themselves as distinct entities existing over time. The class of mentally developed beings diverges considerably from the class of human beings: "Those who attempt to eliminate this divergency by forging some logical link between these two classes will make themselves liable to the charge of speciesism." The smallest modification regarding the criteria for moral patiency, a modification caused by the desire to protect marginal cases of humanity, means that we must shift from saying that all human lives have unique value to saying that all persons have unique value, pace the previous definition of *person.* One of the problems here is that *human* and *person* are, in everyday discourse, often used as synonyms.[19]

One of the purposes of this initial chapter is to explore in detail the different ways in which two of the AMC's most noted defenders—Singer and Regan—make their cases. At this point in my consideration of Singer, it is worthwhile to indicate his own perceived distance from Regan. If the AMC is a good argument, as he thinks it is, three possible options are open:

1. While retaining our present attitudes to mentally defective humans, we change our attitudes to animals who are not persons, so as to bring them into line with our attitudes to mentally defective humans. This involves holding that animals have a right to life, and therefore should not be killed for food or for the purposes of scientific experimentation.
2. While retaining our present attitudes to animals, we change our attitudes to mentally defective humans, so as to bring them into line with our attitudes toward animals. This involves holding that mental defectives do not have a right to life, and therefore might be killed for food—if we should develop a taste for human flesh—or (and this really might appeal to some people) for the purpose of scientific experimentation.
3. We change our present attitudes to both mentally defective humans and nonhuman animals, so as to bring them together somewhere in between our present attitudes. This involves holding that both mentally defective humans and nonhuman animals have some kind of serious claim to life—whether we call it a "right" does not matter much—in virtue of which, although we ought not to take their lives except for very weighty reasons, they do not have as strict a right to life as do persons. In accordance with this view, we might hold, for instance, that it is wrong to kill either mentally defective humans or animals for food if an alternative diet is available, but not wrong to do so if the only alternative is starvation.[20]

Singer thinks that Regan argues for the first alternative, whereas he himself opts for the third. He could hardly be wrong about what his own view is, but I will be attentive to what Regan has to say to see whether his view is exactly the one that Singer attributes to him.

In any event, Singer claims that we need to change our present attitudes toward both animals and mental defectives because of the following distinction, which is integral to his view: equal consideration of interests is not the same as an equal right to life. Singer defends only the former. Equal consideration of interests allows us to treat different beings differently, but only when their interests differ. Unequal consideration of interests (speciesism) is akin to racism or sexism, whereas equal consideration of two quite different sorts of interest (say, those of a being who conceives of itself as a distinct entity over time as opposed to a being who has no such conception) is not at all akin to racism or sexism. For example, if mentally undeveloped animals are replaceable, as Singer thinks they are, then humans at a comparable mental level are also replaceable. Because Singer's view here will strike some, including Regan and myself, as untenable, it is worth quoting: "Some people carry genes that mean that any children they produce will be severely mentally retarded. As long as the lives of these children are pleasant, it would not, according to the replaceability argument, be wrong to perform a scientific experiment on a child that results in the death of the child, provided another child could then be conceived to take its place. . . . It is our attitudes to mentally defective human beings that are in need of reconsideration."[21] As before, Singer thinks that only persons have a *right* to life, in the strongest sense of the term that can be used by utilitarians, but not all human beings are persons (self-conscious beings aware of themselves as distinct entities over time). Sometimes even persons (whether human or animal) can be "sacrificed" in medical experiments, given results weighty enough to benefit other persons. In short, sentient beings with undeveloped mental lives (whether human or animal) should be treated alike, and those with comparably developed mental lives should be treated alike.

From 1975 to 1991 Singer insisted in published writings that species in itself cannot make a moral difference. One consequence of this view, as I have shown, is that brain-damaged human infants may legitimately be allowed to die or be killed. Our willingness to euthanize unfortunate animals may constitute the one and only respect in which we currently treat animals better than we treat human beings. Just as we have progressed beyond the blatantly racist ethics of slavery and colonialism, so might we now progress beyond the blatantly speciesist ethic that has hitherto been operative, except perhaps when animals were in need of euthanasia. The progress for which

Singer hopes includes rights for animals, at least if all human beings have rights. He is skeptical of the claim that infants and brain-damaged humans have only a "courtesy status" as right-bearers if the criteria for possession of rights are the familiar ones such as rationality, autonomy, self-consciousness, or the ability to enter into contracts or reciprocate. This courtesy status looks suspiciously like an ad hoc proposal meant to insulate conventional attitudes from change. Nor is he convinced by the claim that if we euthanized defective newborns, we would create a slippery slope that would slide directly into a willingness to kill normal but somehow undesirable human adults. Many human societies, he notes, have killed handicapped infants without showing a willingness to do the same to normal adults. There is simply no justification that Singer can think of to permit, for example, the testing of food additives on animals, thereby poisoning them to death, while refusing to even consider doing the same to (orphaned) infants with severe brain damage.[22]

The obvious problem with defending human equality by reference to superior mental capacities is that not all humans possess these capabilities. Newborns may have the potential to develop these capacities, leading some to see them as radically different from the other marginal cases. Arguing from potential is fraught with difficulties, however, for if the potential for rationality is the relevant criterion, then embryos and fetuses must also be included in the class of protected beings—indeed, individual sperm cells would have to be included. In any event, if the potential for a developed mental life is the criterion for moral respect, then there will still be marginal cases to lend support to the AMC. To see rationality (or the potential for rationality) as *essential* to the human species is to use a term redolent of an Aristotelian biology. There is a good deal that should make us suspicious of the suggestion that we ignore individual characteristics and instead judge individuals by the general characteristics of their species, as when women were denied admission to the professions on the basis of their membership in a class that generally was not academically prepared to be doctors or lawyers.

Some Anti–Animal Rights Critics

Before moving to Regan's animal rights critique of Singer's defense of the AMC, it will be helpful to see what three critics—John Benson, Meredith Williams, and Thomas Young—have alleged regarding

Singer's view from their anti–animal rights standpoints. Benson objects to Singer's requirement that before carrying out an experiment on a beast, we should ask whether we would be prepared to carry out the same experiment on a human being with the same susceptibility to suffering and whose life is of comparable value. According to Benson, it is not easy to find a human being who is comparable to the mental level of an animal; a grossly brain-damaged infant may be one of the few examples. Moreover, the side effects involved in experimenting on a human being are usually great, so this grossly brain-damaged human being would have to be an orphan with no one to grieve for it. These difficulties with the AMC, he claims, should prevent us from pressing the parallel between speciesism and racism: "The racist can admit without discomfort that exceptional members of the other race should be admitted to equality, though he usually finds it harder to admit that sub-standard specimens of his own race deserve no better than normal specimens of the other race. But if he managed that feat of impartiality he would not on Singer's definition be a racist."[23] But Benson's criticism here works only if sentient animals are the exceptions to the rule, which they are not. The racist admits that there are a few "exceptional" blacks, Jews, and so on, as Benson notes, and hence the racist smugly retains his prejudice. The speciesist, however, is being confronted by Singer not on the basis of a few of the great apes who may be taught human sign language but on the evidence of almost all animals with central nervous systems or something like them.

Benson is on stronger ground when he observes that some may attempt to use the AMC to empty the institutions in which the hopelessly subnormal are kept and use the inhabitants for medical experiments. I will deal with this understandable concern in due course, but it should be emphasized that the strongest case Benson makes against experimenting on the hopelessly subnormal is based on the special relationships these beings have to normal human beings. Most human beings are programmed by biological inheritance and tradition to treat their own young with special tenderness. To suggest that being retarded makes a child more eligible for conversion into scientific "preparation" is best read, according to Benson, as Swiftian satire. But this criticism plays directly into Singer's hands. By suggesting that the AMC is a piece of Swiftian satire, Benson is assuming that retarded people obviously do have rights, and the point to the AMC is that if the marginal cases of humanity have rights, then animals have them as well. Benson is correct, however, that defenders of the AMC—whether utilitarians or deontologists—are generally skeptical of the view of ethics as arising out of, and justified in terms of, partial affections toward kin and friends and members of one's own species. For Benson,

> partiality for our own species, and within it for much smaller groupings, is, like the universe, something we had better accept. That we care at all about the interests of strangers of our own species or animals of other species results from our extending to them by sympathy something of the concern that we feel spontaneously for those with whom we have closer connections. . . . The danger in this attempt to eliminate partial affections is that it may remove the source of all affections.[24]

In effect, Benson is distinguishing two sorts of speciesism. One sort is objectionable, as when only human suffering matters. A second sort is not objectionable, as when a marginal human is protected "beyond its deserts" by sentiments peculiar to the human community. Later I will discuss one defender of the AMC, Stephen R. L. Clark, who shares Benson's view of partial affections and distrust of the utilitarian and deontological view of ethics as the search for impartiality. Until that time it may be worthwhile to ask the following question: why should our ethics arise out of, and be justified in terms of, partial affections for kin and friends and one's own species only, and not also partial affections for members of one's own nation, race, and sex?

Williams's complaint centers on the distinction between infants and other marginal cases. The former, as already noted, may well have the potential to move out of the category of marginal cases in that they have the potential to form life plans, establish meaningful relations with others, and become rational beings. Retarded and brain-damaged persons do not have this potential. However, her way of protecting these marginal cases for the most part differs from Benson's appeal to partial affections, although she does at one point say that we should decide in favor of brain-damaged humans rather than animals because of our greater sympathy for the former. Williams's dominant view is to claim that only in severe instances will it be true that retarded or brain-damaged humans are no more rational than animals. In effect, she tries to reduce Singer's rather large class of marginal cases (infants, the retarded, the senile, the comatose, etc.) to a rather small class. Moreover, she thinks that in these rare and extreme cases, it is by no means clear that we should treat the individuals as "moral beings," that is, as subject to equal consideration. They can be said to have interests only in an attenuated sense. Contra Singer, Williams alleges that these really marginal cases are already experimented on routinely. (It should be noted here that Singer's call for a rethinking of our treatment of the severely disabled is far less radical than Williams's view is. That is, Singer is not claiming that the most marginal of marginal cases do not deserve equal consideration; as long as they are sentient, they deserve at least this. Nevertheless, on Singer's utilitarian view, they do not necessarily deserve a right to life. It is not necessarily the defender of the AMC who exposes the marginal cases to exploitation.)[25]

Young (along with Evelyn Pluhar) correctly notes that AMC can stand for either "the argument from marginal cases" or "the argument for moral consistency." If one believes that all humans have a right to life, then animals who possess relevant capacities equal to or superior to marginal cases also possess a right to life. The AMC leaves one with three options, he thinks: (1) all humans and some animals have a right to life; or (2) some humans (the marginal cases) do not have a right to life and some animals do; or (3) some humans and all animals lack a right to life. The efficacy of the AMC is seen when it is noticed that Young, although an opponent of the argument, nonetheless has to exclude the traditional belief that all and only human beings have a right to life. On Young's interpretation, Regan opts for the first option; Singer, for the second option (although Young does not state Singer's view as precisely as it should be stated); and Young himself, for the third. As I will show, defenders of the first option, such as Regan, admit that the AMC is only part of the support for that option; one must also, if one defends the first option, show why marginal humans have a right to life. One may attempt to do this on the basis of any one of several characteristics, according to Young: (a) having a soul, (b) membership in *Homo sapiens,* (c) sentience, (d) rationality and language, (e) self-consciousness (in Singer's sense: the desire to continue living as a distinct entity with a past and future), (f) cognizance of the fact that one can be killed, and (g) cognizance of one's relations with others.[26]

If (a) or (b) are adopted, then the traditional view can be maintained, as Young correctly argues. But justifying (a) philosophically, as opposed to theologically, is notoriously difficult. Furthermore, Young admits that Singer is correct in claiming (b) to be a morally indefensible, speciesist criterion. Young thus thinks that the traditional view is not defensible. Young himself (along with R. G. Frey) is skeptical as to whether (c) is defensible. The possession of sentience might give one the right to be morally considerable but not necessarily the right to life. (Regan's comments on this point appear later.) Young thinks that (d) and (e) are individually necessary and jointly sufficient conditions of (f), which, along with (g), he supports as establishing the case for a right to life. He is skeptical as to whether animals possess (d), (e), (f), or (g), however, and hence Regan's treatment of (c) will be no trivial matter, in that even for nonutilitarians, sentiency plays a major role in the attribution of rights for marginal cases. The AMC, here interpreted as the argument for moral consistency, requires Young to face the fact that marginal humans also have a difficult time meeting (d), (e), (f), and (g); hence Young, like Benson and Williams, justifies our aversion to experimenting on, or killing and eating, marginal humans through certain sentiments that we have and through the difference between the side effects of our killing and eating marginal humans and those of our doing the same to animals.[27] In effect, Young takes back with one hand what he gives with the other. By choosing option 3—some humans and all animals lack a right to life—he indicates that he has in fact been convinced by the consistency requirement of the AMC. His aversion to killing and eating mental defectives turns out to be more than an aesthetic preference, however; it is an indication that at present he thinks it impermissible to kill them for food. Killing and eating them would be permissible only if his own and the felt preferences of most people regarding this issue changed radically.

Regan's View

Now that some of the anti–animal rightists' criticisms of Singer's use of the AMC have been heard, it is time to move to Regan's use of the AMC. By the end of this chapter I hope to be in a position to consider several specific uses of the argument by other authors and to respond to several specific criticisms of the argument. Considering Singer and Regan together in this chapter allows me both to show the force of the argument and to anticipate many of the criticisms of the argument.

As early as 1975 Regan was engaged with the AMC. His approach is not utilitarian but deontological, yet even Regan stops short of saying that all human beings in all circumstances have a right to life, contra the impression some commentators have of his view. That is, early on Regan realized that the most marginal of the marginal cases—those human beings who never have manifested any interests and never will do so, who apparently do not experience needs, affection, aversion, hopes, or fears—are in a situation quite different from that faced by a retarded human being or an infant. Regan even doubts whether it is accurate to say that these unfortunate beings are in fact human beings, despite the fact that they have human parents.[28] But this gets me ahead of the story a bit. If we say that to have rights, a being must be rational or have free will, then we run up against the realization that mental defectives do not have these abilities. Hence, if we stick with these criteria, we are forced to ask whether we are prepared to say that infants and the mentally enfeebled lack rights.[29] As with Singer, Regan thinks that we cannot account for a creature's possessing moral rights by determining what is true "in general" of the members of the species to which it belongs. Regan wavers, however, between claiming that *if* marginal cases have rights, then animals have them as well, and claiming that since the marginal cases *do* have rights, animals have them as well.[30]

To support the claim that marginal cases have rights, Regan at several places turns to the capacity to experience pain rather than to the capacity for rationality or moral agency. Sentiency

> provides a logically necessary and sufficient condition for a being's possessing the right not to be made to suffer non-trivial pain. This enables us to ascribe this right to infants, severe mental defectives, schizophrenics and the like, provided only that they have the capacity to experience non-trivial pain. Now since we do think that these beings do have this capacity; and since we also think that they have the right in question; and since there does not appear to be any other relevant consideration that could be thought to underlie possession of this right; it seems that a human's capacity to experience non-trivial pain *is* a necessary and sufficient condition for his or her possessing the right not to be caused such pain.[31]

And there are literally thousands of species of animals whose members have this capacity. As before, Regan wavers between the weak version of the AMC (*if* marginal cases have rights, then animals have them) and the strong version (animals have rights because all—or almost all—humans have them). In one important article where Regan restricts himself to the weak version, he goes out of his way to suggest that it might be more accurate to refer to "nonparadigmatic humans" rather than to "marginal humans," in that the latter phrase, in a way, subtly suggests a willingness to see such beings as expendable, a willingness resisted by Regan except in the most marginal of marginal cases. When dealing with marginal cases (or, if one prefers, with nonparadigmatic humans), the principal distinction that must be made is that between basic and nonbasic moral rights. The latter are the sort of rights compatible with utilitarianism in general and with Singer's use of the AMC in particular.[32]

Basic moral rights are those that ground moral obligations rather than vice versa. For example, if A has a basic moral right to life, then A's having this right explains why we have the obligation not to take A's life. Invoking the weak version of the AMC, Regan momentarily wonders whether marginal cases—or anyone, for that matter—has basic moral rights. The problem with the view that marginal cases do not have basic rights is that with it we cannot account for our strong belief or intuition that there are grossly immoral ways of treating marginal cases. That is, only basic rights can account for the strong belief among reflective people that killing and eating severely retarded people is unconscionable. Regan puts his case in two ways, one critical and one constructive. The critical way does not establish what the necessary and sufficient conditions for right-possession are, but it demonstrates what the necessary conditions for right-possession are not:

1. Given certain criteria of the possession of rights, some marginal humans and not just all animals will be excluded from the class of right-holders.
2. However, humans, including those who are marginal, do have rights and so belong in the class of right-holders.
3. Therefore, each and every one of the criteria of which (1) is true must be rejected as setting a requirement for the possession of rights.[33]

R. G. Frey disputes the second premise. I will not attempt to refute Frey here, but Regan does think it to be significant that the assumption that people who are normally considered moral make with equanimity—that there are grossly immoral ways of treating marginal cases—cannot be theoretically accounted for without also assuming that marginal humans have basic rights. The constructive argument runs as follows:

1. Humans, including those who are marginal, have rights and therefore belong in the class of right-holders.
2. However, given the most reasonable criterion of the possession of rights, one that enables us to include marginal humans in the class of right-holders, this same criterion will require us to include some (but not all) animals in this class.

3. Therefore, if we include these marginal humans in the class of right-holders, we must also include some animals in this class.[34]

The methodology in both the critical and constructive arguments above is transcendental: given that humans, including those who are marginal, have rights, how is this possession of rights to be accounted for? Rationality, autonomy, and so on obviously will not do. If we say that marginal cases have rights merely because we stipulate that they do, however, we account for neither the existence nor the strength of our intuition that they can be violated. Sentiency, Regan thinks, lies behind the claim that marginal cases have rights, and if sentiency is a sufficient condition for having rights, then animals have them as well. But is sentiency also a necessary condition for having basic moral rights? If we are to account for another strong intuition that reflective people have—that plants, lacking a central nervous system, cannot be pained, but animals can—then we must assume the sentiency criterion to be more than just a sufficient condition. That is, if we assume that sentiency is a necessary and sufficient condition for having rights, we can explain (1) why we think marginal humans can be the victims of gross injustice, (2) why we can mow the grass without cringing, and (3) why morally reflective people—including meat eaters—cringe when they imagine cows being mowed down in the abattoir. Again, none of this is meant to refute Frey, but it is meant to shift the burden of proof onto those who would treat the suffering of marginal cases and the suffering of animals in radically different ways.[35]

The weak version of the AMC works on the assumption that marginal humans have rights and hence on the presumed reasonableness of sentiency as a necessary and sufficient condition for the possession of rights. Only the most marginal of marginal cases (e.g., the irreversibly comatose) are altogether lacking in sentiency, in contrast to infants and the mentally enfeebled. Regan is obviously open to the charge here that the irreversibly comatose can be treated in grossly immoral ways—say, if they were killed and eaten—although this intuition (that the most marginal of marginal cases can be mistreated) is not as powerful as that governing our treatment of retarded people and the other marginal cases. Later I will consider the role of intuition in moral philosophy, but Regan seems to do no harm in trying to account for our intuitions in a transcendental way. He offers a revised version of his critical argument and a revised version of his constructive argument:

1. Given certain criteria of the possession of rights, some marginal humans who are not irreversibly comatose and not just all animals will be excluded from the class of right-holders.
2. However, humans, including all those who, though marginal, are not irreversibly comatose, do have rights, and so belong in the class of right-holders.
3. Therefore, each and every one of the criteria satisfying (1) must be rejected as setting a requirement for the possession of rights.[36]

1. Humans, including all those who, though they are marginal, are not irreversibly comatose, have rights and therefore belong in the class of right-holders.
2. However, given the most reasonable criterion of the possession of rights, one that permits us to include all non-comatose marginal humans in the class of right-holders, this same criterion will require us to include some, and exclude some other, animals.
3. Therefore, if we include these marginal humans in the class of right-holders, we must also include some animals in this class.[37]

Regan is famous (or infamous) for recommending that the criterion for right-possession be "inherent value," a concept that has three noteworthy features: (i) if X has inherent value, then this value is logically independent of any other being's valuing X; (ii) X's having inherent value makes it improper to treat X as though it had value only as a means; and (iii) X's being good-of-its-kind is logically distinct from X's having inherent value. Several things can be noticed about these features of inherent value. First, Regan obviously has an anticonsequentialist intent here. Second, Regan is taking his cues here from Kant, or better, from G. E. Moore's version of Kant. Third, Regan's criteria for inherent value are remarkably similar to those for basic rights, indicating, perhaps, that a being has basic rights to the extent that it has inherent value. In fact, although Regan does not want to equate sentiency, inherent value, and basic rights, it seems that all three of these stand or fall together in Regan's philosophy, despite the fact that possession of sentiency is a factual matter in ways that possession of inherent value and basic rights are not. Later I will return to the question of what inherent value is for Regan; this is an important topic if only because his three criteria for inherent value tell us only what inherent value is not.[38]

Although it is conceivable that beings lacking even the potential for consciousness or sentiency (e.g., trees) might have inherent value, Regan is not convinced that an argument has been developed to show this. Merely being alive does not establish inherent value on the three previously cited criteria. Whereas merely being alive is too low a criterion for inherent value, however, Kant's criterion seems to be too high. If free will and rationality are the standards, then many human beings lack inherent value. On Kantian grounds we cannot object to using the mentally enfeebled in painful experiments because they have been harmed; we can object only because the mistreatment of the mentally enfeebled makes us prone to mistreat those human beings who are inherently valuable. But why would mistreating marginal cases or animals make us more likely to mistreat moral agents if there is no morally relevant similarity between marginal cases and animals, on the one hand, and moral agents, on the other? In a way Regan is more Kantian than Kant. The mentally enfeebled and animals can be shown disrespect, according to Regan, because they are more than things useful to our ends. They have inherent value because certain types of life are better or worse *for them;* they are subjects of a life that has value for the individual whose life it is, even if the individual in question is not rational.[39]

The claim that all human beings except the irreversibly comatose have inherent value does not entail that they all have equal value. The severely mentally enfeebled, for example, do not so much *lead* a life as *have* one. They cannot really lead a life because they have no possibility of moral agency or moral development; hence normal, adult humans, who have these abilities, have a greater value. (Later I will spell out how, on Regan's view, some beings have greater value without having greater inherent value. As before, inherent value is an all-or-nothing affair: those who have inherent value have it equally.) Once again, as with Singer, sentiency is the threshold, but not the epitome, of moral beneficiary status. In the familiar philosophical examples regarding survivors on a lifeboat, we should decide in favor of normal adults, but these in extremis situations do not necessarily justify those with greater value treating those with less in any way they please. Mentally enfeebled human beings at least *have* a life that is better or worse for them. It is lamentable that the same is not the case for the irreversibly comatose. There is no better or worse *for them;* there is only the being alive. At one point Regan softens his view of the irreversibly comatose: we should not necessarily conclude that they do not have rights; rather, their moral status should remain an open question.[40]

The place of sentience in the grounding of basic rights can now be seen: it is a logically necessary and sufficient condition of some being's leading or having a form of life that is better or worse for that being, namely, the form of life where pleasure outweighs pain or where pain outweighs pleasure. The AMC (in this instance, the argument for moral consistency) requires that any beings meeting the sentience criterion must be assumed to have rights, and it is unreasonable to think that a great number of animals fail to meet the sentience criterion. Perhaps only a few animals (e.g., primates) can lead a life in the previously described sense, but most animals certainly have a life that is better or worse for them, such that when we treat animals as if they had only instrumental value, we act immorally. It should also be noted that to say that animals and marginal humans have rights, including the right to life, is not necessarily to say that all the rights they possess are the same. Some subclasses of animals and of marginal cases carry with them certain capacities that merit certain rights rather than others. For example, if the individual in question (whether animal or marginal human) is capable of intentional bodily movement, it has a right to freedom of movement. This right is violated, say, when chickens are forced to live their entire lives in cages so small that they cannot turn around or when mental defectives are, as they historically were, permanently chained. The key point, however, is that if the relevant respects in which certain marginal humans possess capacities that merit rights also apply to certain animals, then these animals also merit the appropriate rights.[41]

The prominence Regan gives to sentience and his admission that the irreversibly comatose might not have rights might be seen as efforts to bridge the gap between his version of the AMC and Singer's utilitarian version. There are in fact significant differences between the two, however. Regan agrees with Singer that we should prohibit behavior toward mentally defective humans that we now allow toward more intelligent, more self-conscious animals. Nonetheless, he rightly wonders how Singer can justify the AMC on a *utilitarian* basis. The equality of treatment principle (which refers to the belief not that all beings should be treated equally but rather that equals should be treated equally) regarding animals and marginal cases (precisely the AMC) can be understood in utilitarianism in three possible ways, according to Regan: (1) the equality of treatment principle is identical with the principle of utility, (2) the equality of treatment principle follows from the principle of utility, or (3) the equality of treatment principle is presupposed by the principle of utility. Regan thinks that (1) is implausible in that the question of whether treating beings with equal interests equally would be conducive to the utilitarian goal is an open one. It is conceivable that violations of the principle of equality could be optimific.[42]

Regarding (2) Regan notes that some might think of the equality of treatment principle following from the principle of utility either logically or by virtue of certain factual premises, but he thinks that both of these options are implausible. It is possible to affirm the principle of utility and yet deny the equality of treatment principle without thereby contradicting oneself, according to Regan. That is, someone might suggest that we could bring about the greatest balance of good over evil by treating some beings *un*equally. It should be noted, however, that Regan does not emphasize a point that surely would be emphasized by utilitarians: utilitarianism is committed not merely to maximizing happiness but to maximizing happiness for the greatest number. This distributive element in utilitarianism somewhat counteracts some of Regan's criticisms of utilitarianism.

Regan agrees with Singer that we are inconsistent when we allow behavior toward animals that we would not allow toward less-developed humans, but he is not convinced that these violations of the equality of treatment principle are also violations of the principle of utility. Regan is also skeptical regarding (3), the view that utility presupposes equality. If the principle of utility did presuppose the equality of treatment principle, then utilitarianism would encompass a principle more fundamental than that of utility. That result would be inconsistent with utilitarianism, a theory wherein the principle of utility is the "one and only fundamental moral principle."[43]

In addition, as a utilitarian Singer appears to be unable to say that, whatever the consequences of experimenting on and eating animals, we ought not to engage in such practices because they violate the animals' rights. Rather, if Singer's defense of the AMC is to be a utilitarian stance, it must be based on long-term consequences. Regan puts his criticism of Singer as follows: "In a word, then, the dilemma I think Singer must face is this: if he is a utilitarian, then he must give a radically different argument than the one he has actually given; whereas, if he rests his case for vegetarianism on the argument he has actually given, then he cannot continue to believe that he has given a utilitarian basis for the moral obligation to be vegetarian. Possibly the appeal to the rights of animals is not a 'concession to popular rhetoric' after all."[44] Or again, Regan agrees with Singer that we should not treat mentally enfeebled human beings as research machines or as gourmet food sources, but he quite rightly disagrees with Singer's grounding of this judgment. What if such practices using these unfortunate humans should become optimific (as well they might, not so much for culinary as for scientific purposes)? If we have adopted the principle of utility as our fundamental principle, we would have to at least doubt, if not abandon, our view that it is wrong to treat mentally enfeebled human beings in these ways.

It is not only utilitarians whom Regan finds to be problematic. Rational egoists, as well, might agree to the AMC on the grounds that, although marginal humans are not and perhaps can never be rational agents, they can be the objects of sentimental interest on the part of rational agents. But there is no guarantee that they will continue to be the objects of sentimental interest in the future. Or again, the best conjecture we can make regarding what Kant's position would be is that we should not mistreat the mentally enfeebled because this will eventually lead us to mistreat rational, free beings. Nevertheless, there is no reason that this supposed connection between animal cruelty and cruelty to humans will have to hold in the future, assuming, for the moment, that such a connection holds in the present. It is possible that in the future a sharp line will be drawn between rational, free beings and marginal cases for any one of a number of reasons (utilitarian, scientific, environmental, etc.).[45]

Because of the arbitrariness of these and other positions in dealing with the AMC, Regan is "ineluctably drawn" to the idea that (even) mental defectives have certain rights and that we *owe* it to them not to mistreat them. This "ought" does not rely on niceness or sentimental interest, nor is it because animals and the marginal cases provide a sort of "warm up" for the really serious moral game played among free, rational beings:

> It is only, I think, if rights are postulated *even* in the case of morons that we can give a sufficiently firm theoretical basis for our conviction that it is wrong to treat them in the ways in question. . . . For if, as I think, in our search for the most adequate theory to account for our settled moral convictions we are driven to postulate that morons (even) have certain rights, it remains to be asked what there is about them that could serve as the grounds or basis of the rights they have, if they have them. Singer, I think, has argued persuasively that it cannot be the fact that they are human beings . . . that is to mark moral boundaries in a way which invites com-

> parisons to racism and sexism. Nor can it be argued that morons have the rights they do, if they do, because they are autonomous or very intelligent; they are not. Nor, again, will it do to argue that they belong to a species whose members are rational and the like. Rather, if there is some basis for their having rights, *it must be something about the capacities of the morons themselves*. . . . Many, many animals will satisfy the grounds in question. Take, for example, Singer's mention of "the capacity to experience pain and/or enjoyment." That seems to me to be a very strong candidate for grounding rights in the case of human morons.[46]

Regan does not think that utilitarianism should be abandoned; rather, he thinks that it does not account for our *duties* to severely mentally enfeebled human beings. Hence, Regan's own view can be described as Kantian even though he often disagrees with Kant himself on certain key points. By failing to ground our duties to certain *human* beings, utilitarianism, egoism, and so on also fail to ground duties to animals. The straight line from grounding respect (or lack thereof) for marginal humans and grounding respect (or lack thereof) for animals is supported by the following comment by C. S. Lewis, quoted by Regan: "Once the old Christian idea of a total difference in kind between man and beast has been abandoned, then no argument for experiments on animals can be found which is not also an argument for experiments on inferior men."[47] If Washoe and her great ape relatives have greater psychological capacities than severely retarded humans, why should we inflict terrible suffering on chimpanzees but not on less-capable humans? Regan's point is not that we should inflict suffering on retarded humans in research but rather that the sort of respect traditionally given (in Christianity) to retarded humans cannot consistently be denied to animals.[48]

It is quite remarkable that some philosophers think that a proposed analysis is adequate if it fits the normal cases only. A familiar, proper method of testing a proposed analysis in philosophy is precisely to deal with the deviant cases or counterexamples. Conceptual analysis should, Regan thinks, lay bare the conditions that must be met if a given concept can be properly applied. For example, although normal adult human beings have beliefs and can express them linguistically, it does not necessarily follow that only those individuals who can express beliefs in language can have them. It seems that children have the ability to form beliefs before they learn to use a language, for otherwise they could not learn to use one; if humans can have nonlinguistic beliefs, then so can animals. For Regan, the moral community is wider than the class of beings who can express beliefs linguistically. It includes all those individuals who are of direct moral concern, or better, toward whom moral agents have direct duties. Within this moral community can be found moral agents as well as moral beneficiaries, the latter a population whose members sometimes differ in morally relevant ways—normal human beings, obviously enough, are both moral agents and moral beneficiaries.[49] (It should be remembered that Regan hesitates to put the irreversibly comatose even in the category of moral beneficiaries, much less that of moral agents.)

Some moral beneficiaries are conscious and sentient but lack other mental ability; some moral beneficiaries are conscious and sentient and possess other cognitive and volitional abilities (e.g., belief and memory), albeit abilities that fall short of those that make one a moral agent. The latter sort of moral beneficiary typically has the following traits: desires and beliefs, perception, memory, intentional action, a sense of the future (i.e., self-awareness or self-consciousness), a psychological identity over time, and a kind of autonomy (preference autonomy). There is no exact line between those humans who possess these traits and those who do not, but the efforts we make to distinguish human beings with self-consciousness, say, from those who are not self-conscious should be the same efforts we make to distinguish self-consciousness from lack of self-consciousness in animals. A brutal beating of a child is wrong even if the child is not a moral agent, just as attending to the basic biological needs of the senile is arguably right, even if the senile human being is not a moral agent. It may well be the case that moral relations between moral agents should be built on reciprocity. But the relationship between a moral agent and a moral beneficiary is not one of reciprocity; rather, it is one where the former has a direct duty to the latter.[50]

Perhaps it will be objected against Regan that the only duties owed to moral beneficiaries are indirect, not direct. Indirect duty views limit membership in the moral community to all and only moral agents. On these indirect duty views, there are still moral constraints on what we may do to animals or to human beneficiaries. Regan notices that indirect duty views are not necessarily speciesist (even if they usually are), in that it is possible to deny animals entrance into the moral community not because they belong to a certain species but because they lack certain properties necessary for reciprocity to occur. The AMC makes it abundantly clear, however, that for defenders of indirect duty views to avoid speciesism, they also have to exclude some human beings from the moral community. The key question regarding indirect duty views is the following one: which of the alternatives before us is the most reasonable view, that moral beneficiaries are of direct moral significance or that they are not? Those who accept indirect duty views—Narveson, Kant, and so on—must think that some of our strongest intuitions in ethics are mistaken They also have the monumental project of explaining why moral beneficiaries cannot receive harm that has direct moral significance. Animals and marginal humans not only can be but are harmed when, for example, they are caused gratuitous suffering or are denied the opportunity to exercise their preference autonomy.[51]

The issue is not whether killing a moral agent and killing a moral beneficiary are, other things being equal, the same thing: they are not. Moral agents are sometimes moral beneficiaries (e.g., when they are asleep). Hence, to be accurate I should probably refer to moral agents as "moral agents/beneficiaries." For the sake of convenience, however, I will use the simpler "moral agents." The important distinction here is between the object or beneficiary of a moral duty and the one who is obligated by the duty.

Moral beneficiaries lack moral agency. The issue is whether we have any direct duties to them. It is true that moral agents can often be harmed in more ways than moral beneficiaries can be harmed, say, by denying them opportunities for advanced education or by denying them the vote. Still, both moral agents and beneficiaries can obviously be harmed in similar ways, say, by denying them basic nutrition, by inflicting gratuitous suffering on them, or by bringing about their untimely death. If it is clear that moral beneficiaries *themselves* can be harmed, largely because they are sentient and perhaps self-conscious beings, and can be harmed in ways that are similar to the ways in which moral agents can be harmed, then the requirement of impartiality will require that we make fair judgments regarding the harmful treatment of each. As before, indirect duty views are not speciesist *if* they include the notion that human beings who are moral beneficiaries also, in addition to animals, fail as the recipients of direct duties. But it is extremely difficult to deny that children, the retarded, and animals are sentient, have beliefs and desires, and can act intentionally. Hence, it is extremely difficult to deny that they, and not just their masters, can be harmed. On Regan's view, no indirect duty view can command our rational assent.[52] (It should not be assumed, however, that Regan's opposition to indirect duty views automatically puts him in the direct duty camp. Sometimes he uses the phrase "direct duty view" to apply to a version of act utilitarianism or to a view that prohibits cruelty to animals without thereby claiming that animals have rights—stances that he rejects.)

As before, Regan thinks that animals and marginal cases have inherent value, and it is this inherent value that enables us to say that they have rights. Inherent value, as he uses the term, is not to be confused with the intrinsic value that attaches to the experiences of individual animals or marginal cases, for example, their pleasures or preference satisfactions. Inherent value is not reducible to the intrinsic values of an individual's experiences, or better, the inherent value of an individual is not found by totaling the intrinsic values of his or her particular experiences. Those who have more intrinsically valuable experiences, Regan thinks, do not necessarily have greater inherent value as individuals: "To view moral agents as having inherent value is thus to view them as something different from, and something more than, mere receptacles of what has intrinsic value."[53] Regan's view here is once again in opposition to Singer's (mere) receptacle view: for Singer, it is what goes into the cup (intrinsic value) that has value, not the cup (inherent value), as it were. Given the utilitarian (mere) receptacle view, it is difficult to account for utilitarianism's own version of equality, for the individuals in question might radically differ from each other given their vastly different particular experiences (intrinsic values, including pleasures).[54]

By invoking inherent value, Regan is attempting to show that moral patients are ends in themselves. Kant's mistake was in thinking that only moral agents could be ends in themselves, despite the fact that moral patients can receive some of the same harms received by moral agents. Although Regan says that the killing of a moral agent is worse than the killing of a moral beneficiary, and that moral agents have more moral rights than do moral beneficiaries, he does not think that inherent value admits of degrees. To think that the inherent value of moral beneficiaries is unequal to that of moral agents is perhaps to confuse inherent value with intrinsic values, which can in fact admit of qualitative and quantitative differences. The inherent value of moral agents does not wax or wane depending on their comparative pleasant or painful experiences at some particular time; likewise, if some moral beneficiaries have less-pleasant lives than those of certain moral agents, this in itself does not mean that they have less inherent value than moral agents: "Inherent value is thus a *categorical* concept. One either has it, or one does not."[55] Contrary to what might seem to be the case initially, Regan is not advocating a morally egalitarian universe where each individual has equal inherent value. Nonliving things, he suspects, do not have inherent value, nor does merely being alive do the trick. It is not clear how we reasonably could have direct duties to blades of grass or potatoes or to collections of these: lawns or potato fields. Although Regan does not want to go so far as to say that to be a subject of a life is a necessary condition for having inherent value, he is skeptical as to whether a genuine ethic of the environment is possible. Or better, Regan does not think that a defensible account of inherent value in nonsentient nature has yet been produced, even if such an account is needed for a full environmental ethic, as opposed to a view of the environment as instrumentally good for human beings and animals (including the wild ones). Regan is also skeptical as to whether the permanently comatose are subjects of a life, and he doubts whether they have inherent value.[56]

Regan is open to arguments that try to establish different conclusions, but as far as he can tell, only those who are subjects of a life have the distinctive kind of value—inherent value—such that they can be seen as more than mere receptacles. Subjects of a life have beliefs and desires, perception, memory, and a sense of the future; they have an emotional life, including feelings of pleasure and pain, preferences, and the ability to initiate action in pursuit of their goals; and they have some sort of identity over time, such that their experiences fare well or ill for them. Young children and the mentally enfeebled, for example, lack the knowledge to satisfy even their basic needs and desires, but they can fare ill if we do not act on their behalf. Each such individual is a subject of a life who can fare well or ill for him- or herself, logically independently of their utility for us. All moral agents and beneficiaries are subjects of a life; hence, they all have equal inherent value (which is different from saying that they all have equal value); hence, they all have rights.[57]

It should be emphasized that Regan, as a follower of G. E. Moore, does not think that he has committed the naturalistic fallacy. Rather, he seems to be committed to two claims that enable him to avoid it: (1) If marginal human beings have rights, then animals have them, too; this leaves open the question as to what grounds the rights of the marginal cases. (2) When trying to establish the rights of the marginal cases, a transcendental approach is best. That is, the view that certain individuals have equal inherent value is a *postulate* with good reasons behind it. Regan here is quite different from someone who claims that sentiency in beings with a central nervous system itself grounds moral respect: "To postulate . . . equal inherent value provides a theoretical basis for avoiding the wildly inegalitarian implications of perfectionist theories, on the one hand, and, on the other, the counterintuitive implications of all forms of act utilitarianism (e.g., that secret killings that optimize the aggregate consequences for all affected by the outcome are justified)."[58] Once again, intuition plays a fundamental role in Regan's defense of the strong version of the AMC. Once equal inherent value is postulated, it is easy to see why Regan defends what he calls the respect principle: we are to treat those individuals who have inherent value in ways that respect their inherent value. We fail to treat individuals who have inherent value with respect when we treat them as if they were mere receptacles of valuable experiences or as if their value depended upon their utility. Individuals who have inherent value should never be treated merely as means to securing the best aggregate consequences.[59]

Just as individuals can have legal rights they neither understand nor can claim on their own, so also moral beneficiaries can have moral rights they fail to understand and cannot themselves claim. In fact, the less cognizant individuals are of their rights and the less power they have to defend them, the more we must do to help them defend these rights when they are violated. This qualification is needed to avoid the absurd consequences of the claim that we should defend the prey's rights against the predator in wild nature. But wolves, for example, because they are not moral agents, cannot violate anyone's rights. Once again, however, not all right-bearers have equal rights that are threatened with violation. For example, if we had to cast overboard a dog or a normal adult human being, we should surely cast the dog overboard, unless the human being chose to perform an act of supererogation by willingly jumping out. The dog does not have *intrinsic* goodness in its experiences equal to that of a normal adult human being. Nonetheless, this does not imply that the dog does not have rights that, in less extreme situations, deserve preservation: "In exceptional circumstances, we are justified in limiting an individual's liberty (say a man has become temporarily deranged and poses a threat to the security of others, a threat we can cancel only by forcibly restraining him), it does not follow that we would be justified in allowing institutions or practices that *routinely* limit individual liberty."[60] In less than extreme circumstances, all human beings and all animals with a central nervous system—except perhaps the permanently comatose—are the sorts of conscious, sentient beings concerning whom the possession of rights should be taken most seriously.[61]

Although contractarians are normally thought of as rights theorists, they are not necessarily helpful regarding the rights of animals or marginal cases. Young children, for example, are unable to sign contracts, and hence they lack rights, even if they are the objects of sentimental interest by those who bear rights. Contractarians have duties *regarding* young children but not *to* them. Our direct duty is to the parents of the children. Animals, like young children, cannot sign contracts and hence cannot have rights within contractualism. Animals, moreover, like young children, are the objects of sentimental interest. Our duties are to the "owners" of the animals, however. Concerning those animals for whom there is little or no sentimental interest—for example, laboratory rats—our duties grow weaker to the vanishing point. The pain and death they endure are not wrong, on contractualist grounds, if no one cares about them. Regan disagrees both with the contractarian view of marginal cases and hence, a fortiori, with the contractarian view of animals.[62]

The rights view is the most satisfactory moral theory because it surpasses other theories in the degree to which it illuminates and explains the foundations of our duties to one another. The AMC is an important supplement to rights theory because it makes clear that attempts to limit the scope of rights theory to human beings fail. Animals, it is true, cannot read or make gourmet dishes, but neither can many human beings, yet we do not and should not say that these human beings have less inherent value, less of a right to be treated with respect, than do others. The most basic similarity human beings possess is not rationality but sentiency, or more precisely, the fact that we are all experiencing subjects of a life, conscious creatures having individual welfare that is of import to us regardless of our usefulness to others: "We want and prefer things, believe and feel things, recall and expect things. And all these dimensions of our life, including our pleasure and pain, our enjoyment and suffering, our satisfaction and frustration, our continued existence or our untimely death—all make a difference to the quality of our life as lived, as experienced, by us as individuals."[63] Furthermore, all these qualities are also possessed by animals; they, too, have inherent value and are experiencing subjects of a life.

An Initial Criticism

Before moving to some of the detailed criticisms of the AMC in later chapters, I want to introduce a criticism that has been directed against Regan's version, specifically, the criticism of Henry Cohen. Cohen is careful to note, where many scholars have not been so careful, that when Regan uses the term "all humans"—say, when he is arguing or implying that all humans have rights—he more exactly means all humans except those who are irreversibly comatose. Cohen's criticism has to do with Regan's use of inherent value to ground animal rights instead of what Cohen takes to be Singer's simpler and clearer use of sentience for that purpose. To say that an individual can have a life that is better or worse for that individual is reducible, on Cohen's reasoning, to saying that the individual is sentient.[64] It seems to be Regan's attachment to a G. E. Moore–like indefinability to inherent value that gets him into trouble here, in that he never positively describes inherent value. If being sentient and having memory and preferences are necessary and jointly sufficient conditions for the possession of inherent value, however—a view that might not be Regan's even if it seems that it should be—then inherent value can be given a positive description in terms of sentiency and having preferences. From Regan's point of view, although the ability to be sentient in general seems to be an important constituent in inherent value, there is a danger in overemphasizing sentience because it is easy to slide into Singer's view that the value of an individual's life *simpliciter* is to be found in the particular pleasures an individual has, such that the individual begins to look like a mere receptacle for those pleasures rather than a subject of a life. Regan's legitimate point here is close to the Aristotelian one that pleasure is part of the overall good of an individual but not the whole of that good. Hence, despite Cohen's claim, it is not crucial for Regan to develop some sort of algorithm for weighing the value of a human life diminished by becoming a quadriplegic, on the one hand, against the value of an animal's natural mental limitations, on the other.

Summary

Both Singer and Regan defend the AMC. The former's version depends on a distinction between mentally undeveloped human beings and animals, on the one hand, and mentally developed human beings and animals, on the other. Because even the mentally undeveloped are sentient, they are morally considerable and deserve equal consideration by moral agents. Nonetheless, Singer thinks that the mentally undeveloped lie within the sweep of the replaceability argument because they do not have a right to life. Mentally developed human beings and animals (e.g., chimpanzees and pigs) do have a right to life because they are persons; that is, they are self-conscious beings with an awareness of their past and an anticipation of their future. Because they have a right to life, they do not lie within the sweep of the replaceability argument, but this does not mean that their right to life is absolute, for if the consequences are weighty enough, even mentally developed beings can be sacrificed. The key point is that mentally undeveloped beings—whether human beings or animals—deserve equal consideration; mentally developed beings—whether human beings or animals—also deserve equal consideration. Singer thinks that, as a consequence of the AMC, our views of both animals and the marginal cases of humanity need to change. That is, they need to be brought together such that a loftier view of animals results; a reconsideration of the view of human life as sacred is also called for. (1) The lives of mentally undeveloped animals and marginal cases may be taken if there are weighty reasons for doing so, and (2) the lives of mentally developed human beings and animals (i.e., persons) may also be taken if the reasons are weightier still. Perhaps the most problematic part of Singer's version of the AMC is that, in conjunction with the replaceability argument, and as a consequence of (1), some marginal humans are indeed replaceable.

By way of contrast, Regan does not think that our view of marginal cases (excepting the irreversibly comatose) needs to be changed. In fact, his version of the AMC hinges on the traditional respect given to marginal cases. Our view of animals, however—and this on the evidence of the AMC—needs significant modification. He sees the AMC as convincingly showing that the moral status of severely retarded human beings is not superior to that of animals such as dogs and cows. One of the strongest moral intuitions is that killing and eating severely retarded human beings is a moral outrage. But why? Only the possession by the severely retarded of basic rights can account for our moral outrage, as I will show again later in this book. These basic rights are much stronger than Singer's (nonbasic) rights because both animals and marginal cases are subjects of a life, which is argued largely on the evidence of their being sentient. Although it is stated with less than optimal clarity, Regan's view seems to be that because animals and marginal cases are subjects of a life (sentient), they have inherent value as individuals and are not merely receptacles for the intrinsic values of their pleasures and pains. It is this inherent value that grounds basic rights; in short, inherent value makes marginal cases and hence animals ends in themselves rather than mere utilities. We have direct duties to marginal cases and hence to animals as a consequence of the inherent value they possess equally.

Regan's transcendental argument is meant to account for one of our strongest moral convictions in a way that utilitarianism, contractualism, and so on cannot: that marginal cases can be treated in grossly immoral ways. He does not violate another firmly held conviction, however: that normal human beings are of greater value than animals. To *have* a life it is not enough to merely *be* alive. Sentiency seems to be a necessary condition for having a life, but mentally undeveloped beings (to use Singer's language) who have a life do not necessarily *lead* a life, in Regan's sense, for autonomously leading a life requires certain sophisticated intrinsic values in addition to the individual's inherent value. Animals (chimpanzees might be an exception) do not seem to have these sophisticated intrinsic values.

In many ways the differences between Singer and Regan mirror the classic differences between utilitarianism and deontology in general. Nowhere is this more apparent than in Singer's replaceability argument. A telling point in Regan's favor is that he, along with Evelyn Pluhar, criticizes this argument because of a serious implication that it has: if morally undeveloped animals are replaceable, so are human beings with comparable characteristics in like circumstances. According to Singer, no wrong is done if mentally undeveloped animals are killed painlessly and are replaced with conspecifics, but neither would a wrong be done to mental defectives who were raised and killed painlessly, had their flesh stocked for food or experimentation purposes, and were replaced with conspecifics. It should be noted that the problem here is not with the AMC but with Singer's attempt to link it to the replaceability argument. Hence if we shudder at the prospect of canning "moron meat," we would do well to withdraw consent to the replaceability argument, for the AMC in itself carries no implication that marginal cases may be treated thus. Once again, it is Singer and not Regan who thinks that our attitudes toward mentally defective human beings need reconsideration, to the point where marginal cases might be killed for food—if we should develop the taste for them—or for experimental purposes if the marginal cases are raised and killed humanely and are replaced. One consequence of all this is that those, like myself, who are interested in Regan-like defenses of the AMC cannot rest content with the weak version of the argument, where, on the *assumption* that marginal cases have rights, we can then argue that animals, too, have rights. That is, there is a need to defend a strong version of the AMC wherein it is shown *why* marginal cases have rights.[65]

Although I prefer Regan's version of the AMC to Singer's version, I realize that there is something mysterious about his notion of inherent value. His transcendental argument, at least, is clear: to avoid morally unacceptable conclusions, we should postulate that all subjects of a life have inherent value. His nontranscendental account of inherent value is not as clear as his transcendental account, however, although they both lead to the same result, for he is not quite ready to put the matter in the following blunt way: sentient beings are subjects of a life and therefore have inherent value. I contend that he should be so blunt even if the price he has to pay is giving up of his G. E. Moore–like elusiveness regarding the definition of inherent value.

In any event, I share Regan's abhorrence at Singer's replaceability argument in that both of us think of human beings and animals as more than mere receptacles for the intrinsic value that attaches to pleasurable experiences. It is this "more than," it seems, that Regan wishes to secure through his notion of inherent value. My own way of securing this "more than" relies on a view of human beings and animals moving through time asymmetrically, as I argue at the end of this book. That is, Singer's view is overly atomistic in a Humean sense, in that as long as the moment of death is painless, he is willing to consider moral replaceability of animals and marginal human beings. On my view, however, human beings and animals are, albeit short of Aristotelian substances, nonetheless the sorts of beings who to varying degrees have memories of the past and expectations or hopes or possibilities regarding the future, and it is morally bothersome to terminate these as a result of the replaceability argument.

2

Reciprocity

Now that the major thrust and some of the implications of the AMC are on the table, I want to consider the positions of four major critics of the argument—H. J. McCloskey, Jan Narveson, John Rawls, and Richard Watson—all of whom base their opposition on some version of the thesis that only beings capable of reciprocal relations with free, rational beings can have rights. McCloskey, Narveson, and Watson treat the AMC explicitly, whereas Rawls does so only implicitly, but all four have generated responses from AMC defenders including Joel Feinberg, Dale Jamieson, James Rachels, and Evelyn Pluhar. It is my hope both that the complexity of the reciprocity objection will become clear in this chapter and that the persuasiveness of the rejoinders made by the AMC's defenders will become apparent.

The reciprocity objection admits of different forms: some are contractualist, some are based on rational egoism, and some derive from the American pragmatist idea that animals do not have rights because they cannot regulate their attitudes by the institutional norms of rights.[1] There is at least a family resemblance among all these views, however, so that my effort will be to deal with proponents of the reciprocity objection to the extent that they take the AMC seriously. I will not spend time on those such as Tibor Machan who think that the fact of "occasional" borderline cases is simply irrelevant to the issue as to whether rights should be extended from humans to animals.[2]

McCloskey and His Critics

H. J. McCloskey is quite opposed to the claim that animals have rights. He thinks that it is little short of irresponsible to abandon animal experimentation given its benefits. Perhaps the same or greater benefits would accrue if we did the experiments on fetuses, brain-dead human beings, or criminals, but these sorts of experiment raise significant, unresolved moral issues. In fact, he thinks that forbidding experimentation on animals but permitting it on human conscripts (or volunteers) "is morally outrageous."[3] McCloskey is open to the possibility that we have duties concerning animals, but not because they have rights, just as we may have duties concerning the oceans and forests and great works of art even though these objects do not have rights. One argument that McCloskey uses is that animals cannot possess rights because only beings who can possess things at all can possess rights, and animals cannot possess things. Regan rightly objects to this line of argumentation because a right is not exactly a thing, and a being who possesses a thing does not exactly stand in the same relation to the thing as to a right that can be possessed. That is, *possess* is equivocal. In any event, why cannot animals possess things? The question, "Does this bone belong to your dog?" is perfectly intelligible.[4]

McCloskey further attacks the notion of animals' rights by arguing that only a being that has interests can have rights; animals do not have interests, and hence they cannot have rights. Defenders of the AMC agree that only a being with interests can have rights, so that there is no problem with the major premise in this argument. The minor premise, however, where McCloskey peremptorily declares that animals have no interests, is extremely problematic. Regan comments:

> To say that a being A has an interest in a thing X is ambiguous. At least two different things we may mean by this are (1) that A is interested in X or (2) that X is in A's interests. These ideas are logically distinct. A person, for example, can be interested in something that is not in his interests—e.g., Jones might be interested in taking drugs that are injurious to his health. And a person might not be interested in something that is in his interests—e.g., Smith might not be interested in exercising despite the fact that exercise is in his interests.[5]

In the second sense of the term, something is in A's interest if it will contribute to A's good or well-being. Hence, there is both an evaluative overtone in saying that something is in A's interest and a prescriptive overtone: X will contribute to A's good, and X ought to be of concern to A, respectively. An animal might not be the sort of being for which this prescriptive content means very much, in that an animal might not be the sort of being that ought to care or be concerned about anything, but neither is a marginal case of humanity. If we say, "Treatment for worms is in Fido's interests," or, "Jimmy, who is mentally defective, ought to get a tetanus shot," we mean that the prescriptive content is to be directed toward those who have a fiduciary responsibility to Fido or Jimmy. The point is that if infants or the severely mentally enfeebled of all ages have interests, then animals have them, too, contra McCloskey.[6]

It should be clear by now that Regan, in the Kantian tradition, tends more than the utilitarian Singer toward an absolute proscription of certain ways of treating marginal humans and animals. Robert Elliot is one who, like Regan, tries to defend this Kantian approach against McCloskey's attempt to undermine it. McCloskey tries to demonstrate the existence of properties that are possessed (virtually) exclusively by humans and that are the necessary conditions for the coherent ascription of core rights. McCloskey believes that a necessary condition for being a possessor of rights is that one be morally autonomous, and this requirement excludes all nonhumans, as well as many humans. In effect, this is a Kantian case against Regan's and Elliot's Kantian defense of animal rights.[7] Nevertheless, even though animals might not be capable of pressing their claims on their own, reciprocating with human beings, or acting autonomously, as McCloskey requires, these are not necessarily reasons to deny them legal or moral rights, as Joel Feinberg ably argues. McCloskey does not make much of the fact that small children and mentally deficient and deranged human beings are commonly seen as having (Kantian) rights and are therefore commonly represented by trustees when they are incapable of granting consent or entering into contracts. Representation is always of interests, however, so that these marginal cases must have interests to be legitimately represented. Feinberg notices that animals also have custodians whose job it is to look out for their interests. Hence, if we are to be consistent, we must say, in opposition to McCloskey, that animals are among the sorts of being of whom rights can be meaningfully predicated.[8]

Despite the fact that the reciprocity objection is not as pronounced in McCloskey as it is in Narveson, it is nonetheless implicit throughout all his objections to animal rights. Feinberg is in opposition to McCloskey here because it simply does not follow, he thinks, that the intellectual shortcomings that disqualify animals from duties (from reciprocity) disqualify them from rights as well:

> Both law and common sense present numerous examples of the rights of the incompetent. Infants not yet able to walk or talk (much less make promises, sign contracts, appreciate the wrongfulness of their conduct, and so on) most assuredly have moral claims against us as well as enforceable legal rights. So do insane, feebleminded, and senile persons. Even incorrigibly brain-damaged persons are commonly held to have a right to be treated humanely. . . . Animals may have claims against us, but they cannot *know* that they do. . . . One need not *know* that one has a right in order to have it, and . . . animals no less than infants and insane persons can make claims in law courts through proxies speaking in their behalf.[9]

McCloskey's view dies hard, however. Michael Wreen picks up McCloskey's line of reasoning in response to Feinberg by claiming that to be a moral person, one has to have certain mental, not affective, capacities. Wreen is more forthright than McCloskey, however, in admitting that if sophisticated mental capacity is the necessary condition for having a right to life, then some nonhumans have this right and some humans do not. Whereas Williams's list of marginal cases is attenuated, Wreen claims that the list is quite large. Even if the requisite mental capacities are quite elementary, a human being who is an infant, seriously retarded, extremely insane, very senile, or in a coma is not a commonsense person and would not have a right to life on the reciprocity criterion. So also Wreen thinks that many animals are not commonsense persons (implying that at least some of them are). Wreen summarizes his view as follows:

> Exactly how many humans and how many animals, if any, have a right to life will depend, on this view, on how high the standards for commonsense personhood are set. Joel Feinberg's standards, which are moderate, exclude all fetuses and, apparently, all young infants; Peter Singer's standards, which, it would seem, are quite low, include a fair portion of the animal kingdom. Regardless of what the standards should be, however, merely being a live member of our own species, *Homo sapiens*, constitutes no valid ground for the ascription of a right to life. To think that it does would be to be guilty of speciesism.[10]

From this position, however, Wreen goes on to defend speciesism against Singer and Feinberg. That is, Wreen offers a bolder and more forthright version of McCloskey's view. Wreen takes Singer's view to be that a sufficient condition for speciesism is provided when A ascribes a right to life to X, who is a member of A's own species who fails to qualify for commonsense personhood, but A refuses to ascribe a right to life to Y, a member of a different species who also fails to qualify for commonsensical personhood but is otherwise similar to X. Normal adult human beings are persons, but not a brain-damaged human being, a mongoloid, or a human being "who is mentally though not physically a dog." Wreen agrees with Singer that the concepts of "human being" and "person" are not related merely empirically. Nonetheless, it seems to be Wreen's contention that through sympathy or compassion we can show preference to human nonpersons over animal nonpersons (and perhaps over animal persons, too), in that we can recognize that we were once infants, and we could eventually be brain-damaged or comatose. The chance occurrences to which all human beings are subject may well prevent a human being from becoming, or from continuing to be, a person; hence, Wreen thinks, human nonpersons should be ascribed rights. Human nonpersons are in the same class as human persons because we could be, or once were, them, and they perhaps someday will be us. The saying, "There but by the grace of God go I" illustrates the spirit of Wreen's argument.[11]

The difficulties with Wreen's view are ably pointed out by Evelyn Pluhar. She straightforwardly defends the weak version of the AMC: if certain humans with impaired mental capacities have rights, animals with comparable capacities must have rights, too. To deny rights to the latter is to assume that species membership is morally relevant, an assumption just as indefensible as the one made by racists or sexists. Pluhar agrees with Wreen that human beings are not necessarily persons (individuals who are self-aware, sentient, capable of emotions, and able to learn, reason, and plan), even if most human beings are in fact persons. Wreen thinks that human nonpersons are linked to human persons by a "quasi-metaphysical linkage" such that "X is a live human being" is good evidence for the statement "X is a human person." One worthwhile objection that Pluhar makes here is that it is easy enough to imagine a world in which "X is a live human being" is *not* good evidence for "X is a human person," so that the evidential claim cannot be a necessary truth. The best evidence provided by Wreen is that we psychologically identify with human nonpersons in ways that we do not identify with animals. Psychological identification is indeed crucial for taking up the moral point of view, but one must be careful about using this capacity selectively. Pluhar alertly uses the example of Joseph Mengele, who was very fond of "Aryan" children but had no trouble torturing Jewish ones. A great many humans take the same attitude toward animals that Mengele took toward Jews. Her overall point here, however, is that a great many human beings *do* psychologically identify with animals, especially with their suffering, despite what Wreen says.[12]

Wreen's speciesism is built on the belief that human nonpersons have been "denied" personhood, whereas nonhuman nonpersons have the status they have because of something other than bad luck: the shark would not have *been* a shark if it had been a person. Pluhar has us notice that at most Wreen has made a case for the ascription of rights to human nonpersons whose condition is no fault of their own, a view that does not cover the brain-damaged human after a failed suicide attempt or after a motorcycle accident where the human was not wearing a helmet. More important, however, what sense does it make to talk, as Wreen does, about the injustice of nature or about rights being accorded to marginal cases as restitution or compensation for such injustice? Even if one personifies nature, this approach makes sense only if God or nature omnipotently is responsible for every detail in the universe, a view that theists often reject. The crucial point made apparent by the AMC is that, however the marginal cases got here, if they have rights, then animals have them as well. And if personhood—a very high criterion, but one often favored by those who offer the reciprocity objection—is the criterion for moral respect, then many humans will fail to meet the criterion while some animals (apes, dolphins, and whales, Pluhar thinks) will meet it. An animal whose capacities are equivalent to those of humans with advanced Alzheimer's cannot survive in nature, but many animals *do* survive in nature. In any event, Pluhar does not want the criterion for moral respect to be as high as personhood; she is content with Regan's subject-of-a-life criterion or with the plain notion that animals have interests.[13]

Critics of the AMC such as McCloskey and Wreen have a tendency to make the entrance fee for moral beneficiary status and for a right to life rather high and then surreptitiously let the marginal cases in the back door, for they cannot pay the fee. But the question I am concentrating on here is why the entrance fee should be so high. There is an enormous number of cases where a being can have a right but not duties: fetuses in the later stages of pregnancy, infants, the retarded, the senile, the sick, and, according to the AMC, animals. Civil rights such as the right to vote may be concomitant with certain duties, but basic rights such as the right to life and the right not to be made to suffer gratuitously do not necessarily require the performance of any duty.[14]

Narveson and Rational Egoism

Jan Narveson is much more explicit than McCloskey regarding the importance of reciprocity. Moreover, it should be mentioned again that it was Narveson who gave the argument from marginal cases its name. Still, it is not clear that Narveson takes the argument as seriously as he should. Even though Narveson may grant that speciesism is unacceptable, he says the marginal cases provide no "intractable problems." Only free, rational beings really have rights, on Narveson's view, which he refers to as rational egoism or contractarianism. On Narveson's own admission, this theory must classify as not inherently qualified for basic rights any humans who are so far below the standard for our species as to be unable to communicate effectively or react in a rational way to the rest of us. Narveson asks a legitimate question regarding this view: why, then, should we be concerned for the well-being of these beings? We might add, why not allow people to hunt them? Before responding to these questions, however, Narveson reminds us that there has been tremendous variation in different ages and cultures regarding how to treat the marginal cases, including exposure of unpromising infants. It is not *obvious* that the marginal cases have rights.[15]

Nonetheless, Narveson thinks that there are straightforward reasons to extend the ambit of morality to infants and mental defectives. For example, we might extend the ambit of morality to children because (1) we want our children protected, (2) we have nothing to gain by invading other people's children, and (3) we have much to gain in treating other people's children well in that we do not want them to grow up into criminals. Likewise, we might extend the ambit of morality to the feebleminded because (1) we might become so, and (2) we might want to show respect to the rational relatives of these marginal cases. Neither children nor feebleminded individuals pose a major problem, according to Narveson, who also claims that since neither children nor feebleminded individuals have rights, animals do not either. Narveson thinks that the moral status of animals is one of the real watershed issues in recent moral philosophy (but why?), yet animals do not have rights. Or again, animal suffering is a bad thing, but this does not require us to be vegetarians.[16]

There is some legitimacy to Narveson's complaint that Regan uses *moral patient* in too narrow a way so as to refer only to those who are beneficiaries and not agents. Since moral agents are also capable of being affected for better or worse, moral agents are also, in a way, moral beneficiaries. To use the term as Regan does, and as I generally use it throughout this book, as referring to those who are moral beneficiaries only and not also moral agents, should not blind us to the fact that there are passive aspects to moral agents that matter morally. Once again, the basic distinction here is between the one who is obligated and the one who is the direct object of a duty; there are some who are the latter without being the former, and there are some who are both, although all who are the former are also the latter. Moral agents (or, in Narveson's terms, moral agents/patients), however, are not so important that we should agree to Narveson's claim that rules benefiting beneficiaries simply as such have no fundamental appeal: "The pig himself has no rational clout. . . . If we want something out of the pig, and treating the pig well is necessary for getting it, then we shall have reason to treat him well. If we don't, however, or if it isn't, then why should we go to the trouble?"[17] There are many problems with this egoistic orientation, as I will show. One of them is that if the only reason to treat a being well is that it benefits us to do so, then the range of application of this egoistic principle would extend not only to how we deal with pigs but also to marginal cases and, it should be noted, to other moral agents whom we might be able to exploit for our own advantage.

The main argument in Regan's armory, according to Narveson, is the AMC, an argument based on the intuition that there is something wrong about cruelty to infants and mental defectives. Narveson does not accurately report Regan's intuition, however. It is not merely that marginal cases can be treated cruelly when they are gratuitously pained but also that they are shown disrespect in that they are dignified subjects of a life. Narveson might agree that we ought not to treat infants, mental defectives, and animals cruelly, but his reasons for this view would be his desire not to offend the relatives of, or those who have a sympathetic relationship with, the beings in question and the alleged lack of benefit from mistreating animals or the marginal cases. Narveson also uses the argument developed by Thomas Aquinas and Kant that cruelty to animals may make us more likely to be cruel to moral agents (with whom we must reciprocate). In effect, Narveson puts animals and marginal cases in an intermediate status between mere things and rational agents who can and must reciprocate with each other. Members of this intermediate class are eligible for minimally decent treatment not because they *deserve* it but rather because we *give* them this status and this decent treatment because it benefits us to do so.[18]

Regan's primary criticism of Narveson's view is that it automatically excludes from the class of right-bearers any being that cannot enter into agreements. What cannot reciprocate cannot possibly have rights. Narveson himself is quoted as saying that he offers a "frank, . . . heartless rejection of the *relevance*" of animal sufferings. But the AMC makes clear that more than just the sufferings of animals are irrelevant for Narveson; so are the sufferings of the marginal cases themselves. Regan emphasizes the obvious point: marginal humans and animals have the equipment to experience gratuitous suffering even if they do not have the rational equipment to enter reciprocal contracts. Furthermore, Narveson's view would permit treating some mental defectives in what Singer and Regan would see as flagrantly immoral ways. Narveson grants that we might be sympathetic to a mentally enfeebled human being because we might become mentally enfeebled. Does this give us a reason to be sympathetic to a mentally enfeebled human being who is an infant? Apparently not, according to Regan:

> Human beings who, *after* they have reached a level of maturity sufficient to reach agreements based upon one's self-interest, shall have their interests protected if they subsequently become moronic, whereas this protection shall not be extended to those human beings (e.g., morons of one year or less) who are or become moronic *before* they are sufficiently mature to enter into agreements based upon what's in their self-interest. . . . His ability to enter into this agreement insures that *he already is* one of those humans whose interests are to be protected by the terms of the agreement. *He* stands to gain a good deal of insurance, as it were, at very little cost; and the fact that, say, the congenitally moronic stand to lose a great deal need not sway either his reason or his conscience.[19]

Ultimately Narveson's rational egoism does not offer much protection to the interests of marginal cases or animals, nor does it acknowledge the rights of such beings. Some consolation is given to adults who are mentally enfeebled because we might become like them, but none is given to very young individuals with severe mental defects because we will never become like them.

There are also problems with Narveson's claim that there is a good reason to protect the interests of young mental defectives because their rational relatives will have an interest in them. For example, this approach makes the duty to protect the defectives' interests wholly contingent on other beings' having, and continuing to have, a sentimental interest in them. Suppose Smith despises his mentally defective infant, and also suppose that Smith could benefit from having his infant painfully experimented on as part of a trivial research project. Regan correctly asks: "What shred of an argument can the proponent of egoism give as to why Smith should not volunteer his son, or, if it is in my self-interest to help Smith 'close the deal,' why I should not assist him? . . . The gears of right conduct are not so finely meshed with those of self-interest that we cannot profit personally by doing what is wrong."[20] The best response to Regan that Narveson's grounds permit seems to be that we should be opposed to *trivial* research that is painful to animals because it is not in our self-interest: it is a waste of tax dollars. Or again, on Narveson's grounds we should be opposed to trivial research so that neither we nor our loved ones will be subject to it; such opposition is a prudent insurance policy.

But what if some young mental defectives will have no rational relatives who care for them? We would then have no duty to protect their interests. Regan's more defensible view is that it is because pain itself is an evil that we have a theoretical starting point, not the fact that others happen to take an interest in minimizing the pain of such young unfortunates. Our pretheoretical convictions point to the need to posit the existence of individual rights not only to human beings who have high-level rational capacities but also to mental defectives, young and old. It is only on this basis that we can account for our belief that it is wrong to inflict gratuitous suffering on them:

> It is also the case that the principles which can legitimately be appealed to as a basis for overriding this right of humans, if humans have it, must be the same ones that must be appealed to if we are justifiably to override the rights of these animals. Thus, if we would object to using morons routinely as subjects in painful, trivial research because it violates *their* right not to be made to suffer gratuitously, we shall have just as much reason to object to the use of animals in such research on the grounds that it violates *theirs.*[21]

A word is necessary here regarding pretheoretical intuitions. Some might object at this point that Regan-like defenders of the AMC are more than willing to take seriously their pretheoretical intuition that it is impermissible to harm marginal cases but not that it is permissible to experiment painfully on animals if data valuable for human beings cannot be obtained otherwise. There is no necessary inconsistency here, however, for whereas the former intuition is considered, the latter is largely unconsidered. That is, on reflection and after dialectical examination, we certainly do not want to give up the pretheoretical intuition that it is wrong to harm marginal cases, but once examined critically it is by no means clear that we can with equanimity hold onto our pretheoretical intuition regarding the permissibility of painful experimentation on animals. Some, such as Regan and myself, wish to say that this pretheoretical intuition is an inaccurate guide to moral conduct. Even those who wish to follow the lead of this pretheoretical intuition can do so only with a grain of salt or an element of irony. Or better, if they really do consider the pains to animals that are being permitted, they can assent to this pretheoretical intuition, but with a nervous twitch.

Narveson's position contrasts with my view and Regan's. The obvious consequence of this position is that individuals who are unable to enter into contracts and reciprocate with other rational agents cannot possibly have rights. Nevertheless, it would be a superficial reading of his position to think that Narveson is categorically denying moral beneficiary status to marginal cases and animals. He is denying that we have any *direct* duties to these beings. If we protect the mentally enfeebled only because we might eventually become so, however, then this protection will not be extended to those who become mentally enfeebled *before* they are sufficiently mature enough to reciprocate with moral agents. Narveson, therefore, as Regan argues, stands to gain a great deal of insurance by paying very little premium. But the really troubling part is that the mentally enfeebled, who stand to lose a great deal, need not sway Narveson in the least.[22] To treat a being as though it has rights is a far cry from treating it as a right-bearer. Further, this "as though" or "as if" proviso in Narveson's thought on the AMC indicates an inconsistency in his rational egoism, an indication of his implicit acceptance of a moral premise that runs counter to rational egoism.[23] That is, if Narveson were consistent in his rational egoism, he would deny that marginal cases and animals have rights, period.

Dale Jamieson notices another feature of Narveson's stance regarding the AMC, but not one that is favorable to Narveson. Assume that claim making is a linguistic activity that animals lack. Languageless humans also lack this activity, however. Perhaps young children and some mental defectives can make claims, but Narveson and other rational egoists probably cannot concede rights to them, in that young children and mental defectives are not likely to reciprocate. That is, Narveson's criteria for right-possession are extraordinarily high. Not only would he deny rights to the merely sentient, including the right to be spared gratuitous pain, but he would also have to deny rights to those who, although they can verbalize their demands, nonetheless fall short of the ability to enter into contracts. Languageless animals and human beings, as well as some human beings with language, are all denied rights. Because they are denied rights, we can imagine situations where the indirect duties we might have to these beings, on Narveson's view, could be too easily overridden. According to Jamieson, unscrupulous businesses might kidnap mental defectives and sell them to medical schools, and consent forms might be forged (as now occurs regarding animals). The only way to prevent these and other practices is to appeal, once again, to the sentimental interests of moral agents—assuming, of course, that those close to a particular animal or mentally defective human being *do* have sentimental interests. Jamieson's instructive view is summarized in the following lines:

> The moral framework that emerges from rational egoism is inherently unstable. As the beliefs, desires, and circumstances of rational egoists shift, so might their disposition of infants and mental defectives. Ultimately "marginal humans" are no better off than animals from the "perspective" of rational egoism. Both enjoy whatever moral status they do by the grace of rational egoists. Today it might be rational to deny the relevance of animal suffering; tomorrow it might be rational to deny the relevance of the suffering of infants and idiots. Because it is a bad moral theory, rational egoism fails to provide a solid basis for a principled indifference to the suffering of animals.[24]

We would perhaps do well to take Lawrence Haworth seriously, along with Regan and Jamieson, in exploring the possibility that animals and the marginal cases, because they are sentient (and some perhaps even capable of making claims), have rights even though they cannot participate with us in a system of mutual restrictions.[25]

Rawls and the Original Position

Several scholars have treated the relationship between John Rawls's views and animals, but their results are often at odds with one another. The purpose of the present section of the chapter is twofold. First, I will try to bring together for the first time Rawls's thoughts on animals in *A Theory of Justice* (1971), as well as the often contradictory secondary literature on this topic. My hope is that by doing this we will have a reticulative grasp of the whole picture regarding Rawls's view of marginal cases and animals and the problems with this view, not merely one narrow aspect of the problem at hand. Second, I will examine for the first time Rawls's treatment of marginal cases and animals in his long-awaited book *Political Liberalism* (1993). I will be concerned with the degree to which Rawls in this book resolves, or fails to resolve, the problems with his view of marginal cases and animals as pointed out by his critics.

Rawls is abundantly clear in *A Theory of Justice* both that his theory of justice as fairness is not a complete contract theory (in that he is considering only the principle of justice) and that the contractarian idea could be extended to include an entire ethical system. Animals are not included in his particular theory of justice as fairness, but Rawls does not think that there could be a contractarian account of animals even in a complete ethical theory, in that contractarian accounts include only relationships we have with other people.[26]

In *A Theory of Justice* Rawls holds that animals are regulated in a contractarian account of justice, an account that includes the concept of equality; three levels of this concept are distinguishable in the book. The concept of equality applies, first, to the regular administration of institutions as public systems of rules and, second, to the application of these rules. Rawls insists that animals are excluded from these two levels of equality simply because their status is not the same as that of human beings.

It is only with respect to the third level of equality that Rawls indicates what it is about animals that excludes them from consideration. Human beings are moral persons, he thinks, and animals are not; hence only the former are covered by the concept of equality. Moral persons are distinguished by two features: (a) they are capable of having, and are assumed to have, a conception of their good as expressed by a rational plan of life, and (b) they are capable of having, and are assumed to acquire, a sense of justice. Thus, those who have the capacity to take part in the original position are owed equal justice. It should be noted that Rawls seems to assume that all human beings are moral persons with these two features. Or better, he assumes that moral personality is a potentiality that is ordinarily realized in due course. We are not told how we should deal with the extraordinary (i.e., marginal) cases.[27]

The status of extraordinary or marginal cases of humanity is further obscured when Rawls claims that the capacity for moral personality is a sufficient condition for being entitled to equal justice. By "leaving aside" the question of whether moral personality is a necessary condition for being entitled to equal justice, he is able, he thinks, to cover the "overwhelming majority of mankind." In addition, he thinks that there is no serious problem regarding the remaining cases: "We cannot go far wrong in supposing that the sufficient condition is always satisfied."[28] That is, on Rawls's view, even if the capacity for having a sense of justice were a necessary condition for receiving justice, it would be "unwise in practice" to withhold justice on this ground in that such a withholding of justice would pose a risk to just institutions and, presumably, to the normal cases of humanity.

Rawls is correct in noting that the sufficient condition for equal justice, the capacity for moral personality, is not stringent in the sense that no race or recognized group of human beings lacks this attribute. What Rawls does not confront in *A Theory of Justice,* however, is how to account theoretically for those "scattered" individuals who lack the requisite capacity for moral personality, either from birth or by accident. On contractarian grounds one can grant full protection of justice to all those who have a minimal level of moral personality, even to those who have a lesser sense of justice than others. For example, some people can more easily than others marshal arguments and apply principles in particular cases, and some people can more easily than others develop the virtues of impartiality and integrity. Nonetheless, all the guarantees of justice are granted only if some minimal level of moral personality is present.[29]

Equality must apply to some class or other, Rawls thinks, but to which one? He opts for the class of human beings, because members of this class possess the "range property" of moral personality, a property that Rawls sees as a natural capacity. Although he does not want to defend different grades of citizenship, his egalitarianism here depends on a certain minimal level of moral personality being generally filled so as to justify universal application of the principles of justice to human beings. The gap here between what is generally, but not universally, the case regarding moral personality is partially closed when it is realized that Rawls has a capacity in mind and not a realization. Thus, infants who have not yet developed their capacity for moral personality nonetheless receive the full protection of the principles of justice.[30]

It does not escape Rawls's notice that a full discussion of justice would have to take up various special cases of lack of moral personality. For example, those who have temporarily lost their realized capacity for moral personality through accident or mental stress can, like children, be protected, for they still have the capacity, albeit temporarily in an unrealized state. Rawls is a bit glib, however, regarding those whose misfortune is far greater: "But those more or less permanently deprived of moral personality may present a difficulty. I cannot examine this problem here, but I assume that the account of equality would not be materially affected."[31] The glibness can be seen in Rawls's use of the word *may* and in his assumption that his account of equality will not be materially affected by the analysis of the truly marginal cases, those individuals that do not possess even the capacity for a sense of justice. Rawls does not help matters much when he says that "those who can give justice are owed justice" and that it is *only* having a sense of justice that matters regarding the question of who is owed justice. Indeed, it is precisely this sort of contractarianism that gives rise to the problem of marginal cases.

The preceding observations seem to indicate that there is no room for an animal rights position in Rawls, except perhaps if one pressed the AMC on Rawls so as to suggest that *if* he is willing to guarantee equal justice to the marginal cases, he must also be willing to guarantee it to animals that are at the same level of mental, psychological, and affective development as those marginal cases. There is a second possibility, however.

Although no protection is given to animals in Rawls's justice as fairness, it is crucial to note that a conception of justice is but one part of an overall moral view. We do have natural duties in regard to animals, it seems, and perhaps to them directly (Rawls is confusing on these points). Rawls notices that animals can feel pain, and apparently this capacity leads him to say that it is wrong to be cruel to animals: this is perhaps what Rawls means by a duty of compassion *to* animals. Rawls also seems to be committed to a "duty of humanity" *regarding* animals, in Thomistic or Kantian fashion: if we abuse animals, we will be more likely to abuse human beings. In any event, natural duties to or regarding animals are in a sense outside the scope of the contract doctrine. These duties arise from the concept of natural duty itself and from a metaphysical view of the world wherein natural order and our place in it are described. Rawls obviously does not supply such a metaphysics in *A Theory of Justice,* but he does (surprisingly) suggest one in *Political Liberalism.*[32]

The concept of natural duty becomes understandable when we realize that it is redundant to have reasonable contractors promise not to murder each other. We need the reasonable contract for the difficult cases. It is crucial to notice that Rawls himself lists among our natural duties the duty not to harm or injure another and the duty not to cause unnecessary suffering. In fact, these two negative duties are, according to Rawls, stronger than any positive natural duties we might have. These natural duties apply without regard to our voluntary acts, as in those found in the original position, and without regard to our institutional relationships. These features are what suggest the propriety of the adjective *natural.*[33]

If there is a natural duty not to cause unnecessary suffering, it makes sense to suggest that this duty applies to all beings who have the capacity to suffer—say, to all beings with central nervous systems. Although this natural duty does not presuppose an act of consent, it is in Rawls's view "derived from a contractarian point of view," and hence Rawls need not hold that it applies to animals. Natural duties hold unconditionally for Rawls, and they are more fundamental than obligations that arise in the social contract; nonetheless, because they are viewed as fundamental and unconditional *from the perspective of* the social contract, it is not always clear in his account that animals, lacking a moral personality, are owed natural duties. Likewise, this view entails a natural duty to bring about a great good if we can do so easily (otherwise the action is supererogatory), but Rawls fails to indicate clearly whether we have such a duty if the primary beneficiaries of this great good are animals.[34]

Before moving to Rawls's critics, I can sum up what I have alleged about Rawls's view of animals in *A Theory of Justice* as follows: although there does not appear to be room for equal justice for animals as a result of deliberations in the original position, questions remain about (a) the possibility of the AMC being used so as to render Rawls's view more consistent and (b) the possibility of the argument from sentiency being used so as to make greater sense of Rawls's view of natural duty.

Regan notes that in an early work by Rawls ("The Sense of Justice")[35] having a sense of justice is a necessary and sufficient condition for receiving justice; the aforementioned view of animals in *A Theory of Justice* is thus a somewhat more favorable one for animals, for the later work identifies having a sense of justice only as being sufficient for receiving justice. On Regan's view, however, neither the strong view in "The Sense of Justice" (that animals are not owed justice) nor the weak view in *A Theory of Justice* (that it does not *seem* that animals are owed justice) is compatible with what Rawls seems to say about natural duties.[36]

Rawls's position regarding natural duties leads to the following dilemma: either being a moral person is a decisive consideration for determining those to whom we have (or seem to have) natural duties, or it is not a decisive consideration. If it is a decisive consideration, then we have no natural duties to animals, contra what Rawls sometimes indicates. If it is not a decisive consideration, then Rawls might have to defend not only natural duties to animals but perhaps the duty to be just to them as well. Or again, there is some textual evidence to suggest that Rawls thinks that animals ought not to be treated cruelly even though they are not themselves bound by the natural duty not to be cruel.[37] Why not also say, according to Regan, that animals ought to be treated justly even if they are not duty bound to be just?

In addition to pointing out a dilemma regarding Rawls's view of natural duties, Regan holds that the original position should be reconceived. Even if we assume that only reasonable human beings can inhabit the original position, this does not necessarily mean that only they can be incarnated when the veil of ignorance is lifted. That is, the veil of ignorance needs to be thicker so as to occlude vision not only of one's race, class, and sex but also of one's species, as Donald VanDeVeer has also argued. The reason for this thicker veil is that animals have individual welfare in the sense that their experiential lives can go well or ill for them. At the very least, they can be treated cruelly, as Rawls himself admits. As Regan also emphasizes, the AMC can be used against Rawls, in that many marginal human beings that Rawls might want to protect in the original position (Rawls is unclear here) no more possess moral personality than do most higher animals (i.e., those with central nervous systems).

Alan Fuchs's response to Regan is peculiar; Fuchs claims that natural duties are necessarily extended only to moral agents, which leads him to deny flatly that Rawls holds that we have a natural duty of noncruelty to animals. That is, when Rawls speaks of a duty of noncruelty to animals, he is not speaking of a natural duty. The question for Fuchs is this, however: if the duty to avoid being cruel to animals does not arise for Rawls out of the original position (all agree on this point—although some think that it should so arise), and it is not a natural duty (Fuchs's view), what kind of duty is it, given that these two sorts of duty seem to exhaust the Rawlsian options? In any event, Fuchs is to be commended at least for reminding us that the original position has as much to do with Rawls's Kantian view of the status of moral agents (and of their relations with animals) as with a concern for impartiality. The only way for a Kantian or a Rawlsian to acknowledge duties to animals, he thinks, would be to show that some of them (e.g., dolphins or chimpanzees) have the reasonableness and sense of justice requisite for moral agency.[38]

Regan criticizes Rawls in at least three ways: first, he sees a dilemma involved in Rawls's treatment of natural duties; second, he thinks that the AMC can be used to render Rawls's own view more consistent; and third, he sees the need for a revised original position. I want to examine this last criticism more closely.

VanDeVeer has developed a revised original position so as to identify principles that would reasonably adjudicate conflicting claims among all sentient creatures. Remember that parties in the original position must assume that they will turn out to be among the least advantaged, including the possibility of being among the least rational. In fact, they might turn out to be severely retarded. Even if only 1 percent of the human population fails to have a moral personality on Rawls's criteria (a sense of justice and a rational plan of life), we are dealing with a significant number of people, perhaps tens of millions of them: anencephalic infants, the seriously psychotic, a subset of Down's syndrome persons, the severely retarded, the senile, the irreversibly comatose, and so on. There is no reason to think that Rawls would deny that we have duties of some sort to such beings, and as previously mentioned, he explicitly says that it would be unwise in practice to withhold treatment from them.[39]

If we ought to extend treatment to marginal cases even though they are not owed it, we are obviously left with a puzzle. A more efficacious way to deal with the matter at hand is to say, along with VanDeVeer, that the Rawlsian difference principle entails duties to those sentient yet nonrational human beings who are not moral persons, as well as to sentient yet nonrational animals that are not moral persons. Participants in the original position should choose principles for all beings with interests, or better, for all beings concerning whom we can speak of *their own* well-being or ill-being. Rawls's own (apparent) natural duty not to be cruel to animals (contra Fuchs) seems to imply this. To choose in favor of marginal cases but not animals solely on the basis of species membership is, as Regan and others have emphasized, to be speciesist, a failing that is analogous to being classist, racist, or sexist. VanDeVeer puts the matter this way: "If, then, the original position were fully neutral, its participants would not only have to be ignorant of the race, sex, or social position qua participants [in the just society], it would seem that they would have to be ignorant of their species membership as well—subject only to the qualification that they shall have interests as participants [in the just society]. This version of the original position is not that of Rawls. Yet . . . it is not clear why it ought not to be."[40]

If we knew we were to be incarnated as white or black, racist principles would more likely be chosen in the original position than if we did not have this knowledge. Likewise, if we assumed that we would be incarnated as human beings, speciesist principles would more likely be chosen than if we did not have this knowledge. If, however, we assume that we might each be incarnated as a sentient, nonrational being (of whatever species), it would be reasonable in the original position to insist on duties to such a being, provided such a being posed no serious threat to others. It does not help much to respond by saying that animals do not even have the possibility of becoming moral persons when it is realized that permanently retarded or senile human beings do not have this possibility either. However, this revised original position is still compatible with due attention being paid to the more sophisticated interests of rational beings.

Tom Huffman is like VanDeVeer in seeing the need for a revised original position, but Huffman emphasizes the fact that there is something inadequate about the following claim, a claim that is at least hinted at by Rawls and made explicit by other contract theorists: the human species is deemed uniquely morally significant because its members *typically* are moral persons with a sense of justice. But this is precisely speciesism, in that the characteristics of individual animals and human beings are being ignored: "If we start down the road of including beings within our scope of moral concern simply because they are members of some group or another, we may just as easily *exclude* others because of their group membership. This strategy is, of course, typical of racism, sexism and all of the other 'isms' which seek to assign individuals more or less moral value than others based on their membership in some group."[41] The proper task for parties in the original position is to protect any individual with a makeup sufficiently sophisticated to allow it to suffer pain or harm. Even if such an individual might not be a moral agent, there is nothing that logically prevents it from being a moral beneficiary. It is quite common for us to enter into a contract for the sake of another who is not a moral agent, as in a contract with a day care center or with a home for the mentally defective.

Rawls's account of the social contract is much more abstract than traditional (strictly political) social contract theories are. According to Huffman, this helps to explain how the interests of sentient yet nonrational beings could, and indeed should, be considered in the original position. Those in the original position are rational and mutually disinterested, but Rawls himself admits that they might not have these qualities when they are incarnated. The one restriction on the scope of this incarnation is that the being in question can benefit from the decisions made by the reasonable and mutually disinterested parties in the original position: marginal cases and animals can so benefit; rocks and insects and plants (presumably) cannot. An example from fiction is helpful: In *Flowers for Algernon,* by Daniel Keyes, a severely retarded man is made temporarily rational (in fact, a genius) by a miracle drug that eventually wears off. We can easily imagine the demands he would make while rational regarding how he would like to be treated when the drug wears off. It should not be too hard to do the same were the subject in question a chimpanzee, a cow, or a laboratory mouse.[42]

Lilly-Marlene Russow objects to the attempts, like those of VanDeVeer and Huffman, to have some of the participants in the original position incarnated as animals without having properly understood what the original position is supposed to accomplish. The original position, she urges, was set up in response to utilitarianism—specifically, utilitarianism's failure to respect individuality. Individuality involves having and caring about a life plan. Thus, she thinks, participants in the original position can be incarnated only as moral persons, that is, as moral agents. Animals can enter the original position on this basis only if they are moral agents (as may be the case with respect to chimpanzees and dolphins). That is, Russow views philosophers such as VanDeVeer and Huffman not so much as stating what could or should be done with the Rawlsian original position as introducing new themes that are independent of—indeed, contrary to—Rawls's basic ideas.[43]

Russow admits that we cannot be assured that participants in the original position will be as clever in real life as they are behind the veil of ignorance (recognizing valid arguments, grasping economic calculations, etc.). To maintain her focus on the role of moral personhood in Rawls, however, she must also emphasize (indeed, like Fuchs, she must overemphasize) the tentative and equivocal treatment of animals in *A Theory of Justice.* If moral personhood were the whole story in Rawls, he would not even be tentative and equivocal; rather, he would explicitly and unequivocally deny that we have any duties to animals. He does not do this, however, and hence there is an aperture through which VanDeVeer and Huffman can crawl. Further, Regan as much as Rawls can counteract the defects in utilitarianism, but the former can do so without largely excluding animals from the realm of moral beneficiary status.

It is also significant that Russow is not bothered by the fact that, strictly speaking, Rawls does not include marginal cases in his theory of justice. Rather, she is consoled by the fact that the theory of justice is only part of morality, the part that deals with what reasonable moral agents would agree to in a social contract. Nevertheless, at least in the article in question, Russow does little to show how marginal cases and animals at the same level of sentiency are to be protected in a full-blown morality. If they are not included in the social contract, are there natural duties to them? Or will marginal cases and animals be protected by our comprehensive religious, moral, or philosophical views, of which the theory of justice is only a part? In any event, Regan, VanDeVeer, and Huffman have shown that Russow is premature in claiming that those who defend the argument from marginal cases discredit contractarian views from the outset. In fact, these three thinkers have shown an interest in working *within* the contractarian position so as to improve it.

Steve Sapontzis, however, unlike Regan, VanDeVeer, and Huffman, does think that it is precisely the "contractarian attitude" that eliminates animals from Rawlsian concern. The question, "what sorts of beings are owed the guarantees of justice?" is itself prejudicial in that the issue of who is *owed* something ordinarily presupposes that the benefit has to be earned. Hence, the contractarian approach seems of necessity to treat animals (and marginal cases) prejudicially.[44]

I now want to sum up what I think can be learned thus far about Rawls and animals from my treatment of *A Theory of Justice* and from the various commentators on the view of animals in that monumental work.

Eleven points should be emphasized. The first five deal with *A Theory of Justice* itself. (1) Rawls is clear that as a result of the social contract, no duties of justice are owed to animals, in that they are not moral persons with a sense of justice and a rational plan of life. (2) Rawls is not as clear, however, regarding the degree to which an entire ethical system can be produced on a contractarian basis. For example, if even natural duties are owed only to moral persons (i.e., to moral agents), then there seems to be no place whatsoever for duties to animals to arise in Rawlsian theory, not even the duty not to be cruel. (3) But Rawls suggests that we *do* have a duty not to be cruel to animals. (4) Rawls's lack of clarity here is also exhibited when he insists that moral personality is only a sufficient condition for being owed equal justice, not a necessary condition. (5) Moreover, although Rawls offers no theoretical defense of the duty to be just, or not to be cruel, to the marginal cases of humanity, he does indicate that it would be unwise *in practice* to withhold these duties in our treatment of them.

The next four points deal with Rawls's defenders. (6) Neither Russow nor Fuchs offers a theoretical defense of the duties owed to marginal cases, so that this crucial lacuna in Rawls's thought remains. (7) These defenders of Rawls do not clear up the relationship between natural duties and animals. If all natural duties apply only to moral persons and never to animals, as Russow and Fuchs contend, then what sort of duty is the duty not to be cruel to animals, mentioned by Rawls himself? (8) It is not clear that the only sort of individuality relevant in moral matters is that which comes from having a life plan, as Russow implies, for the sort of individuality made possible by sentiency may also be morally relevant, as when we use the phrase "pain in *my* leg." (9) Furthermore, if duties to animals and marginal cases are not the result of the social contract and are not instances of natural duty, are they then due to some comprehensive religious, moral, or philosophical theory wider than but including both the theory of justice and natural duties? (As I will show, Rawls responds affirmatively to this question in *Political Liberalism.*)

The final two points concern Rawls's detractors or reformers. (10) Sapontzis thinks that contractarianism itself is the problem, in that it creates insuperable problems in the effort to protect animals (and marginal cases). (11) Regan, VanDeVeer, and Huffman, however, all indicate (albeit in different ways; e.g., VanDeVeer is not a big fan of the AMC) that Rawls's view could be improved in two significant respects: (a) Rawls could make it clear that the duty we have not to be cruel to animals is a natural duty, and hence it would then have an identifiable place in Rawlsian theory. If Rawls were to do this, the consequences of this duty could be adequately explored regarding several practical matters such as eating, wearing clothes, testing products, experimenting, and so on. In addition (b), duties to animals could be enhanced through a consideration of the AMC, but only after Rawls himself clarified the status of the duties to marginal cases that he seems to have in mind.

These preliminary conclusions are reinforced through a consideration of a debate between Michael Pritchard and Wade Robison, on the one hand, and Robert Elliot, on the other.[45] The former think that a revised original position would enormously complicate the calculations of reasonable persons in that position and that by considering animals we would conflate Rawls's theory of justice (which is applicable only to human beings, they think) with the derivation of morality in general (where animals are presumably included). That is, the proposed change in the original position would entail a fundamental change in Rawls's contractarianism.

Nonetheless, Elliot is like Regan, VanDeVeer, and Huffman in thinking that Rawls's own veil of ignorance is too thin and that Rawls's defenders are unpersuasive in their efforts to keep it thin with regard to knowledge of one's species. Rawls too readily assumes that excluding marginal cases from justice will weaken just institutions but excluding animals will not. He can do this only by confusing a biological classification with a moral one. The regulative ideal provided by the social contract can affect animals in many ways—say, regarding what can easily be seen as their primary goods or their share of the wealth: a livable habitat. Further, Elliot is correct to emphasize that comparative judgments regarding the interests of human beings and animals are not as problematic as Pritchard and Robison suggest. In fact, these judgments might be easier when they concern animals than when they concern human beings, in that animal interests are comparatively more straightforward and less abstract: animals simply want food and the space necessary to express their desires and so on. To give animals their due regarding these basic goods does not contradict the belief that there are varieties of moral concern in addition to those associated with justice, as in those concerns regarding what virtuous people would do in regard to animals in addition to what they would do minimally as a matter of justice.

My task now is to see the degree to which Rawls's treatment of animals in *Political Liberalism* can help to shore up his defenders' efforts and to respond to his critics.

Rawls's Political Liberalism

Not much help is given in *Political Liberalism* regarding how Rawls would deal with the status of marginal cases, a question that he says he will "put aside for the time being." As before, he wishes to deal with an idealized and simplified case—moral persons—in order to focus on what he sees as the main question, which in this case is the question of public political culture. He knows that there are "problems of extension" with which he must eventually deal: extending justice as fairness to future generations, extending it to cover international law, and extending it to cover marginal cases and animals (and the rest of nature). Apparently he thinks that if we start with the principles of justice defended in *A Theory of Justice,* move to the particular area of extension, return to the principles of justice, and so on, we can engage in a back-and-forth procedure that will eventually give us an adequate account of our moral relations with marginal cases and animals.[46]

But Rawls is ambivalent in *Political Liberalism.* On the one hand, he explicitly admits that justice as fairness, in particular, and contractarianism, in general, ultimately might fail the test regarding the effort to extend the social contract so as to include marginal cases and animals. On the other hand, he is (again) glib in his assumption that marginal cases can conveniently be set aside until later. Until that time he is content to deal with the normal cases. Or better, the parties behind the veil of ignorance do not know what natural talents and habits they will have when the veil is lifted, but they *do* know that these talents and abilities will be within the normal human range. What this means is that the attempts of Regan, VanDeVeer, Huffman, and Elliot to revise the original position so as to use the AMC to extend Rawlsian concern from marginal cases to animals (in that the AMC can be rephrased as the argument for moral consistency) are not so much refuted as ignored. Rawls stops this effort to use the AMC in its tracks by leaving the status of marginal cases in a precarious position, the same precarious position found in *A Theory of Justice.*[47]

For Rawls in *Political Liberalism,* the key issue regarding animals concerns when a question can be successfully resolved by public reason. Many questions, it seems, cannot be resolved by Rawlsian public reason, not even by what Rawls calls a "complete" public reason. There are at least four major "problems of extension" for Rawls to deal with in his defense of public reason. One is the problem of extending justice to future generations (i.e., the problem of just savings). A second problem is that of extending it to principles that apply in international law. The third problem is that of extending justice so as to develop principles governing just distribution of health care. Although Rawls does not deal with these problems in any more detail here than he did in *A Theory of Justice,* he is nonetheless confident that they can be reasonably dealt with under justice as fairness.

Regarding the fourth problem of extension, the effort to extend justice to animals and the rest of nature, however, Rawls is ambivalent, as I have shown, and he is not nearly as sanguine as he is regarding the other three problems of extension. He is less optimistic regarding animals because if we take for granted the full status of adult (normal) persons in society, we can easily proceed forward to other generations of such persons, outward to other societies that contain such persons, and inward to consider the health care needs of such persons, but we cannot easily include animals because they are not moral persons (chimpanzees and dolphins aside). According to the principles contained in the revised original position, however, one should also move outward to the least advantaged cases of humanity, to those marginal cases who are nonrational yet sentient, and to be consistent, to animals that are also nonrational yet sentient.[48] That Rawls should altogether ignore the revised original position and the AMC in his later work is a significant omission.

From what has been said thus far, it might seem that Rawls has not advanced his position one iota beyond his view of animals found in *A Theory of Justice.* Nonetheless, in a surprising move he introduces a comprehensive moral view that is far wider than the view that would be agreed on by reasonable persons in the original position trying to establish principles of justice and principles of public reason. That is, what we agree to in the original position will most likely be far less than what is included in our own comprehensive moral view, in that what we are looking for in the social contract is an overlapping consensus that can be reached with those who have moral views that, although reasonable and comprehensive, differ from one's own, perhaps radically so. In fact, it is the existence of reasonable pluralism of comprehensive religious, philosophical, or moral views that creates the need for a social contract and public reason.

Rawls's surprise move consists in invoking what he sees as the traditional Christian view of animals and the rest of nature, a view that is certainly not everyone's comprehensive view. On this comprehensive view animals are seen as subject to our use and wont. Rawls apparently likes this view because it is clear and practical.[49] We can further our own good and that of future generations by using animals and the rest of nature judiciously; we can improve human health through biological and medical knowledge gained through animals and the rest of nature; and by protecting the beauty of nature, we can enhance public recreation and a deeper understanding of the world.

Even if it is reasonable to adopt this stance in the original position (a questionable assumption), it is obviously not the only plausible candidate for adoption, nor does it help Rawls to argue against the revised original position proposed by Regan, VanDeVeer, Huffman, and Elliot. Rawls seems to be attempting to set up a battle between two comprehensive views, between what he sees as the traditional Christian view of animals and a view found in what he calls "natural religion." This latter view he identifies as a stewardship view, in contrast to the anthopocentrism traditionally found in Christianity. Rawls's usual evenhandedness is not in evidence in his treatment of these contrasting views, however. To adopt the stewardship view of natural religion, he thinks, is not a constitutional essential or a basic question of justice *as these questions are specified* in the original position; public reason does not apply to the concern for animals shown by the natural religionist. Natural religionists are free to try to convince other citizens of their (nonpolitical) views, he admits, but they should not assume that reasonable people will or even should agree with them. The question to be asked of Rawls, however, is whether the traditional Christian view of animals that he apparently adopts is to be identified as a constitutional essential or a basic matter of justice any more than is the stewardship view he apparently rejects.[50] Perhaps Rawls treats the traditional Christian view favorably because all the reasons he cites in its favor are anthropocentric reasons for respecting animals and the rest of nature, reasons that are more easily made compatible with the anthropocentrism of his version of the original position.

In addition to the preliminary conclusions reached in the previous section of the present chapter, two additional points should be made in the light of Rawls's most recent efforts to deal with animals in *Political Liberalism.*

First, there is a significant (I am tempted to say invidious) ambivalence in Rawls regarding animals. On the one hand, he sometimes assumes that marginal cases and animals can be put aside and that their moral status can eventually be clarified. On the other hand, he sometimes admits that his version of justice as fairness, in particular, and contractarianism, in general, might eventually fail in the effort to protect marginal cases and animals. His confidence regarding efforts to extend justice to future generations, to principles in international law, and to the health care needs of moral persons and his lack of confidence that it can be extended to animals indicate this ambivalence. Another indication lies in Rawls's decision not even to consider the revised original position as developed by several critics in the quarter-century or so since the publication of *A Theory of Justice;* it is hard to imagine that the efforts of all these critics could have escaped Rawls's notice. It is ironic that these critics have a great deal of admiration for Rawls's work; they think that he, like Columbus, has made a great discovery, but he is mistaken about the precise character of that discovery.

Second, Rawls compounds the felony committed in *A Theory of Justice.* In that earlier work he is not entirely clear about whether animals, left out of the original position both as moral agents and as moral beneficiaries, might be acknowledged as having some status as moral beneficiaries as a result of natural duties that antedate the social contract. In *Political Liberalism* he is equally unclear about the extent to which animals are to be primarily understood in terms of a comprehensive religious view that postdates the original position. That is, Rawls could be clearer both with respect to his Promethean foresight regarding which comprehensive view should succeed the original position and with respect to his Epimethean hindsight regarding the natural duties that precede the original position.

The fact that Rawls prefers one comprehensive view (the traditional Christian view, which he sees, perhaps erroneously, as anthropocentric)[51] to another (the stewardship view found in what he calls natural religion) seems to confirm what all the defenders of the revised original position have suspected: anthropocentrism is assumed from the outset in Rawls's original position and presumably constitutes a fundamental axiom that is not amenable to criticism. At the very least, one would hope that the deeper understanding of the world made possible by a study of animals,[52] a deeper understanding noticed by Rawls himself, would encourage him to put his anthropocentrism on the table for discussion.

VanDeVeer, Again

Something more needs to be said about VanDeVeer's view and some of its critics. Although VanDeVeer's commitment to modifying the original position so as to consider animal rights issues is firm, his commitment to the AMC is not strong. Only chimpanzees, he thinks, have greater morally relevant capacities than human persons with Down's syndrome; rabbits, for example, are not comparable to these persons.[53] But VanDeVeer realizes that this issue is complex. Consider the following argument:

1. If (a) human beings have a right not to be made to suffer gratuitously and (b) humans have it solely because they can suffer and pain is an evil, then animals which can suffer have a right not to be made to suffer gratuitously.
2. Assumptions (a) and (b) are true.
3. Hence, animals which can suffer have a right not to be made to suffer gratuitously.[54]

A critic might object to this argument by saying that part of (1) is false because human beings do not have such a right *solely* in virtue of their capacity to suffer. Rather, it might be alleged, human beings have such a right because they have some joint property, such as the ability to suffer *and* significant rational capacities. To hold this objection, however, means that infants with Tay-Sachs disease, who are not and never will be rational, cannot be made to suffer gratuitously. Such an objection cannot be sustained.

Although the old classification of retardates as idiots, imbeciles, and morons is outdated, VanDeVeer notes that morons were assumed to have an IQ of between 50 and 75; such individuals are typically capable of tasks as complex as running certain machines and laying brick. That is, despite the Tay-Sachs example cited by VanDeVeer himself, there is a question as to whether this example is much of a concession to the defender of the AMC: "One general point here is that moronic human beings are typically far superior (in terms of psychological capacities) to all or virtually all animals raised for food and all or virtually all animals raised for experimental research. For certain purposes this seems a relevant difference. Morons and humans with even lesser capacities differ from most of the more intelligent animals with respect to their range of capacities to suffer in certain ways."[55] Remember that both Singer and Regan take pains to distinguish among the different sorts of marginal cases. Regan, for example, seems to exclude the irreversibly comatose from the argument altogether, and he also distinguishes between those remaining marginal cases who have some mental and volitional abilities and those who are conscious and sentient but who do not even have these minimal mental and volitional abilities. Hence there might not be as much distance between Regan and VanDeVeer as VanDeVeer sometimes indicates. That is, idiots and imbeciles, on VanDeVeer's use of these terms, may more easily fit the AMC than morons who can run certain machines do. Furthermore, Regan admits that to the extent that a being has mental and volitional abilities, our duty not to inflict pain on it may rest on reasons beyond those appropriate to our treatment of a being who does not have these abilities—say, if the more advanced being has a greater ability to anticipate and dread the pain. Nonetheless, Regan is not convinced that *any* being who can experience pain is in a less-privileged position with respect to the prohibition against the infliction of gratuitous pain.

Some might object to VanDeVeer's revised original position by asking whether we should not go further and allow the possibility that when the Rawlsian veil of ignorance is lifted, we might turn out to be orchids or poison ivy, since we can intelligibly speak of the well-being of these things. Plants need not be seriously considered even in VanDeVeer's revised original position, however, because VanDeVeer, like Singer and Regan, sees sentiency as a necessary condition for rights. Some things may be "in the interest of" a plant, but only sentient beings have interests in the sense of their being satisfied or dissatisfied with their treatment; only sentient, conscious beings are subjects of their own lives. Hence VanDeVeer rests content with his own revised original position—the preoriginal position, as he calls it—a position that allows him to take animal rights seriously, but not necessarily on the basis of the AMC.[56]

According to Annette Baier, one of the problems with Rawls's work (and VanDeVeer's) is that he only gives the appearance of greater precision in moral theory than is present in an ethics of sentiments, such as Hume's. Baier relies on the Aristotelian principle that we should aim only at that degree of precision that our subject matter admits: "It may be a hard historical fact that the developed formal techniques in decision theory are those developed to meet the needs of capitalists and heads of armies. But that is no good reason to make ethics the moral equivalent of war."[57] Baier seems to exaggerate the strengths of Hume's ethics at the expense of any moral calculus, whether utilitarian or contractarian, but she is correct in emphasizing certain (Humean) virtues that have an impact on how we view both animals and marginal cases: kindness, friendship, good nature, considerateness, benevolence, good sense, and so on. If cruelty should be avoided in our dealings with marginal cases, surely it should also be avoided in our dealings with animals: "To limit one's concern to those sensible beings who are of one's own species is to be part-monster, but such monsters, alas, are not merely fancied ones. . . . Hume's version of human nature is a good basis from which to start, since it encourages us to respect, not to downgrade, the capacities we share with other animals."[58]

Humean theory, according to Baier, extends our moral concern, despite what VanDeVeer insists, from those human beings (future generations, the severely retarded, psychotics) who cannot have a reciprocal concern for us to animals that must fail to reciprocate. Although it seems that Baier, in her corrective efforts of Rawls (and VanDeVeer), is an adherent to the AMC, such is not the case. Rather, she highlights the "delicacy" and "judgment" that are shown when moral agents come into contact with moral beneficiaries, a delicacy and judgment that also indicate differences in the ways we should treat children, the severely retarded, the mentally ill, apes, and lambs. There *is* a moral difference, she thinks, between eating human and other flesh.[59]

In the final analysis, both Baier and VanDeVeer are opposed to the AMC. Nonetheless, VanDeVeer is helpful in the way he loosens up Rawls's version of the original position, wherein reciprocating moral agents are given almost exclusive attention. In addition, Baier is helpful in the way she recovers the Humean belief that reason alone cannot discern what is right. It should be remembered that Regan's transcendental argument is meant to explain how we can best account for our *intuition* that marginal cases can be treated in grossly immoral ways. Utilitarians such as Singer have a notoriously difficult time accounting for what Kai Nielson sees as a moral truism, that is, as something we just intuit: other things being equal, pleasure is good and pain (especially the gratuitous infliction of it) is bad.[60] Although moral philosophy might begin with intuitions, it certainly cannot end there. Narveson is correct to point out the following service done by Singer and Regan in applied ethics: they do not begin with a definition of ethical concepts and high-level pronouncements, but, as the AMC indicates, their method is to "identify what seem to be the major outlines of our considered moral beliefs, and then to bring logical analysis to bear on these to see whether they square with our apparent unconsidered attitude toward the particular matter under investigation."[61] This effort is rational to the core.

Rawls's requirement of reciprocity may initially seem plausible, but there are good reasons to reject it, as James Rachels argues. Having a moral obligation is quite different from being the beneficiary of one. Normal adult humans have the obligation not to torture each other, but we do not hold severely retarded human beings responsible for their actions, even if we think that torturing them would be treating them immorally. Animals, like retarded human beings, lack characteristics necessary to have obligations, even if they can be the beneficiaries of obligations. This is not to deny that there is the germ of a plausible idea in Rawls's reciprocity argument: if a person is capable of considering our interests and refuses to do so, then we may very well be released from any similar obligations we might have had to him, or at least our obligations to him are diminished, as Rachels rightly argues.[62]

Watson and Reciprocity

Richard Watson resembles most of the other thinkers criticized in this chapter in holding that the notion of an entity's rights makes sense only if that entity can fulfill reciprocal duties. If reciprocity is taken as being central to the concepts of rights and duties, then only a few animals have rights and duties in an intrinsic or direct or primary sense, even if they can be assigned them in an extrinsic, an indirect, or a secondary sense in connection with human interests. The animals that Watson has in mind for possible possession of primary rights and duties include chimpanzees, gorillas, dolphins, and dogs. Obviously the mere possession of sentiency is not enough to justify the primary rights and duties that Watson has in mind as a reciprocity theorist. However, Watson tries to protect his view by denying that beings without a right to life can be killed for trivial reasons. Like Singer, Watson believes that marginal cases and animals may be morally considerable without having an absolute or near absolute right to life.[63]

Like Watson, Peter Miller tries to push the case as far as possible for a morality confined to reciprocity relations. Such an effort is necessarily incomplete, however, as Miller emphasizes in the following list of beings (mostly moral beneficiaries) outside reciprocity relations: "A society of moral agents can attend and respond to other intrinsic goods apart from their own welfare. Our 'moral milieu,' for example, prescribes moral behavior toward amoral animals, idiots, and infants (avoid cruelty); toward immoral adults (turn the other cheek); and toward those too weak, powerless, incapacitated, or remote to reciprocate in kind (liberate the downtrodden and oppressed, feed the hungry, and preserve a viable world for future generations)."[64] The intrinsic goods found in these beings are ignored by reciprocity theorists, and as far as I can tell, those who defend the AMC receive little consolation from reciprocity theorists who say that marginal cases and animals can be the objects of indirect duties. As Lawrence Johnson points out, the parents of a slightly brain-damaged infant *might* be pained by the plight of their child, but then again they might be pleased if the infant is eliminated. Indirect duty views such as Watson's rather arbitrarily place the fate of marginal cases and animals on the shoulders of beings whose psychological and cultural assumptions are largely the result of contingent factors.[65] It is for this reason that Watson's view should be criticized.

On the Naturalistic Fallacy

All the reciprocity theorists indicate that rights cannot be grounded apart from agreements made by rational agents. In a way, the weak version of the AMC is compatible with their overall point, for the claim that animals have rights only if marginal humans have them does not commit these theorists to any natural property that grounds these rights. On the strong version of the AMC, however, where it is asserted that marginal cases *do* have rights, and hence animals have them as well, it is not so clear that we can avoid the naturalistic "fallacy." Perhaps the marginal cases, and hence animals, could be granted rights by virtue of attention being paid to them by rational agents, but as I have shown, there are problems with this position. For example, this view cannot explain why we think that even orphans and abandoned dogs can be mistreated. Hence, it makes sense to focus on the sentience of marginal cases and animals as being the grounds for our belief that they ought not to receive gratuitous pain. That is, to fully respond to the reciprocity theorists, some sort of response to G. E. Moore is required. It should be noted that the naturalistic fallacy, as Moore portrays it, consists in attempting to *define* moral predicates in terms of nonmoral ones; it does not consist in holding that certain factual characteristics may give rise to moral value, a view that Moore agrees with, as the last chapter of *Principia Ethica* makes clear.

Mary Midgley has done an excellent job of showing that there is no major problem in arguing from facts to values; the difficulty arises in getting both the facts and the values right. That is, *good* is problematic not because it is evaluative but because it is such a general term. I agree with Midgley that the naturalistic fallacy is a stuffed dragon and that philosophers should stop marching around with its head on their spears. Further, there is hyperbole in Moore's boast that he has discovered a single, simple fallacy so widespread as to vitiate almost all earlier moral reasoning. For Moore the *cordon sanitaire* around goodness is established by its being an ultimate simple, but a far more defensible view is that it, like any general term, is explainable in terms of its uses and provinces. For example, when Nietzsche says that war is good or that malice is a good quality in philosophers, we might say "Prove it" or "Explain yourself! Why are these things good?" Goodness is not so much something that is a clincher meant to conclude discussion as something that begins it. Moore erected a quasi-logical barrier meant to save him the trouble of arguing for his view of goodness.[66]

The weblike nature of language and of conceptual connectedness makes Moore's view of logical and metaphysical atomism quite unattractive today, in that it is integrally connected to a Humean, empiricist metaphysics wherein all beings in the universe, considered in themselves, appear entirely loose and independent of each other. It is this sort of approach, for example, that makes it possible for representatives of the tobacco industry (one of the greatest abusers of animals) to say that no amount of statistics can ever reveal causality between smoking and cancer. One pays quite a price for this view, as one does if one adopts Nietzsche's previously mentioned views. But what about the view that the infliction of gratuitous pain is a bad thing, as is torturing a being, starving it, or humiliating it? What we can notice here is that fact is opposed not so much to value as to unsubstantiated opinion or conjecture. Midgley uses Geoffrey Warnock to point out that it makes perfect sense to say that there are facts—even well-established ones—regarding evaluative matters. To say that inflicting gratuitous pain is wrong is not to say something that is infallible or complete, but to deny this claim is at the very least, like the previously cited Nietzschean claim or the one alluded to regarding the tobacco industry, to indicate in a rather bold way where the next conversation has to begin. Goodness is a determinable that can be instantiated in many ways, but it is exceedingly difficult to imagine how it can be associated with the view that it is morally permissible to inflict avoidable pain, and it is exceedingly difficult to imagine that one could get into trouble by associating it with pleasure that is conducive to the long-term well-being of a being capable of such pleasure. Perhaps there are certain mysteries about goodness, those treated by Plato, but they do not concern its general logical status, and they cannot be solved by trying to use the term without natural specifications.

Midgley is helpful not only in her attempt to put the naturalistic fallacy in its place but also in her attempt to encourage humility among animal rightists, in general, and defenders of the AMC, in particular: liberators historically have had a tendency to get puffed up with their accomplishments so as to fail to see their own oppressive acts.[67]

It will be helpful at this point to reiterate the connection between my treatment of the naturalistic fallacy and the AMC, on the one hand, and between this "fallacy" and reciprocity theorists, on the other. Regan is serious in claiming that *facts themselves* about animals impose duties on us. But if it is the (natural) fact that marginal cases and animals are sentient that gives rise to our moral duties to these beings, then Regan is dangerously close to holding the naturalistic fallacy to be no fallacy. I want to make it clear that this procedure would not bother me, in that I do not see the naturalistic fallacy as a problem. Nevertheless, it should bother Regan, for he is a latter-day defender of G. E. Moore. Again, the weak version of the AMC avoids Moorean criticism in that it states that if marginal cases have rights, then animals have them, too. I showed in chapter 1, however, that to avoid Singer's replaceability argument, one has to show that marginal cases do have rights. Neither Rawls nor any other contractualist or rational egoist is of much help here, in that marginal cases do not reciprocate. Regan correctly argues that our strong conviction that marginal cases can be treated in grossly immoral ways can be supported only if they have basic rights. But what lies at the end of this trail of justification from intuition or conviction to the postulation of basic rights, to inherent value, to subjects of a life, to . . . what? The end point must be sentiency.[68]

Even Rawls agrees with Regan here when he says that the capacity for feelings of pleasure and pain imposes some of our duties on us. Most moral philosophers who deal with the origin of basic moral concepts end up claiming that there is some objective component to such concepts contributed by nature and some subjective component contributed by moral agents. Extreme moral realists and extreme nominalists are hard to find. Regan, the G. E. Moorean, nonetheless points to the "facts themselves" about animals that "impose" certain duties on us; Rawls, the quintessential contractualist, nonetheless points to the capacity for pain that "imposes" some of our duties on us.

3

Frey's Challenge

Now that the AMC's complexity is apparent (chapter 1), and several criticisms of the argument from the perspective of the reciprocity objection have been considered, along with certain criticisms of this objection (chapter 2), I want to move to perhaps the most significant critic of the AMC, R. G. Frey. In this chapter I will also treat some other Frey-like critics and offer some rejoinders to the points made by these critics and by Frey, rejoinders that will rely on Stephen R. L. Clark's use of the history of philosophy to defend the AMC. I will nonetheless indicate how Frey's challenge to the AMC is to some extent similar to that offered by certain defenders of animal rights—Steve Sapontzis and Mary Anne Warren—who are, however, in different ways skeptical of the argument.

Frey's Criticisms

R. G. Frey begins by noting Tom Regan's analogy between what is in an animal's interest, even though the animal is not in a position to do anything to meet such interests, and what is in a baby's interest (e.g., a blood transfusion), even though the baby cannot itself secure such an interest. If there is a prescriptive or action-guiding overtone to "Treatment for worms is in Fido's interest," it applies not to Fido but to some other competent being. Frey responds to Regan's analogy by observing that eventually the baby will be in a position to see to its treatment, whereas Fido never will. Frey notes one of Regan's rejoinders to this view, but not a second possible one. Regan's rejoinder (a compelling one, I think) is that Frey has ignored the baby's present state in his potentiality argument. Even more important, however, is the charge that Frey speaks too confidently about the outcome to future contingencies when he says that babies *will be* rational adults. Perhaps they will, but perhaps they will not. I will return to the issue of time as asymmetrical at the end of the book.

It is easy to excuse Frey here for his confusion in replacing a contingent feature with a necessary one. More serious, however, is his belief that on Regan-like grounds marginal cases and animals would not have interests at all if there were no human beings around, a view that, if Regan held it, would surely be counterintuitive. According to Frey, if the prescriptive overtone of interest ascriptions in the cases of babies and animals is directed at and applies to competent (past, present, or future) human beings, and not to the possessors of those interests, then doctors cannot decide whether vitamin C is in a baby's interests until they first determine whether there will be people in the future who will look after the baby (here Frey does treat the future as contingent).[1] I have already shown, however, that Frey does not accurately report Regan's view, for there are at least two different senses of *interest:* (1) something can really be in an animal's or a marginal case's interest, quite apart from whether the animal or the marginal case notices this fact, and (2) a being can be "interested in" something. Frey does not accurately report (1).

Frey describes the AMC as follows:

1. Criterion X, while excluding animals, also excludes babies and the severely mentally-enfeebled from the class of right-holders;
2. Babies and the severely mentally-enfeebled, however, do have rights and so fall within this class;
3. Therefore, criterion X must be rejected as a criterion for the possession of rights.[2]

One point Frey chooses to emphasize regarding this argument is that it is negative and indirect, for it does not seek to establish that animals have rights; rather, it tries to undermine criteria whose application yields the result that animals do not have rights. Frey also mentions a second and perhaps contradictory point, however: the argument fails because it does try to establish something positive, as in the second premise. The second premise is suspect because it is not an open-and-shut case that babies and the severely mentally enfeebled have rights; to claim that they do requires defense. Frey does not think that such a defense is likely to be forthcoming, in that the three most likely defenses all fail.

First, one might try to include babies within the class of right-holders by means of a potentiality argument. Despite what seemed to be the case in an earlier article treated in chapter 1, in *Interests and Rights* Frey argues against the potentiality argument. Or better, he clarifies his earlier view: the potentiality argument does not establish that babies have rights, but the fact that the baby has potentiality for rationality puts it in a moral category different from Fido's. That is, Frey does not think that animals have rights, but he is also content to admit that, if actual rationality is the appropriate criterion for the possession of rights, then babies do not have rights either, even if they are in a different sort of moral relation to us than animals are. (In contrast, Regan and Dale Jamieson claim that if being rational means being able to make inferences, select the most efficient means of achieving certain ends, symbolize, and recognize instances of general concepts, then even some infant primates are potentially rational.)

Second, one might try to include the severely mentally enfeebled within the class of right-holders by means of the similarity argument: the severely mentally enfeebled have strong physical similarities to the remainder of our species, and it offends members of our species to deprive such similar creatures of rights. The similarity argument fails on the rationality requirement, but like the potentiality argument, it nonetheless distinguishes the severely mentally enfeebled from Fido, who does not bear anything like sufficient physical similarities to ourselves. Frey knows that he will be accused of speciesism here, in that he enshrines the active discrimination against other species in favor of our own. His defense of this active discrimination relies on an extremely misleading example, however: if we can save either a drowning human being or a drowning dog but not both, we should save the human being. This is not speciesism, however, for we can justify saving the human being not because the human being is a human being, which is a blatant begging of the question, but because the human being has, to use Peter Singer's language, a developed mental life with plans for the future, and so on, that the dog lacks. Put in Regan's terms, the human being and the dog have equal inherent value, yet the human being is more valuable than the dog because of the enhanced intrinsic values of the human being's experiences. (Once again, Regan and Jamieson think that in some cases animals will show stronger similarities to paradigmatic human beings than will nonparadigmatic human beings who are deformed.)

The third way one might try to include both babies and the severely mentally enfeebled is by means of a religious argument: they have immortal souls. Once again, Frey rejects this argument, and once again, he is quick to point out that the argument nonetheless separates both babies and the severely mentally enfeebled from animals. In other words, babies, the mentally enfeebled, and animals are alike in not being right-holders, hence premise 2 is false. Frey thinks that he has cast doubt also on premise 1, however, in that if any of the three attempts to establish that marginal cases have rights succeeds, then premise 1 is false. Since these attempts do not succeed, however, premise 2 is the main object of Frey's attack.[3]

Defenders of the AMC will no doubt be surprised that Frey has thus far ignored an argument for marginal cases and animals possessing rights on the basis of their being sentient and that when he does introduce such an argument, he does so in a highly skeptical mood. According to Frey, merely citing sentiency as a criterion for the possession of rights neither shows that it is one nor even creates a presumption that it is. Frey is at odds here with Kai Nielson, whom I cited earlier as holding as a moral truism or basic ethical axiom that sentient beings who can suffer ought not to be forced to suffer gratuitously. Frey (incredibly) wants us to show *why* the infliction of gratuitous suffering is wrong. Frey is correct, however, in suggesting that one needs to explain the implications that possession of sentiency has for the class of right-holders. Suppose being sentient makes one morally considerable; does this also give one a right to life? Singer thinks not, unless sentiency is buttressed by developed mental capacities. If *sentiency* merely refers to "reaction to stimuli," then a sentiency criterion for rights compels us to concede rights to plants and even to litmus paper, which are ludicrous results. On a slightly higher level, if *sentiency* is taken to mean "reaction to sensory stimuli," then a sentiency criterion compels us to concede rights even to the lowest forms of animal life, and most people would need a great deal of convincing that flies and ants have rights. On a higher level still, if *sentiency* is taken to mean the "capacity to feel pain," as it is taken by defenders of the AMC in the strong version, then many animals and all human beings must meet the criterion. The irreversibly comatose pose one possible exception, as Regan argues in distinction from Mary Anne Warren.[4]

Another possible exception, Frey thinks, is found in a human being who lapses into and out of a coma, thereby leading Frey to wonder whether this person's rights pass into and out of existence. This need not be the worry Frey thinks it is, however, if the comatose being is not only a potentially sentient being but also a past sentient and rational person who, if he or she recovers consciousness, will recover his or her memories and hopes, as well as the ability to experience pain. Surely this individual has rights even while in a coma, for the present comatose state is like dreamless sleep: both are moments in a life that is valuable.

It is not hard to see how sentiency in the sense of capacity to feel pain is grounded biologically. It stems from the possession of a central nervous system, a property that is not valued because any animal that exhibits it is thereby similar to us, as Frey alleges. Nor is this property problematic because there might be persons who follow us who might not have a central nervous system, as Frey hypothesizes. Rather, a central nervous system is morally relevant *because it makes possible pain states that are morally relevant if anything is morally relevant.* We are back to Regan's transcendental argument regarding the importance of postulating a subject of a life to account for what Karl Popper, along with Nielson and Regan, thinks is perhaps the strongest moral intuition we have: that cruelty is wrong. A sentiency criterion for rights is not merely, as Frey alleges, a lowest common denominator approach that is assumed so that the AMC can be rigged to ensure that animals will have rights. Quite apart from the AMC, there is massive evidence that the inflicting of gratuitous pain is immoral, and the AMC builds on this to point out that this evidence has implications for how animals ought to be treated. Severely disoriented and retarded yet sentient human beings surely desire things, even if they do not have beliefs on Frey's rather high-level criteria for possession of beliefs, and these desires have implications for how we ought to treat them.[5]

Frey would probably be unimpressed with Regan's transcendental argument that we must postulate X to account for Y, assuming for the moment that Frey does not believe in Y. If Y stands for the pretheoretical intuition that it is wrong to inflict gratuitous pain, however, then perhaps even Frey would agree with Y, if not with the postulation of X: marginal cases and animals are subjects of a life. In any event, even Frey would agree that any infliction of pain requires justification (only sadists, it seems, would disagree).

As a utilitarian Frey is willing to concede part of Singer's case. Animal life has some sort of value; at least higher animals deserve some moral consideration. Frey is much more intent to establish that not all animal life has the same value, however, a point that Singer and Regan are willing to concede with qualifications. In my view, however, Frey moves too quickly from the claim that animal life is not as valuable as normal adult human life to the claims that "serious" medical research can go on as usual and that eating chickens, say, is unproblematic. Chickens rarely achieve any individuality in our eyes, he thinks, such that one is pretty much as good as another. It is not clear that Frey could make this case regarding dogs or, for those who are familiar with them, with pigs or cows. Nonetheless, even with respect to mentally undeveloped beings such as chickens, it is important to notice, contra Frey, that it is not a Platonic Chickenhood that suffers but this or that particular (i.e., individual) chicken. We can think up a case, he holds, where we might prefer to save a bright dog over a human being who is terminally ill, irreversibly comatose, or morally corrupt, but in normal circumstances our preferences are quite different.[6]

There is nothing speciesist in seeing normal human life as having a higher quality and greater richness than animal life. Frey is correct regarding why this is so (even if his example of mating and parenting does not provide a clean break with animals, nor does his example regarding music, in that birds may very well enjoy their songs):

> Some of the things which give life its richness we share with animals; there are other things, however, which can fill our lives but not their's. For example, falling in love, marrying, and experiencing with someone what life has to offer; having children and watching and helping them to grow up; working and experiencing satisfaction in one's job; listening to music, looking at pictures, reading books, and so becoming acquainted with our cultural past and present; wondering where we have come from, where we are going, and what explains what happens around us; experiencing humour, delight, and fantasy; making plans and striving to realize them; striving to make something of one's life, in terms of one's purposes and goals; seeking through years of training and hard work excellence in some athletic, artistic, or academic endeavour; these are the sorts of things, more in some lives, less in others, which give them their fulness and texture.[7]

As we deviate radically from ordinary human lives, however, whether through severe mental or physical deformity or through an irreversibly comatose state, the quality and value of a human life plummet drastically, Frey thinks, to the point where it makes sense to wonder whether the life in question is worth living. It should be noted that

Singer would agree with Frey here, as would Regan regarding the irreversibly comatose if not regarding those others with severe mental or physical deformity. One of Frey's ways of putting the point can appeal only to his fellow utilitarian Singer, however: as the value of human life plummets drastically, it becomes amenable to tradeoffs with other values. Frey states: "As the quality and value of human life plummets and continues its downward course, it can approach and even fall below the quality of life of some quite ordinary animals. In cases of the latter sort, if we are confronted with the choice between saving the human or saving the animal, then we should be bound in terms of consistency to regard the animal's life as of greater value and to act accordingly."[8] In general it can be said that human life is more valuable than animal life, but not all human lives have the same enrichment or scope for enrichment (normal babies have scope for enrichment if not enrichment itself). "Some people lead lives of a quality we would not wish even upon our worst enemies."[9]

Frey's consideration of the differences in value among the lives of human beings makes it problematic to say that we should automatically test vaccines on animals. Unlike Regan, who moves from the rights of marginal cases to the rights of animals, Frey moves from experimentation on animals to the possibility that there be experimentation on marginal cases, those whose quality of life is so low as to be exceeded by that of healthy animals or at least to approach it:

> What is needed, in effect, is some reason for thinking that a human life, no matter how truncated its scope for enrichment, no matter how low its quality, is more valuable than an animal life, no matter what its degree of enrichment, no matter how high its quality. I myself have and know of nothing with which to satisfy this need; that is, I have and know of nothing which enables me to say, a priori, that a human life of any quality, however low, is more valuable than an animal life of any quality, however high. Perhaps some readers think that they can satisfy this need; I am receptive to suggestions.[10]

In effect, Frey is persuaded by a good bit of the AMC: we cannot, with the appeal to benefit, justify painful animal experiments without justifying certain painful human experiments. However, Frey makes the defender of the AMC who is also a defender of animal rights painfully aware of the fact that one can move in either of two directions: "On the one hand, we may take the fact that we cannot justify animal experiments without justifying human experiments as a good reason to re-examine our whole practice of (painful) animal experiments. The case for antivivisectionism, I think, is far stronger than most people allow. . . . [Or we might] condone experiments on humans whose quality of life is exceeded by (or possibly equal to) that of animals. . . . The choice before you is either antivivisectionism or condoning human experiments."[11]

If the appeal to benefit (e.g., to utilitarianism) exerts its full attraction, we may find ourselves unable to choose antivivisectionism, just as Regan and Clark allege in their critiques of Singer. That is, as utilitarians Singer and Frey have more in common with each other than would initially seem to be the case. As Frey puts the issue:

> Accordingly, we are left with human experiments. I think this is how I would choose, not with great glee and rejoicing, and with great reluctance; but if this is the price we must pay to hold to the appeal to benefit and to enjoy the benefits which that appeal licenses, then I think we must pay it. I am well aware that most people will find my choice repugnant in the extreme, and it is easy to see how I can appear a monster in their eyes. But I am where I am, not because I begin a monster and end up choosing the monstrous, but because I cannot think of anything at all compelling that cedes all human life of any quality of greater value than animal life of any quality. It might be claimed by some that this shows in me the need for some religious beliefs, on the assumption that some religious belief or other will allow me to say that any human life is more valuable than any animal life. . . . This appears a rather strange reason for taking on religious beliefs (i.e., believing in the existence of God and of God's gifts to us in order to avoid having to allow experiments on humans).[12]

Of course, the side effects of such experiments—say, if massive numbers of people would be outraged—might sway Frey away from painful experiments on marginal humans, but these side effects do not provide an absolute prohibition against such experiments.

In a recent article Frey makes it clear why he, as a peculiar defender of the AMC, is not also a defender of animal rights, except on an attenuated utilitarian version of "rights." Frey is convinced that autonomous beings are in a special or privileged class, an assumption that can be found in versions of Kantianism and contractarianism as well. Nonautonomous beings such as infants, the seriously mentally enfeebled, the seriously brain-damaged, the irreversibly comatose, and animals are to be judged against the standard set by autonomous beings. Once again, however, the question is not so much whether autonomous beings have a privileged status as moral agents but whether they deserve it as moral beneficiaries as well. In one sense everyone can agree that autonomous agents are in a privileged position. Where the *suffering* of a being is concerned, however, autonomy does not matter, as when boiling water is poured over a severely handicapped infant or a dog, as Frey notes. On the other hand, where the *killing* of a being is concerned, Frey, like Singer, thinks that autonomy—the ability a continuous self has to see itself existing over time and to have desires with respect to the future—does matter. Still, Frey is not convinced that even Singer's "mentally developed" animals are autonomous, and hence Frey's view opens up the possibility both for infanticide of severely handicapped newborns and for the killing of animals. Hence, these killings can be enacted on the basis not of species membership but of the richness and quality of life—or better, the lack thereof.[13]

One obvious way to respond to Frey here is to specify a weaker sense of autonomy or to suggest that autonomy admits of degrees. This is precisely what Regan does when he sets out to show that animals are autonomous beings in that they have memory of the past and expectations regarding the future, including the desire to keep on living. That is, in some sense they have continuous selves and are not indifferent to what will happen to them. Frey's worry is that we would drain the word *autonomy* of its meaning if animals could be said to be autonomous, but the same sort of "drain" would occur if we viewed marginal cases as autonomous. Not all human life is of equal value even if one concedes, as Frey does, the difficulty of determining when a life is no longer worth living. Some cases are not difficult: a life wholly and irreversibly in the grip of senile dementia is not worth living, and infants born with hardly any brain whatever have lives not worth living. Significantly, Frey misinterprets Regan as saying that all human beings have equally valuable lives when in fact Regan is committed only to the view that all human beings (excepting the irreversibly comatose) have equal inherent value. Hence Regan would agree with Frey at least to this extent: the severely mentally enfeebled lead lives less valuable than those of individuals who are only mildly retarded and who fall just short of the intellectual level needed to build a bookcase. According to Regan, however, and in distinction from Frey, the severely mentally enfeebled still have a right to life, because they are subjects of a life that can be overridden only in extremis.[14]

It is not clear to Frey that we show respect to a severely handicapped child by keeping him alive to the age of four by a series of eleven operations in order to let nature kill him. From this skeptical view of the claim that all human lives are of equal value, Frey concludes that the AMC as an argument for animal rights must fail. If euthanasia of marginal cases is morally permissible, he seems to be saying, then the AMC as an argument for animal rights does not work. However, as I will show in the chapter that deals with James Rachels, euthanasia is justified only when the being euthanized is killed for its own good, when the killing is a sign of respect for the one who is killed. Euthanasia may well be compatible with the view that all human beings have equal inherent value, if not equal value. Hence Regan's appeal to the equal inherent value of all human life still has force in the effort to have us concede the equal inherent worth of animal life. (As before, by *inherent value* I mean not the G. E. Moore–like mysteriousness in Regan's position but rather the view that subjects of a life are valuable not merely because they have individual pleasurable and painful experiences but also because their lives are reticulated through memories of the past, expectations or hopes for the future, etc.)

Frey correctly points out that elderly people wholly in the grip of Alzheimer's disease, those suffering from all kinds of mental illness (including paranoia and other psychoses), and so on do not have lives as valuable as those of normal human beings; hence, in extremis we can kill them rather than kill normal human beings. If the marginal cases have inherent value equal to that of normal human beings, however—that is, if, qua their status as subjects of a life, it makes a difference to them whether they are treated well or ill—then they can be euthanized only if doing so is compatible with their being treated as ends in themselves. I am not necessarily claiming that this is Regan's view of euthanasia; rather, this view of euthanasia is both compatible with Regan's view of inherent value and ably counteracts Frey's attempt to move from the moral permissibility of euthanasia to the refutation of the AMC as an argument for animal rights.[15]

Like many utilitarians, Frey does not share contemporary "enchantment" with moral rights, but he is quick to point out in one article that nonautonomous beings come out at risk on certain rights theories as well as in utilitarianism. In fact, despite his efforts to derail the AMC as an argument for animal rights, Frey is much closer to it than are any of the reciprocity theorists treated in the previous chapter. This point is seldom appreciated. He disagrees with those who would make autonomy a necessary condition for admission to the moral community in observing that "suffering is suffering and so an evil," even if the one suffering is not autonomous. (This conflicts with what Frey says regarding the need to show why suffering is an evil.) Here Frey is indistinguishable from Singer. The two part company, however, when Frey says that the lives of autonomous, adult humans are *incomparably* richer than the lives of defective humans and animals. For Singer, normal adults and marginal cases are in fact comparable: normal adults have mental lives of greater complexity than those of marginal cases or animals; how great depends on the marginal case or animal in question. Frey tries to divide and conquer when he alleges that Regan and Clark shy away from Singer's attribution of self-consciousness to animals; when it is realized that by *self-consciousness* Singer means having a concern for one's past and one's future, then Regan and Clark are seen to agree with Singer even if they do not use the word *self-consciousness* to refer to these abilities.[16]

In the previous paragraph I implied that Frey is at odds not only with the animal rightists but also with reciprocity theorists. In fact, he is bothered not only by the reciprocity theorists' belief that autonomy is a necessary condition for moral rights but also by their attempt to slip marginal cases and animals into morality through the back door via autonomous agents' interests. In effect, the reciprocity theorists at once grant too little and too much to marginal cases and animals. They grant too little by failing to acknowledge that marginal cases and animals, as sentient beings, should be the direct objects of moral concern, as in utilitarianism. They grant too much to marginal cases and animals by allowing their proxies to make judgments for them that presuppose knowledge the proxies cannot have:

> A person who is now slowly passing through the stages of Alzheimer's disease or senile dementia has a past life we can draw upon in order to see the sorts of things he chose in the past and the sort of life he made for himself. A proxy who now acts for that person has something to go on, something which, however tenuously, we can see as setting guidelines for the proxy to follow so as to enable us to see the choices of the proxy as the choices of the person in question. . . . To be sure, the proxy can make choices *for* the enfeebled person or animal, which can be to their advantage or disadvantage; but he is not choosing in the ways that or what they would have chosen. Rather, he is choosing, *according to his own lights.* . . . And

> it would be as well not to be overly sanguine about what the proxy's view of their best interests will be.[17]

The reciprocity theorists are correct, Frey seems to be saying, in thinking that a right to life hinges on autonomy as integrally connected to agency (contra Regan and Clark) but incorrect in thinking that a right to moral considerability also hinges on autonomy and agency:

> From the fact that animals are members of the moral community, it by no means follows that the lives of animals are of roughly equal value to the lives of normal adult humans; yet, anything less than this will leave animals with less (in fact, markedly less) valuable lives and so at risk. Merely admitting animals into the moral community does not *per se* so alter the value of their lives. . . . Emphasis upon agency in our moral theories will always leave animals at risk. . . . There are plenty of humans who are members of the moral community but whose lives are of a much lower quality, and, therefore, value, than the lives of normal adult humans. Indeed, if we think of certain kinds of cases, such as patients in the grip of Alzheimer's disease or senile dementia, whose lives have so drastically declined in quality, then we may come to think that a life of such very low quality is not worth living. Its value we rate quite lowly, with the result that the threshold for taking this life has been lowered. Yet, there is no suggestion that such patients have ceased to be a part of the moral community or that we do not have to trouble ourselves, morally, about what happens to them. My point, then, is that one cannot use some presumed equality in the value of lives between defective humans and normal adult humans in order to underwrite an equality in value between animal and human life; for there is no such presumed equality in the defective/normal human case.[18]

Frey's Influence

Frey's view of the AMC has been influential both for the AMC's defenders and for its detractors. For example, a defender of the AMC such as Regan has been forced to clarify the relationship between animal interests and the prescriptive overtone associated with animal interests. If there are no competent persons around, then we can still speak of what is in baby Jane's or Fido's interests in the sense of what would contribute to their well-being (and perhaps also in the sense of what they are interested in), but we cannot thereby issue a prescription concerning what someone ought to do. In short, the case of Fido's having rights is as weak or as strong as the case for baby Jane's having them, in that both can have interests even if there is at present no prescriptive meaning associated with those rights.[19]

Somewhat closer to Frey's approach to the AMC is that of Holmes Rolston. It is easy to blur the cutoff points on a spectrum of individuals when it is realized both that human beings are sometimes infants, insane, senile, or ignorant and that some animals are quite bright. Retarded human beings do not defend theories, and chimpanzees are perhaps more self-aware than infants. According to Rolston, however, the problem of fuzzy set edges is a pseudoproblem, in that capacities for value richness are statistical marks of the human species. This emphasis on the richness of (most) human lives is very much like Frey's, but Rolston's speciesism is generally not characteristic of Frey. Rolston defends his view as follows: "It is not, technically, the species to which humans belong biologically that makes moral demands on us; it is the personal, psychological capacities that exclusively (on this planet) and characteristically emerge in *Homo sapiens,* short of mental retardation or other malfunction. It is existential personality rather than biological humanity that we find superior to other species, but it is of course biological humanity that sponsors this existential personality, so to honor the one is to honor the other."[20] Rolston's mention of mental retardation and other malfunctions here shows that he has thought through the AMC, but his position is that we can group marginal cases with normal adult human beings by acknowledging the marginal cases' "potential or tragic loss." Several writers previously discussed, including Frey, place infants in the same moral class as that of normal adult human beings because of their potential or nascent rationality or autonomy. Rolston is distinctive, however, in the way he tries to include some marginal cases in the class of moral human beings because they are "broken humans who but vegetate." He thinks that we should include these humans for historical reasons, namely, their descent and the fact that they have "lost" distinctively human properties: "The criteria for normal humanity remain unchanged. This might call for some extra kindness, going further in consideration than can really be justified by strict attention to their failed or aborted humanity, a kindness that pities their brokenness. We do not respect them for what they are but respect the full humans they were or might have been; we repair the tragedy by charity, rather than do strict justice to their tragic condition."[21]

There is admittedly something disarming about Rolston's approach. It is hard to criticize a view that is so obviously infused with kindness and sincerity. Nonetheless, the best parts of Rolston's view of the AMC have already been included in Regan's version. Retarded human beings *should* have their rights respected, but not because they are members of a species whose members are typically characterized by greater value richness. As many science fiction episodes have illustrated, if we ever come across a being from another planet whose intellectual abilities do not exceed those of a retarded human being but whose sentient abilities are just as acute as those of a retarded human being, then that being will deserve respect even if it has never met any other members of its species and even if we know nothing of its heritage. That is, Rolston's kindness is admirable, but it is put to service in the cause of a bad (speciesist) theory. Our knowledge of the criteria for developed human beings perhaps is operative when we pity retarded human beings (in that such pity indicates that we think of them as defective versions of us) but not when we feel compelled to be kind to them or to acknowledge their rights (in that they deserve such kindness because in a way—they are sentient—they *are* like us).[22]

Rolston admits that in a lifeboat situation he might prefer to save a panda bear over Hitler. (Is there any real choice here?) These anomalies, however—human beings who are less than persons or who are notoriously demeritorious—have to be understood against a background provided by paradigm "class descriptions based on the type-species." In other words, class rules can be useful despite exceptions. Rolston is frustrating here because he himself provides several of the reasons that should dissuade him from holding onto his blatant speciesism: "justice" has a way of slipping into "just us"; "different rules" do apply to those with "superior talents," but not all human beings possess these "superior talents," so there is something arbitrary in having these "different rules" apply to them. Further, he extrapolates in an extremely questionable way when he claims that the killing and eating of animals in culture are still events in nature; they are ecological events no matter how superimposed by culture. Human consumption of animals, even animals raised on factory farms, is still analogous to predation, he thinks. A refutation of Rolston regarding these claims is beyond the scope of this book, but the following are several (admittedly leading) questions with which Rolston would have to deal adequately: are human beings naturally predators, as Rolston alleges, or are they the sorts of beings who can be predators, omnivores, or vegetarians or vegans, beings who can go on a hunger strike or become bulimic? The options seem to be more numerous than Rolston admits. Are the modern factory farm and the abattoir all that "natural," or are they just as much parts of the modern industrial or postindustrial state as the Chicago commodity exchange, where, as the cliché has it, even pork bellies are reduced to their exchange value?[23] There is nothing wrong with Rolston's trying to "follow nature," but it is not clear that he has fairly considered all the possibilities that nature makes available, nor has he carefully enough teased out the cultural elements infused in what he takes to be "natural" events.

Gerald Paske, like Frey and Rolston, does not think that a being has a right to life if it does not possess any rational faculties, but this view does not necessarily leave animals totally out in the cold. Rational abilities are (contra Frey) a matter of degree, and hence the "higher" animals (primates, but not cows, dogs, or cats) might approach a level that validates a right to life. In addition, marginal humans (excepting infants, who have the potential to become rational and to become moral agents) perhaps ought to receive treatment overlapping that owed to the higher animals. In fact, if nothing but ethics were involved in how we ought to treat one another, then some marginal cases would legitimately be treated less well than some animals. This is not much of a concession to the defender of the AMC, however, for two reasons: (1) only members of Paske's truncated list of "higher" animals would be given such treatment; and (2) Paske thinks that other, nonethical factors can legitimately enter into the question as to how we ought to treat each other, so that ethical conclusions might be trumped by these other factors. His view is as follows: "Marginal humans (and animals) either do not have a right to life (if rationality is a necessary condition for the right to life) or, if marginal humans (and animals) do have a right to life, that right cannot be based upon the same considerations that generates the right to life of normal humans. Of these two options, I suspect that the former is correct."[24]

Clark's Response

One philosopher who has criticized Frey on the AMC deserves special attention not only because he defends the AMC as an argument in favor of animal rights but also because he thinks that Frey, like utilitarians and Kantians in general, mistakenly assumes that moral philosophy consists in the search for an impartial moral standard. Stephen R. L. Clark believes that in a crisis, if he had to choose between saving his wife's life and saving his cat's, he would save his wife. But then again, on Clark's (or John Benson's) grounds, if he had to choose in a crisis between his wife's life and his neighbor's, he would still save his wife's. Universalizing Kantians (such as Regan) and utilitarians (such as Singer or Frey) would make the same choice, he thinks, although in theory they should be as willing to save the neighbor as the wife: "But what if the choice lies between, say, a chimpanzee and an incurably comatose human? Is the choice *so* easy? And how comatose must the human be, or how close to human the animal before we can defend the less racist [speciesist] choice?"[25] Or again, consider that if a man is forced to choose between saving his mother or his girlfriend, he really is in a dilemma. Suppose we say that he should save his mother. Would this make it legitimate for him to kill his girlfriend to obtain something that would save his mother's life? Analogously, even if human beings are more worthy of moral respect than animals, it does not follow that animals exist solely for us. Most zoophiles, including Clark, are willing to distinguish morally between human beings and animals. The question is whether speciesists can distinguish between cats and cabbages. Hierarchical order is not to be confused with licensed tyranny, according to Clark, with "hierarchical order" diminishing in importance the further we get from household and friends.[26]

A hierarchy between human beings and most animals on the criterion of rationality is fair enough, I think, as long as such rationality does not attempt to take on a life of its own apart from the heart's affections, affections that are the highest expressions of many members of our own species (the marginal cases) as well as of most animals. Some animals are (ridiculously) treated better than some children, but these pampered pets should not blind us to the fact that to be an unowned animal is still largely a capital crime. If rationality is the sole criterion of value, then even pets could be tortured along with "food animals," psychopaths, and mental defectives. However, Clark's fideism may be overextended when he flirts with the idea that we sometimes ought to try out alternatives to the ideal of rational consistency. This sort of language gets him into trouble with his critics without advancing his own claims regarding animals.[27]

Plutarch notes in his *Moralia* (965b) that boys will throw rocks at frogs in play but that the frogs die in earnest. Should we exonerate the boys by noting that the frogs did not exhibit (perfect) rationality? And what are the consequences of such an exoneration? Clark apparently would answer, "the consequences dictated by the AMC"; "we are absolutely better than the animals because we are able to give their interests some consideration: so we won't." Adherence to the rationalist myth regarding moral beneficiary status has as its consequence a willingness to put the sick and feebleminded beyond the moral law. How much more fruitful and humane, he thinks, to adopt as a myth regarding moral beneficiary status the lure of "irrational affection, artistic imagination, loyalty."[28]

There are sentient beings all around us, and to assume that the intelligence of some of them, however intelligence may be defined, licenses abuse of animals also makes it possible for any intellectual elite (God, the angels, extraterrestrials, or the Nazis by self-proclamation) "to treat the rest of us like trash." The AMC makes it apparent that if we are willing to mistreat animals, we should also be willing to mistreat the severely retarded. Frey comes close to adopting this view when he claims that the marginal cases do not really have rights, but we act as if they do because we are squeamish about abusing them. Clark notes, however, that some of us are reminded of our own condition by animals and are squeamish about abusing them as well:

> But suppose we did not feel squeamish about tormenting, say, microcephalics or brain-damaged orphans? A good many people, indeed, probably do not. And many more, if they thought that some advantage could safely be won for the rest of us by torturing such defective humans [would do so]. . . . I see no reason to suppose that squeamishness on its own is much of a barrier against the exploitation of the human weak. . . . Secretly, I suggest, we know that we ought to care for the subnormal precisely because they are subnormal: they are weak, defenceless, at our mercy. They can be hurt, injured, frustrated. We *ought* to consider their wishes and feelings, not because we will be hurt if we don't, but because *they* will be hurt. And the same goes for those creatures like them who are of our kind though not of our species. . . . The *descent* of our potential victims has nothing directly to do with their susceptibility to injury.[29]

Clark, contra Frey, wishes both to defend the AMC and forthrightly to defend mongoloid children: "A mongol child is not an imperfectly embodied Human, but a genotypic variation within the boundaries of the human population that does not seem to be capable of separate, sustained existence . . . not defective embodiments of an Ideal Essence: they are simply what they are. . . . We no longer have the metaphysical assurance that imbeciles are really rational souls and chimpanzees are not."[30]

Again, if it takes possession of *nous* to enter the community of moral concern, then some human beings are not in the community, and to state that it takes membership in a species (the human one) to enter the community of moral concern is to defend a position (speciesism) that is very close to racism or sexism:[31] "The evils of sexism are that females are denied the opportunity to live authentic lives. . . . A nonsexist society is one in which people are not oppressed, exploited, and manipulated to fit sexual stereotypes. The evils of speciesism, similarly, are that creatures are robbed, assaulted, and killed, not simply that they are distinguished from members of our own species. It is right so to distinguish them. . . . What is wrong is to use them with cruelty and disrespect."[32] It should be emphasized that Clark does not think that mentally defective human beings are really "marginal" human beings, and hence he prefers not to refer to the argument under consideration as that from marginal cases. In fact, he finds the designation somewhat offensive: "Children, imbeciles, lunatics and the senile are not marginal to society, any more than the domestic animals. Society does not exist to serve the purposes of self-seeking rational adult individuals but to maintain the households within which we all grow up."[33]

Each human being is an individual organism having largely unpredictable similarities with others. This unpredictability should not be surprising when it is realized that scientific taxa are not the same as folk taxa, as in "weeds" or "fish" (including whales). There is no set of properties such that all weeds and only weeds have them, nor is there such a set of properties for trees. In contrast, scientific taxa consist in genealogically related individuals rather than in a "Platonic" or perfect type that individuals imitate. Folk taxa are not foolish inventions, however, in that for landscaping purposes it makes sense to talk of trees and weeds, but these taxa should not be allowed to do our work in morality for us, say, by *stipulating* that "humans" have rights and "animals" do not and then by resting content with the assumption that a real or a metaphysical distinction has been made. The folk taxon "human beings" embodies an a priori concept of normality that contrasts one group to those who are less than normal. In this regard folk taxonomy ends up with a serious problem: human beings universally are the sorts of beings who deserve respect, but human beings are essentially or normally rational. Opponents to the AMC are saddled with precisely this problem in that marginal human beings are not rational. In scientific taxonomy, however, every being in a given taxon is as much a member of the taxon as any other, no matter how atypical or "marginal" it is. That is, Clark thinks that we can learn a moral lesson from scientific taxa even if, for pragmatic purposes, we cannot do without folk taxa. In fact, it is true that all human beings belong to the same species in the sense that there are no barriers (social, geographical, or physiological) to interbreeding among human groups. It is also a fact, however, as Clark notes, that there are biological grounds for claiming some sort of unity among all mammals, primates, and so on, in that they belong to the same class, order, or superfamily. An awareness of these unities militates against the prejudice that human persons should consider any conspecific to be worth more than any individual from another species.[34]

From a biological point of view, the unity of humankind rests not in the possession of a common, essentialist "nature" but in being a common breeding population, and this sort of unity does not support the case for speciesism. For example, it does not support the case for the Kantian variety of speciesism wherein only rational agents are of moral worth, a view that has as one consequence that "some creatures of another species might turn out to be 'human' in the morally significant sense; many of our species might turn out to be 'sub-human.'"[35] Clark does find the Kantian view to be laudable in its focus on one morally relevant feature of many human beings—but only one: "The price of this laudable insistence on moral humanism is a profound unease . . . about any attempt to treat the characters and talents of human populations as explicable in something like the way that we might explain the behaviour of baboons or horses. It is asserted, in advance of any evidence worth mentioning, that our species has somehow escaped from the nexus of evolutionary selection, and become pure mind, governed only by the laws of reason."[36] These Clarkian considerations regarding the differences between folk and scientific taxa and the inconsistencies found in the former are meant to drive home the importance of the AMC, an argument that Clark defends without naming it:

> The problem, notoriously, is that the harder we make it to meet the qualifications of "real humanity" (so as to exclude dolphins, chimpanzees, squids and honeybees), the more creatures of clearly human descent we also push beyond the pale. In the end either only the Wise are worth troubling about (and they, so far, are found only among the biologically human) or any individual with feelings and purposes of its own is a proper moral object. Either most human beings may rightly be treated "like animals," when we deal with them at a practical level, and when we try to explain their behaviour, or a good many animals should not be treated like that either.[37]

Clark is correctly urging us to judge certain categories, traditional within Judaism, Christianity, and Islam, but not within the Greek world, as merely artificial: "Once we have acknowledged that a species is not a natural kind—not a set of individuals who share a common, underlying and causative nature—we can afford to allow that other linguistic communities have other views on who are 'people' (i.e., respected members of their community). . . . The question is . . . why do we make so much of any differences there are?"[38]

Clark's frustration with Western anthropocentrism is in evidence when he criticizes the (surprisingly) still prevalent Cartesian view. It is an

> oddity that those moderns who regularly seek to dissociate themselves from these older doctrines of the soul (which they characterize as dualist or Cartesian . . .) still wish to maintain the moral divisions that only made sense upon the assumption of a distinctively human soul. If there is no such soul . . . then there is no reason to distinguish sharply and generally between domestication and slavery, flesh-eating and cannibalism, the killing of an ox and the slaying of a man. Liberal humanists need to believe in the myth of a common nature, but have abandoned belief in the human soul, and so equate that imagined natural kind with the human species. They should think again.[39]

That is, Clark's defense of the AMC is a part of his conservative critique of modern liberalism, a conservativism that reaches back to Aristotle, who, although not a great defender of respect for animals, nonetheless thought that humans were characterized not by some one essential property but by complexes of resemblances and homologous structures: "As we advance upon the Aristotelian road . . . we have steadily less excuse for believing that the presence of our biological species can be detected simply by discovering instances of tool-making, food-sharing, exogamic structures or verbal activity."[40] The moral Clark draws from this Aristotelian lesson is that drawn by Aristotle's pupil Theophrastus, to which Clark gives the following contemporary articulation:

> We live in a world of mutually dependent and competitive organisms, such that there are relatively enclosed gene-pools, and relatively stable species-forms. . . . We cannot assume that all "human" communities should be explained one way, and all "non-human" communities another, as if chimpanzees and whales were more like worms or amoebas than they were like humans, and all human groups more like each other than any of them are like baboons or chimpanzees. . . . We should not assume that slavery or

> cannibalism needs some special explanation, different from the sort of explanation we give for domestication or flesh-eating.[41]

Creatures other than the biologically human might be persons, if by *persons* we mean either those who wear the mask of moral beneficiary status or, in Singer's sense of *person,* those who have a sense of their own past and future.

It should be clear by now that Clark is at odds with Frey's belief that the severely retarded are treated as if they have rights not because they really do have rights by virtue of the same features that animals possess but because we are squeamish about eating them or experimenting painfully on them. Perhaps Frey is calling attention to the fact that marginal cases cannot compel us to recognize them, in which case what he says is obviously true. What is not so obvious is why it is only our squeamishness that makes it bothersome to eat or experiment on marginal cases. Even the early Cartesians were willing to admit that we ought not to torment and kill animals if they have feelings; today we (including Frey) are more confident than the Cartesians were that animals do have feelings. It is the office of philosophical argument, Clark thinks, to call attention to the myopia whereby it is not noticed that cows and cats can be as oppressed as microcephalics. Frey's squeamishness is due to the fact that marginal cases remind us too much of us, but Clark is correct to ask why animals do not also remind Frey of us. As it stands, Frey's view is in one sense like that of the reciprocity theorists: marginal cases matter as parts of our spiritual exercises; we should care for them (and, to a lesser extent, for animals) in the way we might want children to care for their toys: "It is difficult . . . to devise principles that protect imbeciles and not chimpanzees. It is a *moral* argument that draws our attention to what is *wrong* in mistreating, say, imbeciles: not that it offends us but that it injures sentient, appetitive, partially communicative beings. So does the torture, imprisonment and slaughter of, say, chimpanzees. If the one is wrong (as surely it is), so is the other, for they are, in moral terms, the very same act."[42]

If we have no right to force mental defectives to serve the greater good against their will—say, by forcing them to be subjects in painful experiments—then it is difficult to see how we could acquire such a right to do the same to an animal. If our criteria for ascribing wills are broad enough to cover all marginal cases, then we must ascribe wills to animals as well. "Sacrifice" of animals in painful experiments infringes on their right to refuse, their right to rather be doing something other than participating in the experiment: "Those who think, by the way, that children and mental defectives are not primary right-bearers, but are protected only for the sake of parental squeamishness, might like to explain why parents should not have the right to sell, say, brain-damaged or mongoloid or microcephalic children—you can see the posters already: 'A Parent's Right to Choose.'"[43] Obviously much of what Clark says about the AMC does not apply to Frey, but some of it does. On the surface, he notes, Singer and Frey differ simply in their calculations of the utilitarian greater good, but Frey also differs from Singer in thinking that there is little one can do as an individual to ameliorate mistreatment of marginal cases or animals. Clark, however, thinks that if Frey is correct here, then there is something fundamentally flawed about utilitarianism itself, in that nothing one can ever hope to do in any area of life can be expected to have a big effect on the general welfare. Clark is nonetheless like Frey and Singer in not placing much importance on the notion of rights. As an Aristotelian, virtue ethician, what interests him are not so much abstract deontological or utilitarian rights as concrete historical ones. Hence, it is not so much animal rights that he wishes to establish on the basis of the AMC as the "rights" of our domestic partners (pets) or, at most (in that Clark is British), the "rights" of British beasts.[44]

Partial Affections

Lawrence Becker is like Clark in defending a virtue-based approach to ethics, but he holds that the traits constitutive of virtue typically lead one to give priority to the interests of members of one's own species. Animals have some of the same interests human beings have (e.g., seeking pleasure and avoiding pain), yet we treat them quite differently from human beings. Becker admits that in some cases (i.e., the marginal cases) there is no morally relevant difference between human beings and animals, but he claims that this does not necessarily signal the success of the AMC, for there may be no need to find a morally relevant distinguishing characteristic for human beings to justify preferential treatment in their favor. Becker agrees with Clark that when hard choices have to be made, one is expected to rank the interests of one's family over those of friends, those of friends over those of neighbors, and those over neighbors over those of strangers. Then Becker extends his reasoning in what he thinks is an original way to suggest that for virtuous people, the interests of human beings are greater than those of members of other species. There is nothing original here, however, for all the defenders of the AMC treated in this book agree that in extremis we should favor the interests of normal human beings over the attenuated interests of animals. In normal circumstances, however, there is no need to sacrifice animals for our sake.

Certainly there is no need to sacrifice animals so that we eat healthy diets, and it is at least doubtful whether progress in medical science would end or even be attenuated if we refused to continue to sacrifice animals in laboratories, although it must be admitted that biological scientists would have to be more imaginative than they have been in some time. Modern biology started in the seventeenth century on the assumption that animals were mere machines; when Descartes's followers at Port Royal literally vivisected animals by nailing them to a wall and cutting them open, the moral issue was evaded in the following explanation: the screams the animals make are like the sounds made by scraping parts in an unoiled clock. On this assumption great progress was made, however, such that it is difficult for some contemporary scientists to stop treating animals as machines even if they are no longer thought of as such.

Another interesting case is the following: should we favor the interests of a marginal human being over the comparable interests of an animal if we were forced to choose in extremis? Perhaps (and I prefer to be tentative here) this is where the greater social distance between normal human beings and animals compared to that between normal human beings and marginal cases comes into play in such a way that we can favor the marginal cases—unless perhaps the animal is a pet, in which case the social distance between a normal human being and a marginal case might be greater than that between a normal human being and the animal. (Given the greater number of pets than marginal cases, this is a significant consideration.) In any event, the AMC seems immune to Becker's criticism.[45]

Becker distinguishes four sorts of speciesism, however, and he wishes to defend only one of them. *Absolute* speciesism holds that any human interest, even a trivial one, outweighs any sum of nonhuman interests. This is a straw man in that on any plausible version of human virtue, some human interests are to be subordinated to animal interests. *Resolute* speciesism holds that any significant human interest outweighs any sum of animal interests. Virtuous people will also reject this position, Becker thinks, because it allows a massive number of animals to be sacrificed to fulfill a significant interest (e.g., physical health) of even one human being. At the other extreme, *weak* speciesism holds that when human and animal interests are equivalent (and, presumably, we can satisfy one but not both), then the human interests are to prevail. Most defenders of the AMC would be in favor of this view, but they would not be willing to call it "speciesism," albeit weak. It is not really speciesism because the operative criteria at work here would likely be rationality, autonomy, and so on rather than mere species membership. Finally, there is the view Becker wishes to defend, *moderate to strong* speciesism, a position that seeks to determine in some nonalgorithmic way how many animals may be sacrificed for the sake of human beings. Unfortunately Becker does not mean that these "sacrifices" can occur only in extreme, "forced choice" situations; rather, they can occur on a routine basis. In addition, and again unfortunately, Becker does not indicate how his moderate to strong speciesism is a consequence of virtue-based ethics, unless the "moderate" nature of this view is somehow supposed to be Aristotelian.[46]

Roger Paden, like Becker, shares some of Clark's general ethical views but not the particular conclusion Clark deduces from those views. Clark, like Singer, thinks that because animals, like human beings at the same mental level, are incapable of giving informed consent in an explicit way, we must act toward them as we would toward those human beings who cannot give explicit informed consent. That is, we can inflict harm on them only if we are paternalistically intending ultimately to help them. Paden's concern is that these "morally controversial entities" (animals, comatose humans, fetuses, etc.) are difficult to include into the "moral community" because membership in the moral community is not the function of the possession of some essential moral characteristic, a view that Paden disparagingly refers to as "moral essentialism." There are two sorts of moral community, he thinks, with the best community consisting in a combination of the two. In a rationalistic or theoretical moral community the membership is homogeneous and the rules are universal. For utilitarians it would include all beings capable of feeling pleasure and pain, for many Kantians it would include all rational creatures, and for most Aristotelians it would include all beings with internally determined purpose. The second approach is not ideal but empirical; it refers to the actual moral community in which we dwell. Paden's problem with Singer's and Regan's positions is that they rely exclusively on the first sort of moral community and assume that their rationalistic ideals should automatically be forced on our actual moral community. Frey and Clark, however, in different ways, rely on the second sense of moral community.[47]

In fact, Clark seems to use both sorts of community in a way that Paden, at times at least, urges us to take seriously. If it were not for partial affections, we would have no affections at all, and hence morality must at least start in the second sort of community. However, actually existing moral communities are notorious for excluding beings who should, from a rational point of view, be included in the community, as the history of classism, racism, sexism, and speciesism indicates. That is, even given Paden's qualifications, there are good reasons for taking Clark's position seriously. Much less helpful is Keith Tester's (Foucauldian) view of society, wherein moral principles are reducible *simpliciter* to power relationships. (He is unhelpful in part because he reports the views of others inaccurately.) On this view animal rights are merely a fetish, in that Singer, Regan, and Clark are looking for "immutable" natural truths regarding animals. Not only are there no such truths regarding animals, according to Tester, but there are no truths at all "out there." Further, Tester inaccurately claims that for Clark, the moral status of animals is precisely the same as our moral status and that Clark is dishonest in claiming that his theory applies to all animals, whereas it really applies only to mammals. On all these points Tester is unhelpful. Paden, at least, even though he does not adopt the AMC, is at least helpful in his view of the two sorts of moral community and in locating the AMC in the interplay between these two.[48]

The efforts of Clark, Becker, and Paden to reintroduce some of Aristotle's views are successful if they are seen as ancillary to, or as partial correctives of, deontological and utilitarian ethics. Nonetheless, they fail as efforts to completely reorient moral philosophy and to replace attempts to achieve impartial ethical standards with partial, communal affections. Furthermore, Becker and Paden have not done much to indicate how their partial affections are more consistent (assuming for the moment that affections can be consistent or inconsistent) than Clark's. Given Clark's criticisms of Frey, let me return to the effort to move the actually existing moral community to accept the AMC.

Dale Jamieson defends the AMC by claiming that there is no distinctive moral status enjoyed by all and only human beings. Suppose that all and only human beings do share some distinctive moral status. What would it be? It cannot be membership in their species, for this is not a morally relevant consideration. Rationality, capacity for pleasure and pain, or the having of interests all fail, in that these proposed bases either do not exclude all animals or do exclude some human beings. Thus, there is no reason to believe that there is a distinctive status possessed by all and only human beings. There are two basic negative responses to the AMC, thinks Jamieson. One is to try to show that there is some basis for supposing that all and only human beings have some distinctive but overlooked moral status, although this response does not look very promising. The other is Frey's response, that we should deny that all human beings share some distinctive moral status. Jamieson's question for Frey is a direct one: on this basis, why should not "idiotburgers" find their place on restaurant menus, except for the fact that we would probably not enjoy their taste?[49] Or again, and perhaps more realistically, why should not marginal cases be experimented on painfully?

Jamieson thinks that the AMC is the strongest philosophical challenge yet delivered against our ordinary treatment of animals. He criticizes Clark for not engaging with this argument, a criticism that is somewhat misdirected in that Clark does engage with the AMC. Perhaps Jamieson is bothered because he thinks that Clark does not adequately respond to Narveson and Frey. For both thinkers, the sentimental interest rational human beings have in marginal cases is the source of protection for the latter. Hence, if I care for both my mentally defective infant and my cat, my neighbor should not be permitted to molest either. If I have no interest in the infant, however, is it morally permissible to sell the infant to a medical school for experimental purposes? Perhaps other members of society will have a sentimental interest in the infant, but this is by no means ensured if sentimental interest is a contingent phenomenon. Consequently, the defender of the AMC is intent on bringing marginal cases into the moral community in their own right.[50]

Animal Rights Skepticism

Some animal rightists are opposed to the AMC, but not necessarily because they agree with Frey. For example, Steve Sapontzis is intent on responding to this question: is it possible to have a right to something that affects one's interests of which one is ignorant? He thinks it is obvious that one can have such a right, as in having a right to an inheritance of which one is unaware. Severely retarded, brain-damaged, and senile people have all sorts of rights that they are incapable of understanding and valuing. The job of the AMC is to handle at least these marginal (but real) cases, if not the fantastic ones invented in the style of certain analytic ethicians. The key issue regarding the AMC is whether it is inconsistent, once one has granted rights to the marginal cases, to deny them to animals or whether it is legitimate to deny them to animals on the basis of the claim that the marginal cases are nonetheless members of a species whose normal members are rational and the possessors of rights in the strongest sense. Much hinges on whether marginal cases and animals value things. It seems arbitrary to cut off valuing at a high intellectual level. Infants and many animals are obviously capable of preferring, desiring, grabbing for, pursuing, or "valuing" those things that bring them pleasure or happiness. The burden of proof is on those who think that linguistic or intellectual ability are better indicators than sentience or the ability to be an independent evaluator, "and that burden cannot be met by a stipulative definition." What an independent evaluator values is not merely lying in the sun but his or her lying in the sun, as when the agent chases away other individuals to take their place.[51]

In his book *Morals, Reason, and Animals,* however, it becomes clear that Sapontzis is troubled by the AMC. Sapontzis's general view is that although Singer's use of the AMC is a masterful piece of reasoning, it is too exclusively utilitarian to satisfy any but the most dedicated of utilitarians. And Regan is so zealously anti-utilitarian that he goes to the opposite extreme. Sapontzis's self-proclaimed modest approach steers between these two extremes. This "modest" approach is as follows:

> By far the most common defense of our exploiting animals—and the one that is best supported by our moral tradition—is that we are rational beings, while they are not. Other animal rights philosophers have, of course, attempted to overcome this defense, but this has been only one small part of what concerned them in their books. Too often, these refutations have been little more than reciting the now famous "argument from marginal cases," that is, pointing out that we do not consider it morally acceptable to exploit nonrational humans, such as the severely retarded and brain-damaged. Unfortunately (for the animals), the argument from marginal cases is not that compelling; basically, all it does is show that most of us are sentimentally attached to members of our own species to a degree great-

> ly exceeding our attachment to members of other species and that morality is more complex than one might have thought.[52]

Sapontzis tries to escape the AMC by deemphasizing the place of reason in morality, regarding both moral beneficiary status and moral agency. Two points need to be made here, however: (1) Sapontzis's grounds for thinking that animals can perhaps be moral beings need to be explored, and (2) his case against the AMC also needs to be explored. Further, (1) is related to (2).

We are all familiar with the following argument:

> 1. Only rational beings can be moral.
> 2. Animals are not rational.
> 3. Therefore, animals cannot be moral.[53]

Sapontzis points out that *moral* can mean either: (a) "moral-n," agent-neutral action in the sense of moral actions considered independently of the agent's relation to the action, or (b) "moral-a," the moral value of the agent's understanding of the action and his or her motive for doing it. Animals are at least capable of moral-n actions in that they care for their young and sometimes aid those in distress:

> When a dog pulls a child from a fire, it is not acting blindly, like an insect reacting to a chemical mating stimulus, nor does it seem to have ulterior motives. If anything, animals seem to be much less deceptive than humans; the sincerity of their compassionate, courageous, etc., actions is seldom, if ever, an issue. The only real issue here is whether animals recognize the moral-n goods and evils of a situation and respond to them or whether they simply react on the basis of instinct or reflex conditioning. When instinct and reflex conditioning are mentioned we usually think of cases like salmon compulsively swimming upstream in mating season and Pavlov's dogs salivating at the sound of a bell. . . . Maternal instincts and moral-n habits are responses to the moral-n goods and evils of the situation. . . . Not all moral-n actions of animals can be accounted for by instinct or conditioning. The cases of porpoises helping drowning sailors must be spontaneous acts of kindness. There is no reason to believe porpoises have developed an instinct for saving humans.[54]

That is, for Sapontzis the gap between animals and human beings is bridged not merely by, or even primarily by, marginal cases but rather by the animal-like nature of our own morality, and hence Sapontzis has less need of the AMC than do other animal rightists.

It is because animals are assumed to be amoral beings, Sapontzis thinks, that their incapacity for moral rights is alleged to follow. Sapontzis is, like Clark, Aristotelian here, in that Aristotle was quite comfortable with the belief that horses, say, can be ethical beings who can be trained to have the habits (*ethoi*) necessary to do all that they should do, even if horses are not self-reflective enough to understand why they ought to do these actions.[55] *Recognizing* moral rights and duties is a fairly abstract moral accomplishment that many human beings, in addition to the marginal cases, fail to reach. That is, Sapontzis agrees with the AMC at least to this extent: in spite of the inability of infants, the severely retarded, and the brain-damaged to recognize the rights of others and to act out of respect for the duties correlated with those rights, it is not necessarily the case that they lack moral rights. But Sapontzis has two objections to the AMC. First, it is not a telling argument when a refined version of the reciprocity argument is formulated: "Those who will be able to, are to at least a threshold degree able to, may again be able to, or did respect the rights of others are entitled to moral rights."[56] On this formulation of reciprocity, only the severely and incurably retarded or the psychopathic from birth are outside the pale, and this small, sequestered group, he thinks, can be plausibly treated as honorary right-holders out of deference to the feelings of species affinity most of us have.

Two comments are in order here. The first is that Sapontzis's use of the reciprocity argument is not so refined that he escapes all the criticisms of that argument. For example, on Sapontzis's grounds, the severely and incurably retarded do not have basic rights. Hence, if one of these is the child of a single mother who is a drug addict and could benefit from selling the child to a medical researcher, it is not clear how Sapontzis could mount any strong objection to her doing so. Perhaps it will be objected that this child would be protected because people in general do not want to exploit marginal human beings. Once again, however, this is a contingent affair; marginal human beings have been exploited in the past. To say that human beings, including the marginal cases, and animals have rights is an attempt to show emphatically the indefensibility of such exploitation.

Second, Sapontzis's effort to protect these especially marginal cases (not to be confused with the most marginal of marginal cases: the permanently comatose) "out of deference to the feelings of species affinity" is an example of speciesism that he would otherwise oppose in his great book. Sapontzis's response here regarding the severely retarded is that "we cannot infer from our practice in such special cases to what our common moral principles are. Just as this distinction between ordinary and extraordinary cases and the differing moral principles employed in each of them undercuts 'them or us' counter-examples to animal liberation, so it undercuts 'marginal cases' defenses of animal liberation, once those marginal cases have been seriously reduced in number."[57] No doubt there are some similarities here, but the dissimilarities are far greater than Sapontzis admits. The extraordinary cases often posed as counterexamples to animal liberation (e.g., what would you do if you could only save a normal human being or a pig but not both?) are in extremis in nature and hence necessarily tragic in that someone must suffer. But the AMC deals with marginal cases and animals in situations where no one has to suffer, so that these extraordinary cases and the marginal cases are not on a par.

In addition to claiming it not to be a telling argument, Sapontzis has a second objection to the AMC: it is not insightful. Specifically, it is not insightful regarding why the reciprocity requirement has such intuitive appeal. This appeal is due, he thinks, not to species prejudice but to a matter of fairness:

> A's having a right against B is correlated with B's having a duty to A; it would be unfair for B's liberty to be thus restricted without A's liberty also being similarly (or otherwise appropriately) restricted. For example, if Alice has a right to the fruits of her labor, then Bob is obligated (*ceteris paribus*) not to go into Alice's field and take her corn. It would be manifestly unfair, then, for Alice not to be obligated to respect Bob's right to the fruits of his labor and to remain free to go into his field and take his corn.[58]

The Achilles heel of this argument, as Sapontzis himself notes and as I have already argued, is that it cannot provide a basis for the obligations of the powerful to the powerless. Only those strong enough to pose a threat can gain rights against us.

Sapontzis takes a unique approach to the reciprocity requirement; in fact, it is exactly the opposite approach to that taken by Narveson, Frey, and others. Sapontzis thinks that the reciprocity requirement generally does not apply to dealings between human beings and animals, and therefore the reciprocity requirement generally does not pose an obstacle to extending moral rights to animals. To say the least, this transition needs more support than Sapontzis gives it. Regarding the AMC, however, it should be emphasized that Sapontzis is opposed not only to Singer's and Regan's use of it to defend animals but also to Frey's peculiar use of it against animals. As before, he equates extraordinary (i.e., in extremis) cases and marginal cases, and he thinks that both are largely irrelevant to human-animal relations.

Regarding this view, it is best to remember Regan's claim that one of the things that one expects from moral theory is an account not only of the easy cases but also of the alleged counterexamples, extraordinary cases, and marginal cases.[59]

Mary Anne Warren is like Sapontzis in defending animal rights but not necessarily the AMC. (Warren, however, is obviously much more qualified in her defense of animals than is Sapontzis, although both of them are—to some extent legitimately—critical of Regan's notion of "inherent value.") Putting animals in the same moral category as the severely retarded or the brain damaged is highly counterintuitive, she thinks. There is no reason to put nonparadigmatic human beings (like Clark, she avoids the phrase *marginal cases*) on a moral par with animals if there are many reasons for extending strong moral rights to the former. For example, infants and small children are potentially autonomous beings and are already partially autonomous beings. Unlike baby chimpanzees, she argues, human children are already learning the things that will enable them eventually to be autonomous beings. This makes it likely that their minds have more subtleties than their speech (or lack of it) proclaims. This is an interesting point, it seems to me. Less convincing, however, is her treatment of other nonparadigmatic humans who do not have the potential for moral autonomy. It must be granted that some mentally defective human beings are more apt to achieve moral autonomy if they are valued and cared for well. Nonetheless, those who truly lack the potential for moral autonomy can be made to have stronger moral status than animals only if we think it crucial that they are the friends, relatives, and conspecifics of human beings. Warren does think that these relations are crucial.

Warren holds the now-familiar view that "their rights are based not only on the value which they themselves place upon their lives and well-being, but also on the value which other human beings place upon them."[60] But she holds this view in a more tentative way than Frey or the reciprocity theorists treated in the previous chapter. For example, nonparadigmatic human beings are different from expensive paintings and gemstones (which do not have rights) precisely because severely retarded or senile human beings have value not only for other human beings but also because they have their own needs and interests. Unlike Sapontzis, Warren is not so much opposed to the AMC as she is intent on moving beyond it so as to put it in what she thinks is its proper place: "The sentience of nonparadigm humans, like that of sentient nonhuman animals, gives them a place in the sphere of rights holders. So long as the moral rights of all sentient beings are given due recognition, there should be no objection to providing some of them with *additional* protections, on the basis of our interests as well as their own."[61] That is, Warren is between opponents to the AMC such as Sapontzis, on the one hand, and defenders of the AMC, on the other. Her intermediate status is due to her belief that conferred rights are not necessarily any weaker or less binding on moral agents than are "natural" rights. To the extent that she does believe in "natural" rights (the cautionary quotation marks are hers), however, even she can be seen as a defender of the AMC.

Conclusion

In this chapter I have shown Frey rightly push the defender of the AMC to think through some of the implications of the possession of sentiency, but I have also shown his inconsistency regarding the issue of whether possession of sentiency is all that important in the first place. At one point he wonders why the infliction of gratuitous suffering is wrong; at another point he defends the moral truism that suffering is suffering and hence evil. Concerning the latter tendency in Frey, it is crucial to notice that the sort of sentiency he has in mind is not merely reaction to stimuli, or even reaction to sensory stimuli, but rather the ability to feel pain. That is, the AMC builds on the fact that a central nervous system makes possible pain states that are morally relevant *if anything is morally relevant.* In this regard the utilitarian Frey is not only like his fellow utilitarian Singer but also like Regan. Nevertheless, whereas Regan, on the basis of the AMC and the sentience of human beings and animals, moves from the rights of human beings to the rights of animals, Frey moves from the present permissibility of certain painful experiments on animals to the permissibility of certain painful experiments on marginal human beings.

Clark, Becker, and Paden all explore the possibility that the legitimacy of partial affections in human beings has implications for the AMC. Only Clark among these three defends the AMC. Becker tries to move from the claim that in extremis we can legitimately show preference for those close to us, including those in our own species, a claim that defenders of the AMC would grant, to the bothersome claim that in normal circumstances we can still show such a preference, even to the point were we can kill and eat animals, a claim that defenders of the AMC would not grant. Paden is also opposed to the AMC based on his distinction between the actually existing moral community and the theoretical, ideal community. The latter should not be forced on us by defenders of the AMC, he thinks. The problem with too much concern for actually existing moral communities, however—and this problem affects Clark as well in an odd way because of his concentration on pets and British beasts—is that it may result in a reification of certain traditional prejudices, as in classism, racism, sexism, and speciesism, as well as certain forms of patriotism.

There is much to be learned, however, from Clark's defense of the AMC and from his opposition to Frey. It is true that if I can save only my child or my neighbor but not both, I should save my child. Nonetheless, this hierarchy of judgment or partiality of affection does not license tyranny such that I may kill my neighbor so as to benefit my child. Clark is also instructive regarding why intellectual superiority does not license tyranny, for on this reasoning, beings intellectually superior to us (God, the angels, or the Nazis by self-proclamation) could then eat us or painfully experiment on us, as well as doing so with marginal cases and animals.

Frey's influence, however, has not stopped because of Clark's and other critics' opposition. Even some animal rightists agree with Frey on some points. Sapontzis greatly reduces the number of human beings who are marginal cases and then claims that species affinity can be used to protect the rest. That is, Sapontzis is in some ways like Frey and especially the reciprocity theorists. Sapontzis derives a strange conclusion from the insights of reciprocity theorists, however: because reciprocity theory does not really deal with animals, it poses no obstacles to animal rights. Warren is also a bit like Frey and especially the reciprocity theorists in seeing the capacity for autonomy as crucial in determining what sort of moral beneficiary a being can be: infants are partially autonomous, and marginal cases who are properly cared for are also more likely to be partially autonomous. Warren is correct to suggest that if we accept the AMC, it is nonetheless important to note that once the minimal rights that the AMC affords to marginal cases and animals are acknowledged (e.g., the right not to receive gratuitous suffering or the right to life), it is still permissible to put in place additional protections regarding marginal cases. That is, partial affections are legitimate in morality as long as they are ancillary to, rather than replacements for, impartial ascription of basic rights.

The Criticisms of Leahy and Carruthers

In this chapter I highlight two recent critics of the AMC: Michael Leahy and Peter Carruthers. Before moving to these critics, however, I consider the related objections of several of those critical of the AMC. I will argue that neither these critics nor Leahy and Carruthers refute the AMC. In the effort to defend the AMC against Leahy and Carruthers, I will rely on the thought of several scholars. My hope is that by the end of this chapter, I will be in a position to examine in detail the connection between the AMC and the great ape project and euthanasia, which I attempt to do in later chapters.

Several Critics

L. Duane Willard thinks that the AMC is nonsense on stilts, to borrow a phrase from Bentham. Human beings, marginal or otherwise, do not possess rights as properties in the way they possess red hair or lungs, nor do they possess rights in the way that they have interests or pains. "We 'have' or 'possess' rights only in the sense that we decide to ascribe them to ourselves and others." That is, Willard develops the Wittgensteinian belief that rights are not independently existing facts "out there."[1] Hence, on Willard's view, most animal rightists base their views on a kind of natural law theory. As I have shown earlier in this book, I tend to agree with Willard here, but I do not necessarily think that Singer and Regan et al. are wrong in deriving values from facts if the facts to which they refer are the relevant ones and if the values derived from these facts are defensible ones. This is not to say, however, that we ascribe rights to marginal cases or animals prior to, and independently of, all moral judgment. Rather, I am defending, and I think other supporters of the AMC implicitly are or at least ought to be defending, the more moderate (Kantian) view that there is both a subjective and an objective component in the attribution of rights.

Willard's version of reciprocity puts him at odds with the "natural law theory" of most animal rightists, and he forthrightly denies rights to infants, the feebleminded, and animals on this basis. We might have rights *against* the feebleminded, he thinks (say, if they pose material harm to us), and we might have rights against animals or against the human beings who own the animals. But they do not have rights against us, according to Willard. Infants and the feebleminded deserve more respect than animals, Willard thinks, because they are our children and because they might not be totally devoid of the capacity to grasp moral beliefs, whereas animals are not our children and do not have this grasp in any way. Willard wants to be clear here that he grants a favored status to infants and the feebleminded not because of some facts about them that imply rights but because the fact that they are our children is what we have decided to be relevant. "Facts never wear their relevance on their face." What is missing from Willard, however, is some indication as to why some of our decisions are better than other decisions. Why not say, for example, that we have made a legitimate choice if we choose to take care of red-haired retarded children but not brown-haired ones? Willard's view unfortunately does not seem to prohibit such a choice:

> The fact that the feebleminded and infants (with the potentiality of rationality, autonomous will, and self-concept) are our children does not, in or by itself, imply they have rights. Rather, we ascribe rights to infants and the feebleminded because we decide or judge that their being our children is the kind of fact which is relevant to the ascribing of rights to them . . . because of our purposes, intentions, and values regarding them. Similarly with regard to interests and sufferings—whether of infants and the feebleminded, or normal adult human beings, or animals—those facts do not, in or by themselves, imply rights for any of these beings. If we ascribe rights to any of these beings, it is because we decide or judge that having interests and suffering pain are facts relevant to the ascribing of rights to them; but having interests and suffering pain are facts relevant to ascribing rights to these beings because of our purposes. . . . Thus it is that some people claim that animals have rights, for they decide or judge on the basis of their purposes, intentions, and values regarding animals that the interests and suffering of animals are relevant facts. . . . But other people can and do decide or

judge on the basis of their purposes, intentions, and values regarding animals that the interests and suffering of animals are not facts sufficiently relevant to ascribing rights to them.[2]

Granted, it is normal adult human beings who decide which beings have rights, but are there no facts to which we can appeal when making this decision? Willard seems to have illegitimately moved from the claim that human decision making is a necessary condition for there being rights to the claim that it constitutes a sufficient condition for there being rights. He notes that many people view suffering as intrinsically evil, but others think that suffering is essential to the building of character. A better way to make this point is to say that all sane people view suffering as a bad thing, other things being equal. When other things are not equal, however—for example, when the experience of some suffering is necessary for the attainment of a greater good—then some people will tolerate or even welcome suffering without violating their belief that suffering per se is a bad thing.[3]

Michael Fox, who has written the last decade's most influential book defending animal experimentation, is committed not so much to the claim that defenders of the AMC base their defense on natural law theory as to the view that defenders of the AMC such as Singer and Regan have not explained why mongoloid babies ought not to be used as mere means to someone else's ends. Fox is correct regarding the weak version of the AMC, which starts from the assumption that mongoloids ought not to be mistreated. Singer is not agnostic regarding the reasons that legitimate this assumption, however (sentience is crucial), and neither is Regan mute on this topic (see his transcendental argument and his own treatment of sentiency). Fox himself thinks that autonomy is a necessary condition for possessing rights, and hence he may be in a worse position than Singer or Regan in the attempt to explain why we should not mistreat mongoloids. He notes that a fully developed horse may be more reflective (and more autonomous) than a brain-damaged child; a chimpanzee, more skilled in language than a newborn infant; and a cat, better able to reason than a comatose accident victim. However, he thinks it would be morally insensitive to refuse to use the horse, chimpanzee, or cat for any purpose for which we would not feel equally justified in using an underdeveloped or deficient human being.[4]

Fox defends the following strange view: if human beings are allowed to have feelings of kinship with members of other species, then we should be equally allowed to have such feelings for members of our own species. This view is strange in that it seems to imply that some philosopher or other holds that our feelings of kinship for animals are or ought to be greater than those for human beings. But no one holds this view. Regarding the AMC itself, Fox notes that infants are potentially autonomous and that individuals who are senile, comatose, mentally ill, or incapacitated by disease or accident generally were once autonomous:

> In the case of children who are severely retarded, autistic, and so on, however, we are dealing with people who may never achieve a semblance of autonomy. In deciding how we ought to look on all these classes of individuals, a reasonable position to take would seem to be that here membership in our own species ought to count for something, in the sense in which a charitable attitude toward these less developed or less fortunate than ourselves, for whom we feel some especially close kinship, is particularly compelling to a morally mature person. Just as our untutored moral sense tells us that we have very strong obligations to members of our immediate families, so it seems that preferential treatment should, under certain circumstances, accordingly be granted to members of the human family.[5]

An obvious question for Fox at this point is the following one: if these marginal cases deserve fair treatment from us only because of certain sentiments on our part, why not acknowledge those sentiments many people have for animals as fellow members in the family of sentient beings? Fox's response seems to be that this connection is not as strong, direct, or morally compelling as that which ties us to marginal cases. There is nothing necessary about this connection to marginal cases, however. For some human beings, it is not an easy matter to feel a close kinship to those human beings who are less fortunate. For example, some human beings cannot establish an empathetic relationship even with a healthy infant. These facts, noticed by Fox, should make him leery of establishing a position based solely on sentiment, regardless of whether marginal cases or animals are the primary recipients of that sentiment. It is crucial, he thinks, that we have sentimental attachment to marginal cases so as to avoid Nazi-like campaigns against "undesirables," and it is also prudent to have such an attachment in that we might eventually be "undesirable" ourselves. Nonetheless, Fox still has a difficult time explaining why it is wrong, as surely it is, to torture a severely brain-damaged and unwanted infant.

It is correct to claim, as Fox does, that membership in the moral community is not a cut-and-dried matter, in that creatures should be examined on a case-by-case basis. Still, it is not clear why the operative criterion in these examinations has to be affinity to our autonomy, because on a consistent application of this criterion, we would not be able to save as many marginal cases as Fox thinks. Human "vegetables" and "basket cases," Fox argues, might eventually become autonomous if we continue to experiment on animals (not marginal cases) in the effort to eliminate the maladies found in these marginal cases: "A cure is not just around the corner for every severe handicap. But the examples that can be cited should give us pause when we feel inclined to lump together as without hope a whole range of diverse conditions affecting normal human functioning and autonomy."[6] From this we can see Fox's ambivalence regarding line drawing. The line between human beings who are full members of the moral community and those who are not is a permeable one, but the line between human beings in general and animals is impermeable in that not even a yet-to-be-discovered wonder drug will bring autonomy to animals. He bends over backward to give the benefit of the doubt to marginal cases, and he goes as far out of his way as possible not to include animals within the scope of moral concern. This is worse than being ambivalent; it is outright inconsistency. If we are charitable, benevolent, and humane, he correctly notes, then we should extend our moral concern to the marginal cases. But Fox has no argument that I can see to show why these same charitable, benevolent, and humane people should not extend the scope of these virtues to animals.

A similar sort of ambivalence (at best) or inconsistency is found in Ruth Cigman. She says that it is "an empirical fact" that human beings and animals have the capacity to feel pain, but not every being that experiences pain necessarily has the capacity to be a subject of the misfortune of death. She, like Fox, bends over backward to leave open the possibility that the comatose and the insane have the capacity to see death as a misfortune. Furthermore, and again like Fox, she goes out of her way to deny that possibility to animals. We may be somewhat uneasy about ascribing certain conceptual capacities to marginal cases, but it is absurd to make such ascriptions to animals: "A case can be made (albeit, perhaps, a poor one) for describing the former but not the latter as possible subjects of the misfortune of death."[7] The implication of this ambivalence or inconsistency is that all human beings are at least candidates for the right to life, even though some of them are unable to sustain this right because of their inability to realize the capacity to see death as a misfortune. Strangely, no animals are even candidates for such a right to life.

Philip Devine at least initially seems to be more friendly to the AMC than is Willard, Fox, or Cigman. He is prepared to grant that it is wrong to kill, maim, or inflict pain on a chimpanzee except in those circumstances where it is right (permissible?) to do these things to human beings. One doubt Devine has here concerns euthanasia, for he sees fewer objections to killing an incurably ill chimpanzee than to the killing of a similarly ill human being. I will show that Devine's preference for human beings is his dominant view. It is worthwhile noting his belief that chimpanzees are to be distinguished from chickens, presumably because chickens lack developed mental abilities. Further, he thinks, making concessions regarding chimpanzees does not amount to much in that we do not eat their flesh. (Devine does not mention that the paucity of chimpanzees in the world is at least partly due to human interest in using chimpanzees, if not in eating them.) There are two kinds of human being to which chimpanzees, not chickens, can be compared: infants and the severely retarded. Even painless infanticide, much less the use of infants in cancer research or the killing of infants for food, is impermissible precisely because of the infant's potential, he thinks, just as it is impermissible to do these things to sleeping, reversibly comatose, or curably mad human adults.[8]

The severely mentally retarded, however, lack even the potential to achieve the capacities we invoke to treat normal adult human beings and infants differently from animals. Devine admits, contra Fox, that the appeal to potentiality here is unpersuasive, but he nonetheless thinks that we should not use the severely retarded for food or for cancer research. They should be treated as persons even if they are not such. Devine justifies this approach largely on prudential grounds, however, rather than on some principled basis. First, to experiment painfully on the severely retarded would exact too great a cost in anxiety among the mildly retarded and their relatives; second, by making the human/animal distinction the relevant criterion for ascribing a right to life, we have a clear line with which to make decisions in nearly all cases. One wonders, however, whether Devine has noticed the anxiety caused to a great number of people when animals are experimented on painfully; second, one wonders whether the ease of application of the human/animal distinction automatically signals an ethical justification. Devine is on firmer ground when he says that being treated as a person is not always a benefit—for example, if being a person prevents one from getting a merciful death when such a death is requested.[9]

Devine moves beyond a merely prudential defense of the severely retarded to the claim that it is "morally imperative" that we defend them even if the human being lacks the intelligence of a pig. He asks why employment of biological concepts such as "species" is bothersome in ethics. Devine considers and rejects one possible objection, one concerning the analogy between speciesism, on the one hand, and racism and sexism, on the other. Devine's response here is that the racist seizes certain physical differences that are real enough in themselves and then arbitrarily tries to use them for some social purpose. But is this not exactly what the speciesist does as well? There are obvious physical differences between animals and normal adult human beings, but the possession of sentiency is not one of them; there are obvious physical differences between animals and marginal cases, but it is difficult, if not impossible, to think of any that are morally relevant. This is the whole point to the AMC. The problem is not that Devine moves from "is" to "ought" but rather that he does not show how the physical differences between marginal cases and animals (what is) can justify eating and experimenting on the latter (what ought to be, according to Devine). Nor is it clear how Devine can avoid the criticism of a Thomas Nagel–like, antimeritocratic thinker who might say that we no more deserve to be born human than we deserve being born with the particular intellectual capacities that we have.[10]

Devine does not mind moving from "is" to "ought," for he explicitly identifies himself with natural law tradition. Unlike Clark, however, who also identifies with the natural law tradition, Devine infers from this tradition a "normic" sense to the concept of "human." There are, he thinks, "good reasons [that] can be supplied for regarding the lives and interests of nonhumans as of less moral importance than those of humans. If the killing of nonhumans is murder, then we no doubt ought to stop animals from killing each other, not, to be sure, because they are guilty of murder in so doing (they are not moral agents) but on the same grounds on which we stop the activities of homicidal maniacs."[11] He seems to be asking whether animal rightists can be consistent. There is quite a difference, however, as Devine notices, between our killing animals and predators' doing so, in that predators are not moral agents. Equally important is that it is by no means clear that by preventing predation we could save as many animals as we would like or even the animals we intended to save. To take a familiar example: by removing large cats and other predators from a region so as to protect the deer population, we encourage overpopulation of deer such that massive numbers of them starve in winter. To defend the AMC one need not strive for godlike knowledge of ecology. It is obviously a good thing to prevent homicidal maniacs from killing marginal cases, but is it obviously a good thing to bell cats that might otherwise kill a rat? Perhaps so, perhaps not. Cats, both large and small, have their rights, too.[12]

According to Devine, a human life is an intrinsic good, a view that is, with some terminological adjustments, largely compatible with Regan's. But Devine thinks that this view is supported by the consideration that a retarded human being wants to go on living, a consideration that obtains for animals as well, the latter point being entirely missed by Devine but emphasized by Regan. It is not merely "species solidarity" that leads us to protect a deaf, mute, and retarded child. The child also has feelings, as does an animal.[13]

Cora Diamond's rejection of the AMC is related to Devine's. She clearly understands the argument: if we say that animals are not rational, and hence we have a right to kill them for food, but we do not say the same of people whose rationality cannot develop or cannot be restored, we are plainly not treating like cases consistently. That is, the AMC rests on the views that we should give equal consideration to the interests of any being capable of having interests, that the capacity to have interests is dependent on the capacity for suffering and enjoyment, and that we share this latter capacity with animals. Diamond thinks that the AMC is confused, however, in that discussion of human interests in the same breath as animal interests is beside the point. Defenders of the AMC, she notes, ask why we do not kill and eat irrational human beings; this is the wrong way to begin the discussion, because it ignores some central facts: we do not eat our dead, not even after automobile accidents, when their flesh is healthy and edible, nor do we eat amputated human limbs: "Anyone who, in discussing this issue, focuses on our reasons for not killing people or our reasons for not causing them suffering quite evidently runs a risk of leaving altogether out of his discussion those fundamental features of our relationship to other human beings which are involved in our not eating them. . . . *A person is not something to eat.*"[14] Diamond is a vegetarian herself, although she, along with some other animal rightists, might not find anything wrong with eating a cow that has been struck by lightning or a car. Eating a human being is a different matter altogether, she thinks.

We give human beings funerals, but not dogs, although not because human beings have capacities greater than those of dogs. Even an infant who dies after two days deserves a funeral, because not to do so, claims Diamond, is impious. She realizes that the word *impious* does not make for clarity and asks for explanation: "But there are some actions, like giving people names, that are part of the way we come to understand and indicate our recognition of *what* kind it is with which we are concerned."[15] Having funerals for human beings is one of these actions. Or again, people who eat their pets do not really have "pets" in the normal use of that term, for a pet is given a name and is allowed to enter our homes in ways that cows and squirrels are not. That is, a pet is given some part of the character of a person such that not eating it is not due to our recognizing its interests. Furthermore, according to Diamond, it is not respect for our interests that is involved in our not eating each other.

Diamond's view, if I understand it correctly, is defective because it is overly nominalistic. Beings acquire status as moral beneficiaries, she thinks, entirely because we say they deserve such status. Human beings on this view have the Orpheus-like ability to bring moral beneficiary status to life merely by saying that it should be so. The remedy to such an approach does not run to the other extreme, wherein it is assumed that moral beneficiary status is a fact "out there" waiting to be discovered. Rather, human beings are the measur*ers* of nature but not the measure; they are the primary beholders of value in nature but not the only holders of such value, to use Holmes Rolston's language.

Paul Muscari, unlike Diamond but like Devine, questions whether there are many marginal cases whose intellectual level equals that of animals or falls below it. If self-awareness is the criterion of human uniqueness (a questionable claim), then, Muscari argues, schizophrenics and retarded children meet the criterion in that they are self-aware in some sense. Muscari does not specify exactly which sense of self-awareness is exhibited by retarded children but not by mentally developed animals, however.[16] Vinit Haksar puts a Kantian twist to this point. The mentally retarded may seem to lack freedom and rationality, but at some deep, noumenal level they may have these.

Too much sympathy for animals is degenerate because animals do not have this deep, noumenal level. Haksar is a prime example of what I showed Clark discussing in the previous chapter. Some philosophers for moral purposes hang on to an Augustinian soul, a Cartesian ghost in the machine, or a noumenal self long after they have abandoned these in metaphysics. That is, Haksar uses his deep, noumenal level to do too much intellectual work.[17]

Leahy and the AMC

In a recent attack on animal rights, *Against Liberation,* Michael Leahy indicates that it might seem that no matter how low we set the minimal requirement of moral personality for equal consideration of interests, large numbers of human beings will be ruled out of court, most notably infants, the severely retarded, and human beings with severe and irreparable brain damage. Leahy is confident, however: "That problems might beset the minimal qualifications for moral personality ought not to disturb us. The exigencies of life require that we must cut Gordian knots to allow for marginal cases."[18] Leahy claims that infants and the severely retarded may be in different categories, in that the former are potentially normal adults, contra Singer's claim that this is an ad hoc device to keep up appearances: infants are not now at a higher mental level than many animals. Leahy, in contrast to utilitarians such as Singer, does not invoke the capacity to suffer to account for infants and the severely retarded, the "hard cases." Rather, he tries to bolster contractualist accounts.

Parents and relations, cultural and religious sensibilities, are all crucial factors when considering how we should treat mongoloids and animals. These factors hold in check whatever our natural sympathies may push us to do regarding these cases. "Universal" sympathy is not quite as universal as some members of the Scottish Enlightenment thought. According to Leahy, however, we do not need the utilitarian criterion of capacity for suffering to keep passion in check, nor do we need to appeal to Regan's inherent value to do so. Leahy's contractualist account centers on a Wittgensteinian model of language learning that takes into consideration parents, relations, and cultural and religious sensibilities. The vocabulary of moral and legal confrontation (duty, obligation, rights, etc.) is acquired through the gradual process of social interaction. One becomes a moral agent initially through family contacts with parents, siblings, and pets, and then the horizons are gradually extended. The marginal cases obviously do not get too far along this road toward moral agency and the ability to enter contracts. However, according to Leahy, they nonetheless deserve to be the objects of various fair practices because "no theory of moral belief ought to rule out such practices if tradition or special circumstances are generally thought to justify them."[19]

The "natural and tender impulses" of humane people prevent them from treating moral beneficiaries who lack self-consciousness (babies, the severely retarded, and animals) merely as means to an end. But this prevention is not equally enforced. The ability of mature mammals and birds to take care of themselves, care for their children, and interact with members of their own and other species far surpasses that of infants (or anencephalics, who are not capable of language). This seems to be in the animals' favor, but Leahy thinks it crucial that infants will rapidly and without effort cross the language barrier, slowly become self-conscious, and develop incipient moral agency in ways that are impossible for animals. This potential in infants makes Singer's emphasis on sentiency and Regan's emphasis on inherent value seem somewhat exaggerated, he thinks. Leahy has a more difficult time explaining our feelings regarding the mistreatment of the permanently retarded, those with severe Down's syndrome, and those who are microcephalic. These beings, unlike a slightly mongoloid being who has certain plans, do not have much potential. Why not sell them? Leahy's response seems to be that we should not sell them because of the outcry such an act would produce in normal adults, not because of any property possessed by the marginal cases themselves.[20]

The severely retarded can be treated differently from animals because of their "honorary status," according to Leahy, a view otherwise known as "speciesism." Pets and some zoo creatures are the only animals to bear any sort of comparison with the severely retarded who have caring custodians. Leahy says the following about the AMC: "The rather weary drawing of parallels between animals and instances of human retardation diverts attention from their true source of value to us. Animals may be primitive beings but they are not thereby defective ones. . . . Animals . . . are *sui generis.*"[21] Animals are what they are. In contrast, we prefer that there be no mental retardation. This does not mean that retarded human beings should be killed. Leahy's point seems to be that if we are aware of the sui generis character of animals, we are less likely to see them as undeveloped human beings in the way that marginal cases are undeveloped human beings: "The world would be a better place without mental retardation, madness, and senile dementia. But if someone were to claim that it would be a better world without birds and bears, trees and rivers, and the Dani people, then we would have to assume that they were either joking, lying, or crazy. To highlight the *sui generis* nature of animals is not liberationist. It serves only to put their comparison with human imbeciles in proper perspective."[22]

That is, according to Leahy, it is misleading to lump animals, the severely retarded and infants together since infants have real potentiality and the severely retarded have some sort of "human capacity."[23] Despite appearances, however, Leahy's opposition to animal rights is ultimately not due to his opposition to the AMC. The reverse is true: Leahy is opposed to animal rights on a priori grounds, and hence he must oppose the AMC. In the following quotation from the end of his book, he indicates that he would be opposed to animal rights regardless of how strong the AMC is (especially note the last lines of this quotation): "Attempts to convince us that the eating of meat and fish is an evil invasion of the inalienable rights of animals and that it should cease forthwith are a sham. They can only succeed with the help either of opportunistic flights of fancy such as inherent value or *theos* rights, or by otherwise obscuring the differences between creatures like ourselves, who use language, and those that do not."[24] The fact that marginal cases do not use language the way we do is eliminated from consideration by Leahy on an a priori basis; that is, he simply assumes the grounds for the omission of marginal cases.

Carruthers, Contractualism, and Cartesianism

Peter Carruthers's recent book *The Animals Issue* also deals harshly with the AMC. In fact, Carruthers thinks that present concern with animal rights is a reflection of moral decadence, as was Nero's fiddling while Rome burned. His own view involves developing a theoretical framework that accords "full moral standing to all human beings," a view that does not necessarily run afoul of the AMC but that, in Carruthers's hands, does precisely that. Carruthers defends a (qualified) version of Rawls's reflective equilibrium wherein we begin with our considered commonsense moral beliefs (Becker's moral community in the first sense) and then try to construct a plausible moral theory. If the two are in conflict, we can either tinker with the theory or we can give up an element of commonsense belief. In either event, an acceptable moral theory must at least start from common sense. This method of reflective equilibrium is not necessarily bothersome to the defender of the AMC, for the AMC starts from the commonsensical assumption that even severely retarded people have rights and that we ought not to mistreat animals. Further, it offers a theory as to how to deal with these assumptions in a consistent way. Some defenders of the AMC try to argue for the assumption that marginal cases have rights, and some do not. The latter are close to what Carruthers refers to as "coherentists," but both views are compatible with reflective equilibrium. Carruthers believes that only coherentism is compatible with reflective equilibrium, however.[25]

Carruthers is like Tester in seeing any effort to justify the AMC in the strong sense as "foundationalism," a view that, along with intuitionism, he sees as inferior to coherentism. Moral intuitionism does generally vindicate common sense, he thinks, but it is still unacceptable because moral intuitions can and do conflict. Carruthers in one respect is like all the major defenders of the AMC in seeing the need to have moral intuitions backed by moral theory. That is, it is questionable whether Regan is, as Carruthers alleges, a sophisticated intuitionist. All moral philosophers have intuitions, but only the intuition*ist* is willing to have intuitions be self-sustaining or self-authenticating. Regan's (and others') defense of the AMC attempts to render our moral intuitions consistent; Regan attempts a partial defense of, and a partial revision of, common sense. Or better, the defender of the AMC, as I have shown, takes our considered moral beliefs and applies them to unconsidered circumstances that lie scattered in an inconsistent array. What is odd is that Carruthers accuses Regan of being an intuitionist despite the fact that Regan does not use the language of intuition.[26]

The oddity can be explained as follows: in Regan's "intuitionism" one can avoid the word *intuition* because intuition normally appears in the guise of reflective equilibrium. Here Carruthers wants to have his cake and eat it, too. He wants Regan to use more than the method of reflective equilibrium, in that a good moral theory must also give us a plausible picture of the sources of morality. When Regan and others try to go beyond reflective equilibrium, however, so as to explain why marginal cases and animals have rights, they are accused of foundationalism. Utilitarianism fares slightly better, on Carruthers's view, because of its governing conception, which lies in the decisions that would be made by an impartial observer. The utilitarian does not rest content with reflective equilibrium, nor does the utilitarian resort to foundationalism. Rather, utilitarian "morality arises in the first place when the natural impulse towards benevolence is universalized through the impact of reason."[27] It is not so much (experience of) pleasure and pain or preference satisfaction that is at the core of utilitarianism, but rather, as in contractualism, a decision-making procedure. Nevertheless, Carruthers does not like the way Singer uses this procedure in the AMC to claim that the various characteristics that distinguish us as moral beneficiaries from animals—species, appearance, intelligence—are morally irrelevant. Given a contractualist approach, Carruthers thinks, intelligence is not irrelevant. Carruthers unfortunately assumes that the relevance of intelligence in becoming a moral agent is equally relevant in becoming a moral beneficiary. Because intelligence does loom large in Carruthers's treatment of the AMC, he would be bothered if children (potentially intelligent beings) were used in the testing of new cosmetics, but not necessarily if animals were so used.[28]

Even though utilitarianism fares better than Regan's "intuitionism" in Carruthers's view, both stray too far from what Carruthers takes to be the "almost universal human belief" that "the interests of an animal count for practically nothing when set against the suffering of a human being." Of the major ethical theories, only contractualism can approximate reflective equilibrium, according to Carruthers. The thesis that animal suffering and human suffering are of equal moral standing is a type of skepticism, he thinks. But do any of the defenders of the AMC quite think that animals and normal human beings are of equal moral standing even if their suffering is equal? Once again, in extremis situations indicate that Singer, Regan, and Clark are quite willing to be flexible and are not as skeptical of the worth of human beings as Carruthers suggests. Nor do I think that Carruthers is convincing when he makes the typical contractualist move of emphasizing intelligence as an important criterion for moral beneficiary status and then slipping mentally retarded human beings into moral beneficiary status through the back door.[29]

Because animals have far fewer desires for the future than normal human beings do, it is hard for Carruthers to understand how many of their desires could be frustrated even on preference utilitarian grounds. Carruthers furthermore notes (along with Frey) that on preference utilitarian grounds, once one has fed a hungry dog, one would not be failing to fulfill any of its desires by killing it painlessly. According to

Carruthers, dogs and horses are vastly different from (all?) human beings in cognitive powers, and hence they do not deserve the same moral status as human beings. Carruthers thinks that contractualists can respond to the AMC by acknowledging that dogs can be protected by property rights, as are automobiles. It is reasonable that owners' rights of disposal of their cars and dogs should be constrained to some degree, he thinks. What this means, however, is that animals, like buildings, have no direct rights; that animals in principle have a metaphysical status equivalent to nonsentient cars and to nonpreferring buildings; and that unowned dogs everywhere and wild horses—say, in the American West—are fair game for exploitation. At least there are no Carruthers-like reasons to prevent them from being exploited.[30]

Carruthers is at least somewhat aware of the bind he is in. At one point in his book he admits that it is part of commonsense moral belief that duties toward animals can arise in the private as well as public domain. That is, it is easier on contractualist grounds to explain why it is wrong to severely beat a dog in the street than it is to explain why it is wrong to torture a cat in the privacy of one's home. Again, if one owns a painting, even the *Mona Lisa,* one can perhaps use it as a dart board on contractualist grounds, just as one can use one's cat as a dart board as long as those who care about cats do not find out. This last proviso is needed to salvage Carruthers's claim that contractualism gets us closer to reflective equilibrium than do either utilitarianism or Regan's view, even if contractualism cannot accommodate all of what commonsense morality says about animals. Nor can contractualism accommodate all that commonsense morality says about infants, the very senile, or the severely mentally defective. It is counterintuitive, to say the least, that killing an infant or a senile human being is permissible because they have no rights; at most we would be violating our duty to respect the feelings of those people who care about infants (or at least that particular infant) or the senile. As before, contractualists can point to the fact that the infant may become a rational contractor, but this is little consolation to the senile, who are amenable to use as dart boards, test subjects for new detergents, or prey that hunters might chase for sport.[31]

Carruthers explores the possibility of protecting the senile by means of a variation on Rawls's original position: "This is by making the agents behind the veil of ignorance choose on behalf, not just of themselves, but of family lines. . . . Since every human being—whether baby, senile, or mental defective—is the child of (or, at any rate, is descended from) rational agents, the conclusion will be that all human beings have the same basic moral rights."[32] This Rawlsian attempt to protect the senile fails for two reasons. First, not everyone would want to have basic moral rights were they to become senile, but I will defer a discussion of this topic until the last chapter. Second, there is the metaphysical problem of trying to preserve personal identity through cognitive changes as massive as the slide into senility. The physical body would still exist, but it is highly doubtful whether the "I" could still exist. That is, I cannot now in the original position protect the non-I then. The apparent failure to protect the senile leads Carruthers to try one more argument: because there are no sharp boundaries between a normal adult and a severe mental defective, to attempt to accord direct moral rights only to rational agents would be open to dangerous abuse, to a slippery slope:

> In contrast, there really is a sharp boundary between human beings and all other animals. Not necessarily in terms of intelligence or degree of rational agency, of course—a chimpanzee may be more intelligent than a mentally defective human, and a dolphin may be a rational agent to a higher degree than a human baby. But there is not the same practical threat to the welfare of rational agents in the suggestion that all animals should be excluded from the domain of direct moral concern. Someone who argues that since animals do not have rights, therefore babies do not have rights, therefore there can be no moral objection to the extermination of Jews, Gypsies, gays, and other so-called "deviants," is unlikely to be taken very seriously, even by those who share their evil aims.[33]

What is noteworthy here is that Carruthers himself partially attests to the validity of the AMC in his use of the chimpanzee and dolphin as examples. If one assumes the legitimacy of speciesism, then one will be less tempted to abuse marginal cases than one would be to abuse animals. Yet Carruthers thinks that the slippery slope argument is successful in according rights to all (and, it seems, only) human beings.

From a practical point of view, Carruthers thinks that the only way of framing rules that we can live with is to accord all (and, it seems, only) human beings the same basic rights or moral standing. Carruthers nonetheless alerts us to some anthropological evidence that counteracts his slippery slope argument. Many traditional human societies have not accorded the same moral standing to all human beings—say, by practicing infanticide—yet they embarked on no slippery slope. Carruthers's response to this evidence is to emphasize the fact, if it is a fact, that societies practicing infanticide have been teetering on the edge of survival because of poor environmental or agricultural conditions, such that infanticide was a sort of self-preservation. In short, no version of contractualism will accord direct moral standing to animals, although it may accord indirect duties concerning animals. In this regard contractualism cannot explain the commonsense intuition that "unmotivated cruelty to an animal is directly wrong." Contractualists also have an analogously difficult time extending direct moral standing to human beings who are not rational agents, but the slippery slope argument (despite its detractors) proves successful, he thinks, in protecting marginal cases.[34]

Although Carruthers admits that all mammals have beliefs and desires, they are not rational; in fact, no other species of animal even approximates the human one in this regard. Moreover, only human beings have basic rights, because only they can perform correlative duties. Carruthers thus has adopted the Thomistic and Kantian view that the moral value of our treatment of animals is derived from its connection with our treatment of human beings. This belief can escape our notice when we see Carruthers urging the following (persuasive) view: "So the hit-and-run driver to whom it never occurs to stop, in order to help the dog left howling in pain at the side of the road, as well as the one who drives on because late for an appointment at the hairdresser (as well as, of course, the driver who runs down the dog for fun in the first place), will each count as having acted wrongly, on the present account. For in each case the action will show the agent to be cruel."[35] Somehow Carruthers sees this view to be compatible with the denial of direct moral standing to animals, and somehow he thinks that his view represents reflective equilibrium properly understood, even though the denial that animal suffering has direct moral standing is not a part of commonsense but is "a theoretical construction upon it." Again, this sort of theoretical constructivism is precisely the defect Carruthers sees in Singer and Regan.[36]

One of the advantages of contractualism, on Carruthers's view, is that it avoids sentimentality toward animals. (But Clark, Singer, Regan, Sapontzis, Jamieson, et al. avoid this, too.) One of the disadvantages is that it seems to place only indirect moral significance on marginal cases and animals. Hence, Carruthers has to wonder whether he can sufficiently oppose farming babies for their meat or "putting down" aggressive mental defectives the way we put down vicious dogs. He responds to this problem—after admitting that some mental defectives and senile old people frequently have lower levels of mental activity than some animals—by pointing out the "moral salience" in the fact that marginal cases have a "human form." He notes that a crying baby or a senile old woman moaning with the pain of terminal cancer differ only slightly from a suffering normal adult. What he does not note is that the suffering of the baby and the senile old woman also differs only slightly from the suffering of an animal. There may be certain similarities of appearance (this is presumably what Carruthers means by "human form") among all human beings not found among animals, but it is much harder to find similarities of behavior or feeling that differentiate the two. Marginal cases and animals both moan, twitch, scream, and so on when they are in pain. Carruthers asks a perceptive question about his contractualist view: "Some might be puzzled at how I can claim, on the one hand, that sympathy for animal suffering is expressive of an admirable state of character and yet claim, on the other, that those who become desensitized to such suffering in the course of their work need not thereby display any weakness in their character. How can I have it both ways?"[37] His response seems to be that rational people have "contracted" to allow animals to suffer in the contexts of the slaughterhouse and the laboratory and that the cost of increasing concern for farm and laboratory animals is to distract attention away from those who do have direct moral standing: human beings. It seems to me that Carruthers has assumed (erroneously, I think) that moral sentiment is a pie of a fixed size, such that by giving a slice to animals, there will be less for others. In any event, defenders of the AMC such as Clark and Regan are not so much urging that we waste time by doting on our pets, such that no energy is left to alleviate human suffering, as that we keep the same schedules we already have, only that we not eat, wear, or experiment on marginal cases and animals while we do so.

The weakness of Carruthers's contractualist attack on the AMC is indicated by the fact that at the end of his book he tries to supplement his case in a most incredible way. He tries to float a modern version of the Cartesian hypothesis that animals do not really experience pain. To be precise, he thinks that there are both conscious and nonconscious varieties of pain. Although the existence of nonconscious experiences in human beings is widely acknowledged, there are no uncontroversial examples of nonconscious pain experiences in human beings. The obvious reason for this is that painful experiences intrude on consciousness—but not on animal consciousness, according to Carruthers. The psychological connections between our attitudes toward human suffering and animal suffering should be broken, he thinks: "Utilitarians are fond of claiming that if we were perfectly rational we should be equally sympathetic for the sufferings of animals as for the sufferings of ourselves. The truth may be that it is only our imperfect rationality that enables us to feel sympathy for animals at all."[38] This is an incredible view. Carruthers indicates that deep down he, like other contractualists, bases his view of animals on some supposed facts of nature. As before, the problem is not so much the move from facts to values as the effort to get the facts and values correctly. Carruthers does not do this:

> Mental states admit of a distinction between conscious and non-conscious varieties that is best accounted for as the difference between states that are, and states that are not, regularly made available to conscious (reflexive) thinking. Then since there is no reason to believe that any animals are capable of thinking about their own thinkings in this way, none of their mental states will be conscious ones. If this account were acceptable, it would follow almost immediately that animals can make no moral claims on us. For non-conscious mental states are not appropriate objects of moral concern.[39]

This is, indeed, not far from the Cartesian view. Cats screeching in pain when chemicals are dropped into their eyes, it seems, are not "appropriate objects of moral concern."

As evidence that Carruthers does not have his facts straight, consider the following comparison he makes, a comparison wherein the presence of a central nervous system, and the moral difference that system makes, is entirely trivialized: "If insects are not genuinely sentient, then brutish cruelty need not be displayed in one who causes them damage. But then so, too, if the experiences of birds and mammals are non-conscious—those who discount their experiences, in consequence, need not be brutishly cruel."[40] Any "duties" that we have to animals, on this bastardized contractualist/Cartesian account, are given out of respect for the feelings of animal lovers and through the qualities that animals may evoke in us. Any "duties" that we have to human beings who are not rational agents are granted only via Carruthers's slippery slope concerns. Carruthers's view, in sum, is as follows: "The most important practical conclusion of this book is that there is no basis for extending moral protection to animals. . . . Those who are committed to any aspect of the animal rights movement are thoroughly misguided."[41]

Responses to Leahy and Carruthers

Many of the points made in the recent criticisms of the AMC by Leahy and Carruthers were made previously in the 1970s and 1980s, but they also raise new concerns. Both the new and the old points deserve response. A recent article by Sarah Stebbins can be used initially to engage Leahy and especially Carruthers: "As children growing up in an age of Freudianism in the popular culture and behaviorism in the laboratory, my contemporaries and I were encouraged to attribute extremely complex unconscious mental states to the human beings we knew, and we were enjoined from attributing any mental states whatsoever to the nonhuman animals of our acquaintance."[42] With the partial demise of behaviorism, however, largely through the work of scholars such as Donald Griffin and Roger Crisp, we can start to take seriously the evidence from those who have intimate, day-to-day contact with animals: zookeepers, animal trainers, and pet owners. This evidence permits me to sketch four sorts of argument for complex mental states in animals to counteract Leahy and especially Carruthers.

(1) An argument from behavior supports the attribution of mental states to animals because these attributions play a role in the explanation of animal behavior. In fact, the attribution of complex mental states to animals offers the simplest theory regarding the causal origin of complex nonhuman behavior, in that the structures that would be required to produce these behaviors without conscious mental states would demand much more than those involved in the mental states themselves. (2) An argument from evolution supports the attribution of complex mental states, because they would confer a selective advantage to higher mammals in the process of speciation. (3) An argument from neurology uses anatomy to support the attribution of mental states to animals, as in the repeated citation in this book of preferences, pleasures, and pains in animals on the basis of their central nervous systems. This argument from neurology is quite different from an argument from analogy whereby introspectively discovered facts about our own mental states are assumed to exist in animals as well. (4) An argument from other minds tries to reduce to absurdity skepticism regarding animal minds.[43] That is, Carruthers's

doubts about animal sentience should also give rise to doubts about human sentience. All four of these arguments help to support the case for the AMC in making more plausible the claim that the higher animals are as mentally sophisticated or more so than marginal human beings. If, with Richard Sorabji and against R. G. Frey, we can assume that the point to the AMC is to make us recoil in horror at eating or painfully experimenting on the severely retarded and to think again about animals, then the argument looks much stronger than Leahy or Carruthers indicates.[44]

The defender of the AMC must be careful at this point, however. By concentrating too much on the complexity of mental states in animals, one might be tempted by what Colin McGinn calls "intelligenceism." This would consist in a pernicious form of social discrimination whereby inferiority of intelligence makes a being amenable to slaughter or electrical shock treatments for scientific purposes. The obvious consequence of this view is that infants, mentally backward adults, and the senile would lose significantly. In fact, if intelligenceism were adopted, it might make sense to raise genetically engineered "simple" humans for experimental or culinary purposes. Hence, the purpose of attributing complex mental states to animals is not to establish the case that being intelligent is what gives one the right not to be abused. Rather, it is merely to show that animals have mental lives that are complex enough to have preferences, pleasures, pains, memories, and expectations.[45]

Do we really wish to say that monkeys and cows are utterly incapable of reason? Of course not. Are unintelligent beings who are nonetheless sentient outside the sphere of moral concern? Of course not. (Although even retarded human beings may be responsible for their dispositions even if they do not bear full moral responsibility.)[46] The consequence of these leading questions is that if the killing of animals is morally permissible, then the killing of some human beings is permissible, too, as Nicholas Everitt argues. Everitt is even willing to call the killing of animals for food "murder." And murder, or "murder," is obviously wrong even if the one murdered has no family and friends, contra the reciprocity theorists' view of animals. There is a sort of dissonance found in conventional morality, according to Everitt, that consists in the acceptance of the following two propositions:

1. The painless and terror-free murder of a human being where this is not for his own benefit, and causes no loss or distress to any survivors, is seriously wrong.

2. The painless and terror-free "murder" of a non-human, where this is not for the animal's own benefit, and causes no loss or distress to any survivors, is not seriously wrong.[47]

The AMC shows that this dissonance can be removed if one can find some morally relevant feature that all human beings possess and animals do not.

It is difficult to see how the moral difference between murder and "murder" in the previously cited quotation from Everitt can be justified simply on the biological difference between humans and animals. Of course, biological differences can be morally relevant, but only if they provide an empirical base for various other characteristics—say, of a psychological kind—that *are* directly relevant to a moral difference. A mere difference in species in itself does not seem morally relevant, however. Most human beings are mentally superior to animals, emotionally more sophisticated, capable of a greater degree of autonomy and agency, and so on. Everitt points out the following, however:

> The main problem can be stated simply: there is an overlap between the mental characteristics of humans and of non-human animals. If we imagine plotting degree of mental development along a line in terms of increasing complexity, then there will be no point on the line at which all humans will be on one side of the point and all non-human animals on the other. This is most clearly brought out by considering a newly born baby. In terms of mental capacity, the baby is clearly inferior to many adult non-human animals of a wide range of species. At the other end of the human life span, those suffering from gross senility may sink to the level of mental competence lower than that of some animals. So if the wrongness of killing something is supposed to be a function of its degree of mental development, we would expect conventional morality to maintain one or other of two things: (1) the killing of all animals is permissible, and so too is a similar killing of all humans with a lower degree of mental development than that displayed by the most mentally developed animal; or (2) the killing of all humans is wrong, and so too is a similar killing of all animals with a higher degree of mental development than that displayed by the least mentally developed human being.[48]

Some, such as Carruthers, seem to think that a fudge of the mental criterion will do the trick to dismantle the AMC, but Everitt is correct to emphasize that fudging here is not satisfactory for the following reason: there will still be some human beings who will fail to make the grade, such as those with gross mental deficiencies who do not even have the potential to acquire the mental capacities of animals. Everitt is like Clark in suggesting that opponents to the AMC are likely to engage in a sort of mystification whereby all human beings deserve respect because they *are* human beings, possessors of a soul or some sort of immaterial appendix that differentiates them from animals. Suppose, for example, someone believed the following: "It is seriously wrong to kill X (as wrong as murder) if *either* X is a member of the human species, *or* X is mentally equivalent to a normally functioning adult member of the human species."[49] Such a principle is defective primarily because the two disjuncts are unrelated, one appealing to biology and the other appealing to capacities. It is arbitrary to lump these heterogeneous categories together and treat them as one from a moral point of view, yet it is precisely this arbitrariness that characterizes the thought of Leahy and Carruthers. On Everitt's reasoning the weak version of the AMC stands, although he leaves it an open question whether we should push on to defend the strong version or rest content with Frey's admission that the AMC forces us to be willing to perform experiments on marginal cases similar to those now performed on animals.

Edward Johnson is like McGinn in reminding us that there is nothing intrinsically wrong with being relatively unsophisticated mentally; young children are adorable precisely because of their relative simplicity.[50] Too little mental capacity, however—say, the lack of preferences or pleasures or pains—allows one to drop out of the category of moral beneficiary status, at least as a being that could be the recipient of direct duties. Tooley, Frey, and, in a slightly different way, Singer and James Nelson have a somewhat different slant on the issue: possession of sentiency is sufficient to make one morally considerable, but a right to life requires both a cognitive capacity sufficient to conceive of oneself as a continuing subject of experience and the desire to remain so. Some human beings do not have this capacity, and some animals do.[51]

The debate regarding where the lower end of sentiency and moral considerability lies is not part of this book's project (Singer thinks it lies somewhere around the mollusks, whereas Johnson thinks that sentiency might be found even in an amoeba).[52] My concern is with the boundary between human beings and animals at the upper reaches of sentiency, where cows and marginal humans come into play. Kai Nielson is right in emphasizing that if having a right requires being able to claim a right, then neither cows, infants, nor the severely retarded have them.[53] Concentrating on linguistic ability does not help much, for as the Routleys argue, the AMC is strengthened no matter which way one goes:

> For example rationality may be said to be the ability to reason, this being tested by such basically linguistic performances as the ability to do logic, to prove theorems, to draw conclusions from arguments and to engage in inductive and deductive linguistic behavior. But such stringent and linguistically loaded criteria will eliminate far too many members of the human species who cannot perform these tasks. If, however, behavioral criteria for rationality are adopted, or the ability to solve problems and to fit action to individual goals becomes the test—that is, practical reasoning is the test—it is obvious that many nonhuman animals will qualify for rationality, perhaps more easily than many humans.[54]

Scientists would (rightly) be condemned if they experimented painfully on human beings who fared less well on the behavioral criteria for rationality than some animals do. Richard Ryder puts the matter correctly when he says with irony that

> to be cruel to a weak creature but not to a strong one is the morality of the coward and the bully. If some creatures from outer space invaded Earth and proved to be stronger or vastly more intelligent than ourselves, would they be justified in ordering us to be vivisected? . . . One can imagine one of their scientists trying to justify himself in these terms—"Please don't think I am a sadist. As a matter of fact I am very fond of humans and keep several as pets. I can assure you that I would be the first to criticize any experiments that were unnecessary or involved unnecessary cruelty. I agree that fifty million humans die in our laboratories every Earth-year, but most of these are in routine experiments that do not involve severe pain. You really must not allow your emotions to cloud the issue."[55]

No doubt the AMC will offend some people because they will not think that there is any sort of vicious favoritism involved in speciesism, as there is in racism and sexism; rather, it will be alleged, there is a crucial and morally significant difference between human beings and animals. But between *all* human beings and animals? If the difference lies in rationality, then

> we would treat the suffering of people of average intellect as in itself less important than the suffering of highly intelligent people, and the suffering of the retarded as even less important. But surely this would be wrong. Imagine having someone who is far more intelligent than yourself tell you that, because of your inferior intelligence, your pain should count less than

> his, or imagine someone suggesting that since some very retarded people seem less intelligent than some dogs upon whom we experiment, we should feel as free to experiment on such retarded human beings as we now do on dogs or guinea pigs or rats.[56]

As R. I. Sikora notes, this is not a compelling argument. Perhaps it will be said that human beings are *characteristically* rational, but this claim still relies on the assumption that the pain of more intelligent creatures counts more than that of less intelligent ones, an assumption that is questionable at best and cruel at worst. We accept it when insurance companies make judgments about what is characteristically the case regarding drivers in certain age groups, but this sort of "classism" is based on the assumption that it would be too difficult and too expensive to find out exactly which young drivers are the potentially unsafe ones. In the case of, say, the mentally retarded, however, we know exactly which human beings lack the rationality found among many animals.

Conclusion: Harrison and Carruthers

In this chapter I have shown both the inadequacies associated with the Wittgensteinian nominalism of Willard and Diamond, most notably that such a position begs the question as to why it is legitimate to declare that marginal cases deserve moral respect but not animals, and the problems associated with the tendentiousness in Fox and Cigman, who bend over backward to protect all marginal cases yet run away as quickly as possible from the effort to protect animals. Furthermore, Devine's natural law position is problematic not because it is a natural law position but because it assumes both a normic sense of *human* regardless of any characteristics of the particular human in question and a normic sense of *animal* independent of any characteristics of the particular animal in question. In contrast to Willard and Diamond, Muscari and Haksar are not nominalists but essentialists in their positing, for moral if not metaphysical purposes, of a deep noumenal self in human beings. A judicious position should avoid both nominalism and essentialism.

Leahy and Carruthers have these and other thinkers' mistakes from which to learn, but they advance the debate regarding the AMC surprisingly little. Leahy exhibits all the strengths (e.g., an easy account of how we can justify punishing those who have egregiously broken the implicit contract in society) and weaknesses of contractualist doctrine. An example of the latter is Leahy's inability to account for anything but the most indirect duties to marginal cases and animals. He rejects the AMC largely on an a priori basis, in that animals by definition are not rational contractors.

Carruthers's case is much more complicated. He makes a legitimate request that defenders of the AMC move beyond Rawlsian reflective equilibrium, but it is not the case, as he alleges, that they thereby run the risk of becoming moral essentialists or foundationalists in the pejorative senses of these terms. There is always some sort of hypothetical dimension to our theorizing, including our moral theorizing. For example, what are the consequences if we make rationality, sophisticated language use, or ability to enter contracts the criterion for moral beneficiary status? What are the consequences if we make sentiency the criterion? Any hypothesized criterion is open to this question. It is not hard to detect a defect in Carruthers's own resolution of the issue: on the one hand, he makes the level of intelligence necessary to enter into contracts the criterion for moral beneficiary status; on the other, he slips retarded human beings but not animals into the category of moral beneficiaries through the back door. But it is not as clear as Carruthers thinks that abuse of marginal cases is more likely than abuse of animals to lead down a slippery slope to abuse of normal adult human beings.

What is most bothersome about Carruthers's approach is his revival of the Cartesian view of animals as either incapable of pain or at least incapable of pain consciously perceived. Evelyn Pluhar does an excellent job of dismantling this counterintuitive view, doing so by using an inductive argument from analogy to other minds from one's own case. "Beings who are neurologically highly similar to me and who respond in complex, creative ways to stimuli that also elicit my responses are probably conscious just as I am."[57] The argument from analogy has grown stronger since the time of Descartes, for it has been supplemented by centuries of observation (albeit observation often done at great cost to individual animals) that reveals detailed similarities between human and animal vertebrate systems. Many animals have the same pain mechanisms that we do, and their behaviors are consistent with this fact. We fly in the face of evolutionary theory if we assume that consciousness is uniquely human. If Carruthers had his way, scientists might well return to the Cartesian practice of nailing research animals to the wall without the benefit of anesthesia. If this accusation seems to be hyperbolic, it should be remembered that philosophers bear a good deal of the responsibility for the history of animal experimentation since the seventeenth century. Claude Bernard's practice of vivisecting animals is perfectly consistent with Carruthers's theory. Bernard thought it was necessary to take an organism to pieces in successive stages, just as one dismantles a clock; he even vivisected the family dog, to the outrage of his wife and daughters, who founded one of the first European antivivesection societies.[58]

Although he does not treat the AMC explicitly, Peter Harrison is in many ways like Carruthers. Harrison claims to be defending Descartes's view of animals without endorsing Descartes's metaphysics. Although his is not a strict argument against animal pain, in that all pain is essentially private, Harrison thinks that it plausible to deny pain to animals. So-called pain-behavior in animals is no more than an adaptive response. Human beings and animals may be physiologically similar, but this has no bearing on animal "pain" if pain is overwhelmingly a psychological phenomenon, he thinks. One has to have a highly developed ego to have pain. As Pluhar argues, however, neither Harrison nor Carruthers provides independent grounds for denying that animals experience grief, anxiety, or pain. Rather, they assume that conscious experiences play no role in animal behavior. No doubt Harrison is somewhat aware of the implausible view he has elaborated. There is a sudden shift at the end of his article where he reluctantly admits that animals can experience pain, but this pain, he thinks, is not significant. Descartes also plays on both sides of the fence when he assures us that animals can be only automata and admits that animals are capable of sensation.[59]

Harrison's approach has implications for the AMC because Harrison assumes that an animal is like an infant: they are each bundles of discrete sensations incapable of remembering. Significant pain, on this view, requires a continuity of consciousness not possessed by animals, infants, or some mentally impaired human beings. Pluhar treats this inconsistency ironically: "When I avoid the bully who beat me senseless yesterday, I am remembering my painful experience and acting appropriately; when Beauregard Beagle cowers away from the human who kicked him repeatedly yesterday, he is gripped by unconscious instinct!"[60] Although the degree of continuity of consciousness in infants is debatable, it is worth considering that it is "thought by pain researchers that babies and very young children may experience *more* pain than adults, because a 'damping' mechanism which helps to cut down on the severity of pain experiences does not develop until later. Only those who believe that mind and body are hermetically sealed compartments could think that physiology and appropriate behavior (e.g., crying) need have nothing to do with suffering."[61] Harrison's view is more Cartesian than he likes to admit; it is *metaphysically* Cartesian.

Carruthers's view is much like Harrison's, even if his terminology is somewhat different. Carruthers expresses his point by saying that there are pain experiences in animals, but there is no feeling component linked to them. Pluhar understandably sees a contradiction here. How is "painlike" behavior in animals to be understood if not in terms of feelings that animals have? Edward Johnson is like Pluhar in being skeptical as to whether Carruthers can adequately respond to this question. According to Johnson, Carruthers comes dangerously close to reducing consciousness to self-consciousness. Such a reduction has consequences that are disastrous in the light of the AMC. Johnson says the following about Carruthers's view: "If we accept his approach, we have difficulty with babies, as he recognizes, since 'the pains of babies, too, are nonconscious.' Still, he says, 'they should continue to evoke our sympathy' because 'a baby's pains and injuries, and our attitudes toward them, are likely to have a significant effect upon the person the baby will one day become.'"[62] This view of infants is defective because on its grounds there is no need to take seriously the pains of infants who will not survive infancy. (Why not roast them on a spit? Pluhar asks of Carruthers's view.) Pluhar is insightful in stating the following regarding Carruthers: "The real mystery here is how clever, sophisticated philosophers can lead themselves so thoroughly astray. The *ad hominem* fallacy is indeed to be avoided, but one cannot help wondering if Descartes and his modern counterparts would have argued as they did, had they not had such powerful incentives to deny nonhuman suffering as a devotion to vivisection, factory farming, or theodicy, and a common vision of human superiority."[63]

One way to counteract Harrison-Carruthers Cartesianism is to offer arguments in favor of animals possessing complex mental states, as does Stebbins. One must be careful, however, as McGinn reminds us, that emphasis of these complex mental states does not result in a new sort of "intelligenceism," or, as Everitt worries, a new sort of immaterial appendix meant to separate absolutely human beings from animals.

5

The Great Ape Project and Slavery

In this chapter I will try to accomplish two things. First, I will examine the recent efforts of Paola Cavalieri, Peter Singer, and others to gain equal rights for chimpanzees, gorillas, orangutans, and other great apes. Specifically, I will be concerned with how these efforts affect the AMC. Second, I will examine the allegation made by some defenders of both the great apes and the AMC that opposition both to rights for the great apes and to the AMC is often based, explicitly or implicitly, on the belief that animals are, for lack of a better word, our "slaves." That is, defense of rights for the great apes and defense of the AMC are integrally connected to the effort to oppose the view of animals as slaves or increments of capital.

Comparison of Great Apes and Marginal Cases

Christoph Anstotz has noted that it has been taboo to compare the abilities of primates with mentally handicapped human beings because of the fear that the recent progress regarding treatment of the intellectually disabled would be undermined. For example, a United Nations statement declaring intellectually disabled human beings to be morally equal to the rest of humanity did not occur until the 1970s. Discriminations on the basis of race, color, sex, language, religion, political opinion, national or social origin, or property were all condemned before unfair discrimination on the basis of intellectual competence was. Now it is commonly acknowledged that mentally retarded humans share with other humans the same basic rights to protection against exploitation and disrespectful treatment. Even human beings who are severely mentally disabled have basic rights, including individuals who do not communicate or react to other people. In these and other cases, everything that usually makes a difference between human beings and animals seems to be missing. In fact, the most marginal of marginal cases are inferior to animals on several criteria such as rationality, communication ability, and emotional sophistication: "There is nothing that humans with the most serious intellectual disabilities can do or feel that chimpanzees or gorillas cannot; moreover, there is much that a chimpanzee or a gorilla can do that a profoundly mentally disabled human cannot do. This includes the characteristics generally regarded as distinctive of human beings . . . language, intelligence and emotional life."[1] Most of the currently used intelligence tests are not suitable for profoundly mentally disabled people because the tests demand too much. Nevertheless, such tests indicate that more is going on in the minds of the great apes than we had commonly supposed. Julia, a six-year-old chimpanzee, can calculate how to reach a box with a banana in it by means of five separate steps. This ability dwarfs that of, say, a child with strong autistic traits. And so-called unique human abilities, such as language, intelligence, and emotions, are now known to be present in a high degree in the great apes.[2]

One of the advantages of teaching sign language to an orangutan such as Chantek is that we will have fewer questions about what might be in the minds of great apes: "If we keep our expectations realistic and use human children as our model, we can just ask them."[3] Chantek has reached a mental age equivalent of a two- to three-year-old child, with some skills of even older children. We excuse two-to-three year olds from adult moral responsibility, but we nonetheless think that killing them is murder. Likewise, Koko, the famous gorilla, has consistently scored in the 80s and 90s on IQ tests and has consistently tested at a mental age in the 40s (in months).[4] None of this is surprising given that some great apes share with us almost 99 percent of our genes.[5]

Stephen R. L. Clark presents a believable hypothesis as to why, aside from the long history of speciesism, contemporary thinkers continue to deny the great apes basic rights. Clark thinks that all the divisive factors that have torn apart the human species justify subscribing to the United Nations' ideal of the solidarity of the human species. To say that we are all members of one species has never been a primarily biological claim, however, as when we make an assertion about the unity of dogs, wolves, and coyotes. Nor it is a claim about humankind's rational autonomy, in that not all human beings are rational or autonomous. Rather, it is a moral claim, one that aids the AMC if the marginal cases are included within the scope of the claim. Clark, ever the traditionalist, urges that this moral unity largely stems from the fact that human beings are part of a long, variegated lineage in which our habits, gestures, and abilities reveal our common source. But the great apes exhibit many of these habits, gestures, and abilities as well; they exhibit these as much as or more than the marginal cases do. Relying on Kant's term *Realgattung,* a historical collection of interbreeding populations, Clark says the following: "Either we are simply natural products of evolutionary processes or we are not. If we are, then it seems clear that there are no rigid boundaries between species groups, that species, and other taxa, are quite real, but only as *Realgattungen.*"[6]

One of the problems with viewing humankind according to some ideal type, such as rational autonomy, or according to something like a Platonic Form of Humanity, is that only the sage or the saint adequately fits the model. Yet these people have often been more respectful of animals than the rest of us have generally been:

> If saints are the ones who best embody Humanity (as the Platonic tradition would suggest), then we will do the best we can by imitating them. From which it follows that we should respect those other "apes," our kindred. If there are no natural kinds but only *Realgattungen,* then it is reasonable to think of ourselves as parts of *Hominoidea,* "greater humankind." If there are such kinds as Platonists imagine, and "we" here now are partial imitations of the Form of Humanity, let us imitate it better by being humane. . . . If we should respect Humanity in ourselves and others we should, by the same token, respect the other creatures that reflect that Form in however tarnished a mirror. If we are apes, let us be apes together. If we are "apes" (as aping the Divine), let us acknowledge what our duty is as would-be saints and give the courtesy we owe to those from among whom we sprang.[7]

On this line of reasoning, then, to treat the great apes as we would less-gifted humans is a conservative move, especially when it is noted that some "normal" human beings have committed the most horrifying crimes against other human beings.[8] It is something of a commonplace in animal rights literature to imagine what we would say if we were in a powerless position with respect to those who would exploit us—say, if invading aliens did not think that our IQ was sufficient to deserve moral respect, or if vampires thought that human flesh was best, or if angelic or godlike beings decided to treat us frivolously. These fantasies represent the contingency and arbitrariness of our supremacy as a species.[9]

The great apes are, like children and people with a mental handicap, unable to claim their due. Yet it seems to me that they should receive their due, even if what they are due is in some ways below that of normal adult human beings.[10] Remember that Regan holds the basis for this desert to lie in inherent value, a view that he expresses quite clearly and without G. E. Moore–like mystery:

> It remains to be asked . . . what underlies the possession of inherent value. Some are tempted by the idea that life itself is inherently valuable. This view would authorise attributing inherent value to chimpanzees, for example, and so might find favour with some people who oppose using these animals as means to our ends. But this view would also authorise attributing inherent value to anything and everything that is alive, including, for example, crabgrass, lice, bacteria and cancer cells. It is exceedingly unclear, to put the point as mildly as possible, either that we can have a duty to treat these things with respect or that any clear sense can be given to the idea that we do. More plausible by far is the view that those individuals who have inherent value are *the subjects of a life*—are, that is, the experiencing subjects of a life that fares well or ill for them over time, those who have *an individual experiencing welfare,* logically independent of their utility relative to the interests or welfare of others. Competent humans are subjects of a life in this sense. But so, too, are those incompetent humans who have concerned us. Indeed, so too are many other animals: cats and dogs, hogs and sheep, dolphins and wolves, horses and cattle—and, most obviously, chimpanzees and the other nonhuman great apes.[11]

Surely the great apes qualify as being subjects of a life with individual experiential welfare. This is not obvious to some perhaps because (as Rollin argues, echoing Clark) it has only recently been noticed that certain human beings are subjects of a life: women, blacks, homosexuals, native populations, the insane, the handicapped, and so on. One major step toward extending the franchise to the great apes is taken when it is noticed that there exists no good reason not to extend it, "that there is no morally relevant difference between humans and animals which can rationally justify not assessing the treatment of animals by the machinery of our consensus ethic for humans."[12] In addition, Rollin, like Clark, is comfortable with the Aristotelian notion that each animal has a *telos* that can be more easily thwarted if basic rights are not extended to them. Perhaps it is not part of a chimpanzee's *telos* to comprehend English, but the fact that a ten-year-old chimpanzee can comprehend it better than a two-year-old child indicates that the chimpanzee's *telos* must be rather sophisticated.[13]

What giving the great apes their due means is a complicated matter that would require an examination of several key issues in environmental ethics. Perhaps it largely means leaving them alone, setting aside preserves for them with controls on human entrance. Nondisruptive research, some degree of medical care, and perhaps some emergency feeding would be appropriate, since we have already done much to destroy their habitats.[14] Although the great apes are in many ways at the mental level of human children, they are not children but "wild" animals in the sense that their *telos* is not reached in zoos, circuses, laboratories, or any other context where they are seen as someone else's property.[15]

The Slavery Analogy

Thus far by *marginal cases* I have usually referred to either infants/children or human beings who are in some way mentally defective. Nonetheless, the label also applies to adult human beings who have been mistakenly perceived as mentally defective, such as women or slaves. In fact, the presence of the AMC in the ancient world was due not only to the status of animals relative to mentally defective human beings, as the quotation from Porphyry in the introduction indicates, but also to slaves, as some passages from Plutarch indicate.[16] Aristotle refers to slaves as "animated property"; the phrase describes as well the current status of animals. The distinctive feature of slavery is that the being involved becomes property. In the ancient world, the idea that some human beings should be under the absolute subjection of others went virtually unchallenged, just as many people today do not think twice about eating, wearing, or experimenting on animals. There were wide differences in the conditions of slaves, however, in that some of them served in aristocratic households, while others worked in abominable conditions in the mines; similarly, some animals today are pampered as pets, and some are killed for food. Common to slaves and animals is a condition of powerlessness. Like chattel slaves in antiquity (*chattel* is derived from *cattle*), animals largely stand outside the protective moral realm of modern communities.[17]

Paola Cavalieri and Peter Singer emphasize that changing minor aspects of the institution of slavery in the ancient world (e.g., abolishing the gladitorial games) did not greatly affect the institution as a whole. Likewise, replacing hot-iron branding of cattle with less painful means of identification, or using local anesthetics when castrating pigs, does not have much of an effect on the overall condition of animals. Slaves, of course, can rebel in ways that animals cannot, yet few such rebellions in antiquity amounted to much by way of liberation. The most progress occurred by way of manumission, literally a release from the hand of the master. Here the slaveowner unilaterally ended the slave's condition as property: "Just as manumission was the only way out for slaves, so it appears to be the kind of response needed for animals."[18] For example, Epaminondas, leader of the Theban forces, manumitted the helots of Messenia *en bloc.* This collective manumission became a political instrument with tremendous consequences that lead Cavalieri and Singer to desire the manumission of the great apes. No doubt some will worry that concentrating on the great apes implies a sort of intelligenceism that does not bode well for cows or mice. Cavalieri and Singer instead hope that a collective manumission of the great apes is more politically feasible than the manumission of cows and mice, such that treating them as the equals of marginal cases will enhance the situation of all animals, even the ones that are not particularly bright. That is, the animals that are closest to us on the evolutionary tree must be liberated in a decisive way before the plight of other animals, including those raised for the table and laboratory, can significantly improve.

Whereas the collective manumission of Messenian helots led to dramatic social changes, the random manumission of individual slaves did not. Cavalieri and Singer are aware, however, that not even collective manumission is enough. For example, after the American slaves were freed in the 1860s, it took another century until their civil rights were secure. Likewise, although many of the needs of the great apes would be met if they were allowed to roam in a version of Liberia, if the great apes are at a mental level of nonautonomous beings of our own species, they will continue to require our tutelage in some sense or other, as in my previous remarks regarding our destruction of their habitats and their need for the food and medical care that we can give them.[19] (I should emphasize that in no way am I trying to advance the racist comparison of blacks and great apes in terms of mental level. Blacks were treated as marginal cases because of a grossly mistaken assessment of their abilities.)

Slavery and the AMC

The AMC would be greatly weakened if only the great apes were within its scope, but this is not the case. The great apes are of interest here because they often exceed the abilities of the marginal cases by a great distance. If we must prioritize what is politically feasible, it makes sense that those who most deserve basic rights should be acknowledged first. Nonetheless, there is also something to be said for the claim that animals that are routinely killed should rise to the top of the list. In any event, the great ape project can be used to highlight the AMC, but it should not be the exclusive object of our concern while the sufferings of other animals continue. There are still "rational" egoists who have a great deal to gain by exploiting animals *and* children (e.g., children of migrant farm workers).[20]

The greater danger is not that we would establish a gulf between primates (human and great ape) and nonprimates but rather that the present gulf between humans and nonhumans would remain absolute. Even a reflective thinker such as James Nelson still wishes somehow to preserve this latter gulf, although for the understandable reason that he does not wish, in Frey-like fashion, to revise downward the moral status attributed to damaged humans.[21] A defender of the strong version of the AMC can at least partially agree with Nelson when he says:

> I'm not sure that I want to extend to virtuous parents the right to consent to a heart transplant for their children if the donors are children with Down's Syndrome. . . . I have argued that there is a morally relevant distinction between animals and marginal humans: the marginal humans have suffered a tragedy in becoming the psychological equals of animals—a tragedy that animals have escaped. The sentiments properly evoked by the recognition of such a tragedy—pity and compassion—speak strongly against further injury to someone already so afflicted.[22]

In fact, William Aiken thinks that if any human beings should have their moral status revised downward, it is not those with Down's syndrome but violent psychopaths, whose worth as moral agents and beneficiaries is inferior to that of chimpanzees.[23] Or, at the very least, the partial affections of parents toward their children can sometimes override the rights of a violent psychopath more easily than they can the rights of a chimpanzee (the latter, after all, is innocent). Nevertheless, I am not convinced that Nelson can legitimately move from the (defensible) claim that marginal cases should not be the victims of medical research to the claim that animals can be so used. To put marginal cases on a firm moral footing, we need not, as Nelson thinks, distance them from animals.[24]

Mary Anne Warren is like Nelson in having problems with the AMC, but her objection is based on a fear not that we would revise downward our respect for marginal cases but that we would not sufficiently acknowledge the practical and emotional reasons for protecting nonrational human beings (as opposed to protecting animals?) and that we might be tempted to draw a sharp line between those protections that are rights and those that are based on practical and emotional considerations (e.g., family membership). According to Warren, there is no sharp line between rights and these other protections.[25] A rejoinder to this view would be that emotional protection does not necessarily prohibit slavery—for one may be sold into it by one's brothers, as Joseph is in the Hebrew scriptures—whereas no one has the right to sell a being with "individual experiential welfare," to use Regan's phrase, into slavery. Marginal cases are tragic beings, but we should not make their lives even worse by enslaving them; animals are tragic, too, in that they are currently granted such little value that even an exemption from torture is often a step up for these contemporary "slaves."[26]

If it is wrong to test the effects of toxic gas on a severely retarded human being, is it not also wrong to do these things on an animal with equivalent or (in the case of great apes) higher mental capacities? Some might claim at this point that infants have at least the potential for rationality or autonomy and that marginal cases would have had these potentials were it not for their tragic condition, but that animals, including the great apes, have experienced no such tragedy. Evelyn Pluhar asks some interesting questions regarding this claim: "What moral weight could *thwarted* potential have on such a view? Does one's degree of moral significance increase depending on how close to personhood one was when misfortune struck? Does a human damaged as a three-month-old fetus count for less than a child who became brain-damaged after birth? At what point, if any, does a victim of thwarted potential gain a right to life? Perhaps only if he or she had achieved personhood, then tragically lost it?"[27] Pluhar is distinguishing here between a strict potentiality view and a gradualist potentiality view, and she rightly thinks that both are inadequate. Both views have this defect: they can at most allow ascribing a right to life to a nonperson who once was a potential person or potentially rational or autonomous.

Those who were conceived without this potential (say, by having defective genes) have no such potential to thwart. Perhaps it will be objected at this point that a human nonperson has a "species potential" that the animal nonperson does not have (accepting for the moment the questionable assumption that great apes are not persons). Pluhar's response to this objection is crucial because it focuses attention on the question-begging character of much opposition to the AMC:

> Tempting though this line of argument may be, we cannot use it to support speciesism, for it assumes the very point at issue. According to speciesism, membership in a species where personhood is the norm is morally relevant. We cannot *establish* this conclusion by asserting that nonpersons belonging to species where personhood is the norm are thereby more morally significant than nonpersons who are in the normal range for their species. This argument is plainly circular. Thus, however it is interpreted, the thwarted potential argument fails to support any speciesist conclusions.[28]

Pluhar herself, like Regan and Clark, wishes to defend a strong version of the AMC. She is bothered by those who shun abnormal human beings, for example, by abandoning handicapped children or refusing them lifesaving surgery even when the children could have contented lives. Or again: "A 1986 study conducted by the University of Maryland School of Medicine revealed that one-third of the family members who believed that their hospitalized mentally incompetent elderly relatives would not have wanted to participate in an experiment on the adverse effects of urinary catheters nevertheless gave their permission. They reasoned that *others* would 'possibly benefit' from the experiment."[29] In addition to decrying speciesism, Pluhar sees problems with "normalism," the view that abnormal or marginal human beings can be denied basic rights. Steve Sapontzis thinks that Pluhar's critique of normalism is an excellent rhetorical device in that it catches people up short and gets them to think in ways they had not thought before (why is it permissible to vivisect a dog but not a severely retarded orphan?). The charge of prejudice in sexism and racism has to do with typical, standard, or normal cases. Speciesism, he thinks, is not on a par with these unless one can say that animals typically meet relevant moral criteria the way human beings typically do. (For example, it might be alleged that if women and blacks are typically as rational as white males, then it would be wrong to treat them as less worthy of respect than white males are, whereas animals are not typically as rational as human beings.) Contra

Sapontzis, however, animals typically do meet the criteria of sentience and individual experiential welfare in the way human beings typically do, even if they are not as rational or as autonomous as human beings typically are.[30]

Sapontzis is unquestionably an animal rightist, but he is skeptical of both the AMC and the claim that the special intellectual capacities of the great apes should entitle them to a higher moral status than other beings with interests. Pluhar responds to Sapontzis by admitting that the analogy between speciesism, on the one hand, and racism and sexism, on the other, is not and never has been presented as thoroughgoing:

> No nonspeciesist would ever compare blacks or women to mentally deficient white men. The point of the analogy is that it is wrong to treat beings whom one regards as morally similar, be they human or nonhuman persons, or women and men, or blacks and whites, in morally dissimilar ways. The burden is on speciesists to show that their view does not belong in this group. However, *after* one has argued that the right to life is not restricted to persons or to members of personhood-characterized species, it becomes appropriate to raise the analogy between speciesism and racism/sexism in a much more general way, for one would then be entitled to say that normal humans and many other beings are morally similar. In the face of this, continued preference for humans at the expense of others would be just as bigoted, in all respects, as racism or sexism. Current defenders of speciesism can hardly be impressed by this moral general analogy, of course, since it merely begs the question against them. The more restricted analogy which can be drawn in conjunction with the argument from marginal cases has much more sting.[31]

Frey obviously does not want to defend slavery, but he does think that some human lives have less value than others, not because of race or gender but because of factors such as being born without a brain. He attributes to Regan (and presumably to Pluhar), however, the view that all human beings do have lives of equal value, although Regan holds the view that all human beings have lives of equal inherent value (they are not mere receptacles but subjects of a life), even if the intrinsic values of their particular experiences are unequal. The dispute between Frey and the defenders of the strong version of the AMC such Regan, Clark, and Pluhar concerns whether marginal cases have sufficient value (even Frey thinks that they have *some* value if they are sentient) to warrant a right to life: if they have a right to life, then animals have such a right, too; if they do not have a right to life, then neither do animals.[32] Frey does not think that marginal cases have a right to life, and hence they, along with animals, are amenable to at least painless "slavery," even if this is not the word Frey himself would choose to describe the implication of his view. In one sense Frey is not vulnerable to the AMC because he largely sees marginal cases and animals on a moral par; in another sense, however, he is vulnerable to the strong version of the AMC if what it means to have a right to life requires only that one have a future, or at least desires or preferences regarding that future.[33]

Charles Fink, along with several other authors, correctly points out that gorillas or dolphins, say, are not literally mentally defective human beings and that we would misunderstand a gorilla or dolphin if we were to think of them as such.[34] At the least, however, the gorilla or dolphin are equals to marginal cases and normal human beings in being morally considerable, even if the exact rights of each of these differ.[35] John Locke concedes this much, as when he notices similarities between human beings, including the elderly and idiots, and animals.[36] Locke's point can be used to supplement VanDeVeer's efforts to put animal rights on a firm contractualist footing. This effort is worthwhile if only because it is liberalism, broadly conceived, that is largely responsible for the elimination of modern slavery.

As I mentioned in chapter 2, Lilly-Marlene Russow also argues for a liberal theory of justice that is consistent in both letter and spirit with John Rawls's theory. This view has these three characteristics:

1. Rawls is justified in specifying that all those in the original position may assume that they will be moral persons in the society to be governed by the principles which they choose. Thus, the principles of justice which they choose might easily turn out not to cover many who are not moral persons.
2. Nonetheless, some individuals who are not included as moral persons . . . may be moral subjects: our complete moral theory of duties and obligations may show that we have direct moral duties toward some who are not moral persons, e.g., marginal cases and nonhuman animals.
3. It is not a foregone conclusion that marginal cases and nonhuman animals cannot be accorded differential treatment without lapsing into speciesism, but any attempt to justify differential treatment must still be produced.[37]

As before, even though animals cannot be parties to a contract, it does not follow that they cannot be the intended beneficiaries of one in some sense or other.[38]

Tom Huffman is a liberal contractarian who thinks that a contractarian account of morality is consistent with direct duties. At the very least, if we can account for direct duties to marginal cases under contractarianism, then we can do so as well for animals. Species membership cannot be the relevant criterion for moral respect on contractarian grounds, such that animals are left out in the cold, amenable to enslavement. He argues against a tactic often employed to defend such a use of species membership. It is often claimed that species membership represents a family relationship, yet, as I have shown Huffman to argue persuasively, it is difficult to justify which family groupings are significant. For example, why not defend racism or ethnocentrism on this basis? Huffman is particularly interested to refute Michael Tooley's criticism of the AMC, which goes as follows:

> Let John and Mary be two individuals that are not rational beings, and that belong to different species, but which are indistinguishable with respect to their psychological capacities and their mental lives. It is possible that John belongs to a species 99% of which are rational beings, while Mary belongs to a species of which only 1% are rational beings. If species membership is morally relevant . . . , it will be wrong to kill John, but may very well not be wrong to kill Mary.[39]

If the moral community is defined not according to the capacities individuals possess but rather according to the groups to which they belong, then the permissible includes not only "familial" prejudice, as in racism, but also group prejudice, as in sexism. Huffman argues that "one might object, noting that species membership is merely a sufficient, rather than a necessary, condition for inclusion within the moral community; hence, we do not risk this type of exclusion. However, this response misses the point. . . . [It] fails to account for how species membership is relevant in the first place. . . . I know of no remotely plausible explanation for the moral relevance of species membership."[40]

It must be admitted that if a contractarian account includes animals and defective human beings, then it does not closely follow its political analogue, which has liberated slaves but not yet animals. Some defenders of the AMC hope that this contractarian account will eventually have such a liberatory effect for animals. Somewhat unlike Russow, Huffman thinks that there is no guarantee that those in the original position who are rational and mutually disinterested will remain so when the veil of ignorance is removed; as in Russow as well as

VanDeVeer, however, the key issue for Huffman is not who can participate in a contract but who can benefit from one. Furthermore, Huffman thinks that if there is something counterintuitive about the conclusion that animals have rights, this conclusion is nonetheless based on strong intuitions at work in the original position: "The price we pay for aligning contractarian theory with intuitions concerning our duties to defective humans forces us to accept similar duties toward some animals. This latter conclusion, although not strongly supported by intuition, is an inevitable consequence of other intuitions that most of us are reluctant to abandon"—for example, the (Popperian) intuition that to inflict gratuitous suffering is terribly wrong.[41]

Benton and the AMC

The political efforts to get acknowledgment of the rights of the great apes and to ameliorate animal slavery face opposition both from various "conservatives" who would like to hold on to traditional anthropocentric ways and from leftists who are skeptical of the supposedly abstract nature of animal rights. I have examined several of these conservatives throughout the book. (It should be noted, however, that our heritage from ancient and medieval culture is not quite as anthropocentric as some think. If anything, our heritage is theocentric.)[42] Ted Benton, however, is a leftist who in a recent book criticizes animal rights from a different political direction.

According to Benton, Regan and others are to be commended for trying to develop a view of justice that is universal in its application not only to human beings but to anything that satisfies the subject-of-a-life criterion. Benton has a difficulty with Regan's use of the AMC, however. There is a crucial factual premise underlying Regan's use of the AMC, he thinks:

> At least some "mentally enfeebled" humans, and young children, have the full range of subject-of-a-life attributes and powers, but lack the capacity for moral judgement and responsibility. This suggests a view of moral capacity as in some sense a separate faculty, added on, and as detachable by some misfortune, while everything else remains intact. A related structure of assumptions lies behind the thesis of the moral equivalence of human and non-human moral patients. Animals are thought of as like humans in a wide range of capacities and attributes, though they are generally less well developed in these respects, but, like human moral patients they lack only the specific capacities that go to make up moral agency.[43]

The reason for this alleged split in Regan between subject-of-a-life attributes and moral responsibility, Benton thinks, is that there is a huge gap between the level of abstraction at which the AMC is pitched and the practical contexts in which it has to be applied. Oddly enough, Benton the leftist sounds to me like Clark the conservative here. The latter favors not so much the expansion of liberal rights to animals as the expansion of our conception of a household (with its pets) so as to include animals within one's polis; in addition, if it is possible, we should try to include all one's nation's animals (all British beasts, for Clark), or, if the Hellenistic Greeks are correct that the universe is one household, all animals. Both Benton and Clark think that some versions of the AMC prevent any sensitivity to particularity and diversity: "For instance, as between children and the psychologically disabled humans, and the many different species of non-human animals. Regan's style of argument, rejecting as it does human/animal dualism, asserts human/animal continuism in a way which preserves a major weakness of the dualist position—abstract insensitivity to the diversity of non-human animal species and their requirements."[44]

There are several things that can be said on behalf of the impartialist (as opposed to Clark's partialist) version of the AMC. First, if we abandon or deemphasize abstract reason, as Benton and Clark do, then we will have a difficult time criticizing the household or polis where animals are abused, experimented on, or eaten. Second, Regan in particular is willing to make distinctions when they make a moral difference, contra Benton. Consider his distinction between the central marginal cases (if the oxymoron can be permitted) and the most marginal of marginal cases, the latter failing not only the rationality/autonomy criterion but also the subject-of-a-life criterion. And he does notice the obvious difference between a child who is potentially rational and a severely psychologically disabled human being who is not even potentially rational. Once these distinctions are noticed, one can imagine how Regan would respond to Benton's charge that for Regan moral responsibility is some sort of magical, separate faculty. In fact, moral responsibility arises along the continuum of rationality occupied by some animals, some marginal cases, and all normal adults in their various degrees of mental competence.

Benton's view is that the moral status of animals is a function not so much of the kinds of beings they are as of the relations in which they stand to human moral agents and their social practices: "It seems on the face of it unlikely that the single philosophical strategy of assigning universal rights of a very abstract kind to them would be a sufficient response. Is, for example, the moral status of a farm animal, a domestic pet, or a 'wild' animal to be conceptualized in identical terms?"[45]

In one sense, yes. All these animals deserve equal moral consideration of their interests, at least if marginal cases do; in that they have interests, they equally deserve not to be made to suffer or to be killed gratuitously. The question as to whether we also have a duty to prevent other animals from killing wild rabbits, say, is a complicated one that I have briefly treated before. The point to notice here is that wild rabbits are equally deserving to have their interests considered and equally worthy of immunity from torture and death at the hands of human beings, at the very least. In contrast, Benton wants us to believe that pets, farm animals, and wild animals each have a different moral status because of their different relations with human beings; likewise, the moral status of these animals is different from that of young children or mentally enfeebled adults, again because of the different relations these marginal cases have to normal human beings: "All human adult moral agents have been young children, and will have some memory of that state. . . . In the case of mentally disabled human adults there are, again, generally sufficiently powerful subject-to-subject affective bonds to give grounds for thinking that those who campaign on behalf of the mentally handicapped have an authentic sense of what it is the mentally handicapped would themselves campaign for if they were able to do so."[46]

If I understand Benton correctly, he is saying that if mentally enfeebled human beings were rational, they would want to be treated fairly, which is true. But the same sort of conditional claim could be made on behalf of animals.

It is not clear why Benton thinks that appeal to counterfactuals works in the case of marginal cases (e.g., the claims these individuals *would* make if they *were* able to make moral claims on their own behalf) but not in the case of animals. An imaginative leap is required in either case. At base, it seems, Benton is a Marxist who is skeptical of the notion of individualist views of rights for human beings, whether normal or abnormal. It follows a fortiori that he is skeptical of expanding those rights to individual animals.[47] Obviously it is beyond the scope of this book to enter into the debate in political philosophy between liberals and Marxists, but Benton is to be thanked for alerting us to the fact that the AMC is part of a larger liberal political agenda concerning the rights of individuals who have a welfare that is amenable to being harmed. It is precisely this concern for individuals that will be of primary concern in the next chapter. If Benton is to be criticized here, it is in terms of the animal rightist trope to the effect that it is individual cows or chimpanzees that suffer or who lose their lives (just as it was individual human beings who suffered and died under Hitler or Stalin), not a Platonic Cowhood or a Marxist class of chimpanzees who fail to own the means of production.

6

The Nozick-Rachels Debate

In this chapter of the book I highlight James Rachels's recent response to Robert Nozick's criticisms of the AMC. This response has implications not only for the AMC in itself but also for how we should view the connection between the AMC and the right to life as it surfaces in philosophical debate regarding euthanasia. I will also consider other authors who amplify the debate between Nozick and Rachels (or better, the debate Rachels has with Nozick), most notably concerning Rachels's defense of moral individualism.

Nozick's Stance

In *Anarchy, State, and Utopia*[1] Nozick defends a view that he refers to as Kantianism for people and utilitarianism for animals. That is, animals deserve moral respect, but not as much of it as human beings deserve, for animals may be used or sacrificed for the benefit of human beings or other animals, although only if these benefits are greater than the loss inflicted. In a later piece, however, Nozick seems to be somewhat shocked that Regan (and other defenders of the AMC such as Rachels) develops an argument that hinges on placing animals (mentally normal animals of a year or more) on a par mentally with enfeebled human beings. Regan thinks that we can understand the kind of treatment that is due marginal cases only if we allow that they have rights. Furthermore, whatever is on a par with marginal cases—mammals, in particular—also must be granted to have rights. Nozick sees this argument (the AMC) as the central one in Regan, through which Regan threads many subsidiary arguments. There are three troubling aspects of this argument, he thinks: an inflated view of animals, a deflated view of retarded people, and the inference (based on the equating of animals with marginal cases) that animals have (Kantian) rights.

Nozick thinks that Regan (and Rachels) goes too far in ascribing to animals beliefs and desires, perception, memory, and a sense of the future (including their own future), an emotional life with pleasure and pain, preference and welfare interests, the ability to initiate actions in pursuit of their desires, an identity over time, and an individual welfare in the sense that their preferential life fares well or ill for them. Nozick favors a more parsimonious explanation of animals that lacks such a heavy cognitive apparatus, most notably B. F. Skinner's operant conditioning mode of explanation. But this Skinnerian approach runs into some familiar difficulties treated earlier in the book. It is understandable that Nozick would want to avoid the pathetic fallacy, wherein human thoughts and feelings would be unjustifiably transported to animals. It is equally disastrous, however, to commit the "apathetic fallacy," wherein one illegitimately moves from the *methodological* claim that it is best for scientists to detach themselves from the subject matter they are investigating to the *ontological* claim that the animals that are the subject matter investigated lack feeling, mental life, or value. A careful description of animals reveals them to be far more complex, interesting, and affective than is allowed by the boring, apparently parsimonious, account that Skinner and Nozick offer. Even this parsimony is suspect, however, in that such an approach requires a convoluted, highly inefficient explanation for cows' uncooperative behavior at the abattoir, instead of merely saying that they do not want to be there or do not like the smell of blood.

Nozick also thinks that defenders of the AMC deflate the status of seriously retarded people. It is not clear how he sustains this claim if it entails the belief that even seriously retarded human beings have some higher capacities that animals do not have. One wonders whether, on Nozick's Skinnerian basis, even normal human beings have these higher capacities, much less the marginal cases of humanity. Nozick's argument apparently amounts to an appeal to species. In reference to marginal cases, he says that "these people are, after all, human beings, of the same species as we, however retarded or handicapped. Even supposing a particular severely retarded individual turns out to be no more rational or autonomous and to have no richer an internal psychology than a normal member of another mammalian species, he nonetheless is a human being, albeit defective, and must be treated as one."[2] This is not so much to refute the AMC as to beg the question as to whether any beings other than human beings deserve quasi-Kantian respect. Nonetheless, Nozick lends partial support to the strong version of the AMC in arguing for the rights of marginal cases. Nozick's view also includes a legitimate fear that the AMC might lead us not to elevate animals to the level of benevolent treatment of marginal cases, as the defender of the strong version of the AMC desires, but rather (in Frey-like and, to a lesser degree, Singer-like fashion) to treat marginal cases like animals.

Nozick is plainly aware of the difficulties with his position: "It is not easy to explain why membership in the human species does and should have moral weight with us. Shouldn't only an organism's own individual characteristics matter? Normal human beings have various capacities that we think form the basis of the respectful treatment these people are owed. How can someone's merely being a member of the same species be a reason to treat him in certain ways when he so patently lacks those very capacities?"[3] That is, Nozick's view is opposed to what he calls "moral individualism," the view that does not see species membership as "fundamental and essential." Oddly, Nozick himself admits that he lacks an explicit account of why being a member of the human species is important. This is a crucial defect from the perspective of the AMC.

Nozick's only response seems to be as follows: "Nothing much . . . should be inferred from our not presently having a theory of the moral importance of species membership that no one has spent much time trying to formulate because the issue hasn't seemed pressing."[4] Because of the AMC, however, the issue *is* pressing. Being rational is something that has to be respected by all, including any denizens of Alpha Centuri, but the bare species characteristic of being human commands respect only from other human beings. Once again, Nozick seems to rest content with a sort of partialism—specifically, speciesism—rather than to meet the challenge posed by defenders of the AMC. Lions, too (if they could be moral agents), Nozick pleads, should be allowed to put the interests of other lions first. One wonders whether this line of partialist reasoning permits one to believe as the white racist does as long as one is willing to permit the beliefs of the black racist. Is David Duke more palatable because of Louis Farrakhan? The question seems fair when it is realized that for Nozick, speciesism is acceptable because of the texture of human history, human achievements, and family relations. Given these criteria, one wonders whether Nozick can avoid a defense of nationalism or ethnocentrism. Nozick himself is skittish regarding his own partialism: "I have some worries in presenting this type of position, for scoundrels too may seek refuge from criticism in the reply that some differences are too great and complicated to state. Moral philosophers need therefore to develop new tools to handle complex contexts."[5] Nozick does not deliver on this promissory note, however, in that we are not told what these "new tools" might be.

The speciesism defended by Nozick is like that of Leslie Pickering Francis and Richard Norman, who agree that it is wrong to cause animals gratuitous suffering and that major changes are needed in current factory farming. Like Nozick, however, they have trouble with the equal consideration of interests principle, in that they think there are plausible grounds for giving greater weight to human interests than to animal interests. Like Diamond and Benton, Francis and Norman hold that human beings deserve unequal consideration of their interests by virtue not of some differentiating properties but of certain relations human beings have to other human beings. Or better, Francis and Norman think that the traditional differentiating characteristics—rationality, linguistic capacity, and so on—generate acceptable conclusions for most human beings, and the marginal cases are in a special relationship with normal human beings. This moral respect by association, however, at least initially seems to be as unjustified as its cousin, guilt by association.[6] The defender of the strong version of the AMC thinks that marginal cases themselves have properties that make them morally considerable. Francis and Norman might respond by acknowledging that we could develop special relations with marginal cases as well as with dogs and cats, and hence they should not be used for food or painful experiments. There still seems to be something arbitrary in this response, however, if animals as emotionally and mentally developed (or more so) as marginal cases or dogs or cats can be used for food or painful experiments solely because we have not yet made them our pets.

Infants are problematic, according to Francis and Norman, only in the first two years or so of life, after which time the child's mental capacities exceed those of animals. (Although they may be shy by a year or two in comparison with the great apes, the assessment here is generally correct.) Francis and Norman do not see much of a problem even regarding these first two years, however, for very young infants have not only special relations with other human beings but also distinguishing characteristics that animals lack—for example, social interaction and a sense of humor. Francis and Norman here resemble Vinit Haksar in searching for some sort of noumenal, morally relevant property found in young infants but not in even the primates.

We are not told exactly how a one-year-old is socially interactive or exhibits a playfulness or sense of humor that the great apes do not exhibit. To the extent that infants are mentally inferior to animals, even on Francis and Norman's argumentation, to that extent Francis and Norman rely on the special relations infants have with other human beings. Babies are the objects of other people's emotional attachments, especially those of parents, which is a powerful incentive to treat them well. The crucial point here is that some animals, most notably pets, are also the objects of strong emotional attachments for some human beings, and other animals at least could be the objects of our emotional attachments; furthermore, animals (especially mammals) have parents, too. (This last consideration will carry little weight with Francis and Norman.) That is, even if our prime concern should be with the relations a moral beneficiary has with normal human beings rather than with the characteristics of the moral beneficiary in question (a questionable assumption), it is by no means clear that animals fail the test.[7]

Francis and Norman deal with permanently retarded human beings, a category that is, as they note, quite large. They emphasize that there are big differences within this category, however. For example, those who suffer from Down's syndrome may have an IQ between 20 and 80, with the majority clustered around 50. They also have linguistic ability and a great capacity for affection, even if they are not capable of abstract thought. The linguistic ability some Down's syndrome patients have, however—the ability to use tenses and to apply language to situations not immediately present and in the absence of immediate stimuli—does not necessarily distinguish them absolutely from all animals. Thus, the inference that Francis and Norman draw from these abilities—that the possessors of these abilities have interests beyond an immediate sense of physical well-being—seems to apply to some animals as well as to some cases of Down's syndrome. In any event, regardless of how well the best Down's syndrome patients can perform and how well the most advanced animals can perform, it is nonetheless true that the most marginal of marginal cases (e.g., anencephalics, who suffer severe developmental failure of the brain and cranium) clearly fall below the intellectual capacities of many animals. As I have shown throughout this book, there is only a limited gain that can be expected when trying to counteract the AMC by way of making subtle distinctions among the marginal cases.[8]

The point is not that there are no distinctions within the class of marginal cases. There are. Nor is the point that there are no distinctions among animals with respect to mental ability. There are. Francis and Norman serve a legitimate function by reminding us that we cannot treat all animals commensurate with the way chimpanzees, rhesus monkeys, and dolphins, with their developed mental lives, ought to be treated. Nonetheless, even cows, sheep, and chickens have *some* rights worthy of our consideration, in that any morally relevant characteristic they fail to possess is also missing in the lives of some marginal cases. These animals at least have a desire to keep on living, the termination of which by us entails a gratuitous destruction (that is, cruelty) on our part.[9]

Rachels's Rejoinder

Nozick's view (and that of Francis and Norman) is not far from the traditional one, which as Rachels sees it is based on the following assumptions: "At the heart of the traditional doctrine is the idea that the protection of *human* life—all human life—is immensely important. If one is human, and alive, then according to the traditional view one's life is sacred. At the same time, *non-human* life is given relatively little importance. So, in general, killing people is said to be gravely wrong, while killing other animals requires almost no justification at all."[10] Rachels's alternative view is built foursquare on the distinction between having a life and being alive. The biological notion of being alive is relatively unimportant; "one's *life,* by contrast, is immensely important."[11] It is the importance of having a life, and the innocent having of it at that (one does not conquer anyone to get it), that leads Rachels to say that unless one has forfeited one's right to life, one should not be killed by others.

The problem with the traditional view is that it assigns moral significance to a life solely or primarily on the basis of species membership rather than in terms of the distinction between having a life and being alive. At least at first glance the traditional view is based on the possession of rationality, but curiously infants and the severely retarded are included as beings with lives worthy of moral respect even though they do not possess this characteristic (although infants may possess it virtually). The controlling idea, therefore, seems to be that human nature is rational and hence sacred, regardless of one's individual characteristics. Rachels engages in hyperbole in the following quotation, but his general point that the traditional view (as well as the view of Nozick and Francis and Norman) is based on species membership, that is, on speciesism, is legitimate: "As for the other animals, it isn't that their moral status is merely less than that of man—in a strict sense, they have no moral status at all. Traditional thought does not admit that people have *any* moral duties to other animals—not even the duty not to torture them."[12] Rachels seems to be thinking of Thomas Aquinas and Kant in particular.

From Rachels's point of view, there is something extreme in the doctrine of the sanctity of all and only human life, the doctrine that provides the background for Nozick and Francis and Norman. But equally extreme is an Eastern view, particularly the Jain one, that all life is holy. This view makes it difficult to distinguish among kinds of lives; at least in principle, this view puts the life of a bug and the life of a person on a par. Rachels notes that human beings have mental and emotional lives far superior to those of insects. The mistake made by both Western and Eastern traditionalists is in failing to notice the distinction between being alive and having a life. Rachels asks:

> Do animals have lives? Some of them clearly do not. Having a life requires some fairly sophisticated mental capacities, which simple animals do not have. Consider, however, a psychologically complex animal such as the rhesus monkey. Rhesus monkeys live together in social groups; they have families and care for one another; they communicate with one another; they engage in complicated activities; they have highly individualized personalities. And they are clever: one team of researchers noted that they "can indeed solve many problems similar in type to the items used in standard tests of human intelligence." Although their lives are not as complicated as ours, emotionally or intellectually, there seems no doubt that they do have lives. They are not merely alive. It should come as no great surprise that other animals have lives; after all, *we* are animals.[13]

Careful study shows that even animals such as wild dogs and wolves, which live in pack societies, have surprisingly complex and diverse individual lives. Rachels's view is summarized in these words:

> When we consider the mammals with which we are most familiar, it is reasonable to believe that they do have lives in the biographical sense. They

> have emotions and cares and social systems and the rest, although perhaps not in just the way that humans do. Then the further down the phylogenetic scale we go, the less confidence we have that there is anything resembling a life. When we come to bugs, or shrimps, the animals pretty clearly lack the mental capacities necessary for a life, although they certainly are alive. The moral view suggested by this is that animals are protected by the sanctity of life *to the extent that* they have lives. Most of us already recognize the truth of this—we think that killing a human is worse than killing a monkey, but we also think that killing a monkey is a more serious matter than swatting a fly. And when we come to plants, which are alive, but where the notion of a biographical life has no application whatsoever, the moral qualms about killing have vanished altogether. . . . The higher animals ought to have serious moral protection. . . . The protection becomes weaker, however, as we consider progressively simpler animals, until we reach the clams and snails and bugs whose "lives" count for little. Thus, we have found the reasonable middle ground between the two extremes represented by the Eastern and Western traditions.[14]

The complexity of animals matters because one can say much more about a complex being when it dies than one can about a simple being when it dies; there is greater reason to believe that the death of a complex being is a bad thing than there is to believe that the death of a simple being is. This stance might be unsettling to individuals who have not previously thought about the matter when they realize that it implies that the life of a normal human being is to be preferred to the life of a mentally retarded human being in extremis. This is consistent with the claim that each deserves equal moral consideration; once each is given equal consideration, however, we notice some morally relevant factors present in the normal human being not found in the mentally retarded one. This

> *sounds like* an unacceptable denigration of the mentally handicapped. But it does not imply that the lives of the mentally handicapped are to be held cheap, or that they may be killed at will. It implies only a comparison that might come into play in a theoretical situation of "forced choice." . . . I call this the "less radical" implication because it is not quite so contrary to our normal views as it may at first appear to be. . . . Suppose you were to hear of the death of a severely retarded person at the same time as you heard of the death of [a young woman]. Would you think the two deaths equally tragic?[15]

The AMC brings to our attention the fact that severely retarded human beings might have *less* complex mental abilities than those of some animals. On the principle Rachels is defending (contra Nozick and Francis and Norman), there would be reason in these cases to prefer the life of the animal to that of the human in extremis.

Being rational and autonomous are important for human beings, but in itself being human is unimportant. To make this claim, one need not be opposed to all the good causes advanced by the rallying cry that "all human beings have equal rights": the struggles versus slavery, anti-Semitism, and so on. Rather, the principle needed to support these good causes is not simply membership in a biological species. The point can be seen when we imagine a species different from our own—say, from another planet—but having the same capacities we have. To think that members of this other species would not merit the same moral consideration as human beings would be a blatant unfairness based on a treatment of "humanity" as a talisman or magical totem that could by itself do moral work for us. Once again, to deny that species membership is important is not to deny that the interests of human beings are important.[16]

Rachels in effect relabels the AMC as "moral individualism" because it implies that individual characteristics, not species membership, make beings morally considerable. Insofar as animals have the same characteristics as human beings—for example, the capacity to experience pain—they should be treated as human beings are treated. That is, tormenting animals is wrong for *exactly* the same reason that it is wrong to torment human beings: it hurts. However, it is concomitantly true that when human beings have different capacities—and higher ones, such as literacy—they may be, and in some cases should be, treated differently. No one thinks that the great apes should be sent to universities.

It should now be clear how Rachels responds to Nozick's objections to the AMC. It will be remembered that Nozick himself finds it a "puzzle" how someone's merely being a member of the human species could be a reason to treat him or her better than a being from another species, even if the human being in question lacks certain crucial capacities possessed by normal human beings. Rachels addresses Nozick's puzzle in this way:

> When faced with an apparently sound chain of reasoning that leads to a surprising result, we have two options. We could conclude that we have made a new discovery: the reasoning teaches us something (for example, that species membership is not in itself a morally significant matter) that we did not realize before. Or, if we find the surprising result hard to take,

> we might refuse to accept the reasoning. Here Nozick chooses the second path; and so he regards it as a "puzzle" to explain why species membership is in fact important. To say this is a "puzzle" is to *assume* that species membership *is* important.[17]

The issue between Rachels and Nozick concerns a basic matter in philosophic method: do we trust arguments and follow them wherever they lead, or do we trust our intuitions and reject argument when it does not lead in the "correct" direction? Rachels does not adopt the former alternative in an unqualified way, nor does Nozick adopt the latter *simpliciter,* but Rachels does lean toward the former alternative and Nozick toward the latter. Rachels admits that if a chain of reasoning is implausible and leads to a ridiculous conclusion, then it might be wise to distrust the argument and examine it for possible mistakes. There is nothing ridiculous about the conclusion to the AMC, however (or, in Rachels's words, to moral individualism), and hence there is no reason to distrust the argument. In the face of a strong argument to the contrary, it is not legitimate for Nozick to assume that species membership has to be important.[18]

Obviously Nozick is not a racist. In trying to justify discrimination on the basis of species, however, "he has inadvertently produced an argument which, if accepted, would justify racist discrimination as well."[19] Rachels further criticizes Nozick for offering more explanation than justification. It is one thing to explain why human beings feel that human beings are morally special, but justifying this feeling is a different matter altogether. Speaking of his confidence in the AMC (again, what he calls moral individualism) and of the paucity of Nozick's view, Rachels says that the "inability of a thinker of Nozick's ingenuity to come up with anything better than this [puzzlement] only increases that confidence."[20] Belief that species membership is important is a conviction that many people feel intuitively must be true, yet on analysis it turns out to be false.

Just as Descartes's view of animals now strikes most people as ridiculous, so also might current varieties of speciesism eventually come to appear absurd. The only indication of pain in human beings that the vast majority of animals do not have is the ability to tell us that they are in pain, but neither infants, the severely retarded, nor the senile have this ability. Still, not even our ability to communicate that we are in pain differs radically from the ability of animals, for their shrieks, groans, cowering, and so on send messages not too different from the ones sent by human beings in pain. Skinner's view, treated favorably by Nozick, that we can explain animal behavior without attributing such things as desires or beliefs to them is intended to apply to human beings as well. As before, what is needed, according to Rachels, is a "moral individualism" that suggests that "how an individual may be treated is to be determined, not by considering his group memberships, but by considering his own particular characteristics."[21] For example, if we are considering whether we should use a chimpanzee in a medical experiment where the chimpanzee will be infected with a disease, it is not good enough simply to point out that chimpanzees are not members of the preferred group, the human one. Rather, we would have to look at specific chimpanzees and specific human beings.

Rachels's thesis is that moral individualism is an often unnoticed consequence of Darwin's argument, in *The Expression of Emotion in Man and Animals,* that animals experience "anxiety, grief, dejection, despair, joy, love, tender feelings, devotion, ill-temper, sulkiness, determination, hatred, anger, disdain, contempt, disgust, guilt, pride, helplessness, patience, surprise, astonishment, fear, horror, shame, shyness, and modesty."[22] If we think that there is something wrong with treating a particular human being with certain characteristics in a certain way, then to be consistent, we should do the same if a particular animal also has those characteristics. In effect, Rachels advocates replacing the simple doctrine of human dignity with the more complex doctrine of moral individualism. This more complex position is opposed to both "radical speciesism" and "mild speciesism." In the former, even the trivial interests of human beings take priority over the vital interests of animals; if we had to choose between causing a mild discomfort to a human being and an intense pain to an animal, the radical speciesist would choose causing the intense pain to an animal. Moral individualism is also opposed to mild speciesism, where trivial interests of human beings do not outweigh more substantial animal interests; if we were to choose between causing the same amount of pain to an animal or to a human being, however, the mild speciesist would (even outside extreme situations) cause it to an animal. That is, moral individualism rejects mild speciesism because of moral individualism's commitment to a principle of equality (of consideration).

It is doubtful whether Nozick's speciesism is radical, but to say that it is mild is not necessarily to get him off Rachels's hook. The radical-mild distinction deals with the extent of speciesism, not its logical basis. Regarding the latter, there is a distinction between qualified and unqualified speciesism, and Nozick is an unqualified speciesist, which involves the view that mere species alone is morally important. I have shown the arbitrariness on which this view is based. Nevertheless, even qualified speciesism, wherein species membership *plus* some characteristic possessed by members of the species is crucial, is problematic. This view tends to exaggerate the extent to which rationality makes a moral difference. It does make a moral difference, but not always:

> When the issue is paternalistic interference, it is relevant to note whether the individual whose behaviour might be coerced is a rational agent. Suppose, however, that what is in question is not paternalistic interference, but putting chemicals in rabbits' eyes to test the safety of a new shampoo. To say that rabbits may be treated in this way, but humans may not, because humans are rational agents, is comparable to saying that one law-school applicant may be accepted, and another rejected, because one has a broken arm while the other has an infection.[23]

Further, qualified speciesism is problematic because not all human beings are rational agents.

There is a certain appeal to the idea that the way individuals should be treated ought to be determined by what is normal for their species, but on close inspection the idea does not hold water: "Suppose (what is probably impossible) that an unusually gifted chimpanzee learned to read and speak English. And suppose he eventually was able to converse about science, literature, and morals. Finally he expresses a desire to attend university classes."[24] The point here is not that the syntactically complicated language possessed by most human beings—but only rarely, if at all, by animals—necessarily gives them a privileged status. Sometimes intellectual excellence or sophisticated language is relevant—say, regarding the question as to who should be admitted to universities. Regarding the question of torture, however, the victim's ability or inability to speak is an irrelevant consideration. If we compare a rhesus monkey and a fly, we find that the communicative and psychological abilities of the monkey are vastly greater than those of the fly. But the infant with severe brain damage might never learn to speak or to develop mental powers equal to those of the rhesus monkey. Moral individualism would, in extremis, sometimes prefer a marginal human being over a monkey and sometimes the other way around, depending on the individuals in question.[25]

Nor is Rachels in favor of the reciprocity requirement as the basis for moral beneficiary status. The retarded can reciprocate no more than animals can, but that does not prevent them both from being the beneficiaries of those rational beings who can reciprocate with each other. The reciprocity requirement does contain "the germ of a plausible idea," however, which is that "if a person *is* capable of acting considerately of our interests, and *refuses* to do so, then we are released from any similar obligations we might have had to him."[26] Neither animals nor marginal cases are capable of such reciprocity. The fact that most human beings are capable of rationality and reciprocity leads some to *assume* that human beings are more sensitive to harm than animals—say, because of their foresight, which enables them to anticipate painful experiences:

> Nothing in this line of reasoning invalidates the fundamental idea that the interests of non-humans should receive the same consideration as the *comparable* interests of humans. All that follows is that we must be careful in assessing when their interests are really comparable. . . . Suppose we must choose between causing x units of pain for a human or a non-human. Because of the human's superior cognitive abilities, the after-effects for him will include y additional units of suffering; thus the human's total misfortune will be x + y, while the non-human's total will be only x. . . . On the other hand, suppose we alter the example to make the non-human's initial pain somewhat more intense, so that it equals x + y. . . . Where relevant differences between individuals exist, they may be treated differently; otherwise, the comparable interests of individuals, whether human or non-human, should be given comparable weight.[27]

One of the obvious reasons that moral individualism will be difficult for some people to accept is its complexity, which contrasts to the simplicity of the traditional speciesist idea defended by Nozick:

> The fact is that human beings are not simply "different" from other animals. In reality, there is a complex pattern of similarities and differences. The matching moral idea is that in so far as a human and a member of another species are similar, they should be treated similarly, while to the extent that they are different they should be treated differently. This will allow the human to assert a right to better treatment whenever there is some difference between him and the other animal that justifies treating him better. But it will not permit him to claim greater rights simply because he is human, or because humans in general have some quality that he lacks, or because he has some characteristic that is irrelevant to the particular type of treatment in question.[28]

The complexity of moral individualism is made understandable when it is realized that after Darwin, variations (e.g., marginal cases) came to be seen as the stuff of nature, whereas pre-Darwinian naturalists could view variations as mere curiosities, with the standard specimen exemplifying the eternal essence of the species. In effect, moral individualism fits evolutionary theory well, not so much in terms of logical entailment, but in a stronger sense than mere consistency. The principle of equality itself, however, is not a new idea in the nineteenth or twentieth centuries:

> Aristotle knew that like cases should be treated alike, and different cases should be treated differently; so when he defended slavery he felt it necessary to explain why slaves are "different." Therefore, if the doctrine of human dignity was to be maintained, it was necessary to identify the difference between humans and other animals that justified the difference in moral status. That is where the image of God thesis and the rationality thesis came in. They supplied the needed relevant differences. . . . Moral individualism is, therefore, nothing but the consistent application of the principle of equality to decisions about what should be done, in light of what Darwinism has taught us about our nature and about our relation to the other creatures that inhabit the earth.[29]

The moral individualism defended by Rachels, as opposed to the violation of the principle of equality defended by Nozick, dovetails with Regan's view that the value of a life "is, first and foremost, the value that it has *for the person who is the subject of that life.*" I take it that Regan says "first and foremost" because subjects of a life are affected by what happens to their lives more acutely than other beings are; after all, their lives are theirs and not someone else's. That is, something is valuable for such persons if they would be worse off without it. But Rachels seems to have a different emphasis from Regan's regarding the distinction between biological and biographical senses of life. The latter is more important for Rachels, a view that has implications for euthanasia. The following indicates Rachels's view and *perhaps* Regan's, although this is by no means clear:

> Being alive . . . is valuable to us only in so far as it enables us to carry on our lives. This is most evident when we consider the extreme case in which a person, while still alive, has lost the capacity for having a life, such as a person in irreversible coma. Being alive, sadly, does such a person no good at all. The value of being alive may therefore be understood as instrumental; being alive is important to an individual because it enables him or her

> to have a life. This suggests that the moral rule against killing may be understood as a derived rule. To kill someone is to destroy a biological life; this is objectionable because, without biological life, there can be no biographical life. (Being blind makes one's life more difficult; being dead makes it impossible.) The point of the rule against killing is, therefore, to protect individuals against the loss of their lives, and not merely against the cessation of their being alive.[30]

Most human beings are the subjects of lives, not just biological lives, but biographical ones. Many animals with fairly sophisticated mental capacities also have biographical lives, whereas bugs and shrimp do not have these capacities. The sophistication Rachels has in mind refers not merely to the great apes and dolphins but also to a Singer-like list that extends "downward" almost to mollusks and crustaceans, it seems.

Human beings and animals come under the protection of the rule against killing to the extent that they are the subjects of biographical lives. That is, I claim that the wrongness of killing is not an all-or-nothing affair. Killing an animal that has a rich biographical life is worse than killing one without such a life. On this line of reasoning, killing most human beings is worse than killing animals, but this does not mean that the lives of animals are cheap. Consistency (i.e., the AMC) requires that to the extent that animals have lives similar to our own, their lives must be regarded with similar seriousness. Moral individualism requires that the life of a Tay-Sachs infant, which will never develop a biographical life, receive no greater respect than that given to an intelligent, sensitive chimpanzee's. To think otherwise is to be unduly shaped by pre-Darwinian notions.[31]

In his recent book on Darwin, Rachels makes it clear that Darwin himself may not have fully appreciated the implications of his own work. But Darwin's thought is ultimately destructive of speciesism and in the long run supportive of moral individualism (the AMC). The traditional view that all and only human beings have inherent worth, with animals merely a means to an end, began to break up before Darwin, but he completed the job by decisively showing that human beings are not set apart from other animals but are part of the same natural order and indeed are kin to animals. Rachels quotes Singer here: "If the foundations of an ideological position are knocked out from under it, new foundations will be found, or else the ideological position will just hang there, defying the logical equivalent of the law of gravity."[32] The scientific foundations for speciesism have crumbled, and hence it needs to be reexamined. "The heart of moral individualism is an equal concern for the welfare of all beings, with distinctions made among them only when there are relevant differences that justify differences in treatment."[33] It is to be hoped that when the dust settles, a new equilibrium will be found in which our morality can comfortably coexist with our scientific understanding of the world. As it now stands, many intelligent people are in an intellectually schizophrenic position: scientific continuity between human beings and animals alongside ethical discontinuity between the two.

On Species

Once we see that this ethical discontinuity is not sufficiently grounded, we can further appreciate the hollowness of the reciprocity requirement, wherein the distinction between having a moral obligation and being the beneficiary of one is not sufficiently emphasized.[34] Because of the difficulty in establishing the reciprocity requirement regarding animals and marginal cases, those who try to justify animal experimentation, say, must find some way of assigning value to animal life (they must be close enough to us for us to learn from our experiments on them) while still maintaining a large enough gap between them and human beings to justify the research. If we treat animals differently not only in degree but in kind from the way that we treat marginal cases and other human beings, then this value difference should also be of kind rather than degree. No such difference is likely to be found, however, in that secular justifications of such a difference are made in terms of characteristics not possessed by the marginal cases. The categorical difference required to justify painful or lethal scientific experiments is hard to find, at least partly because of our current knowledge in evolutionary theory, genetics, neurophysiology, and psychology, as Susan Finsen emphasizes:

> In fact, recent work in genetics has made it possible to artificially inseminate a female chimpanzee with human sperm. . . . It is not surprising that this experiment was terminated with abortion of the resultant fetus. For, not only could the researchers involved expect moral outrage from the religious and secular community alike, but the creation of such a hybrid would represent a living refutation to the claim that species differences represent important qualitative boundaries. How would such an individual be classified? Should a half-human primate receive the protection ac-

> corded to human subjects, or only the protections of the Federal Animal Welfare Act? What about a ¼ human, or a ¾ human?[35]

The question of where to draw the line is inappropriate, for it suggests that a single line that limits rights to human beings must be drawn somewhere. It may also suggest that if there is such a line, then the marginal cases do not count for much against the general validity of a proposed criterion to justify the line.

Finsen is like Clark in noting that the notion of species is troublesome because it has changed from a real, "Aristotelian," essential, and immutable boundary (or almost so) to a relatively arbitrary one. Descartes's belief that animals lack minds and feelings was based on a notion of species as a metaphysical gulf. Within his framework marginal cases are not even possible. Although it is not clear that the AMC is possible only on the basis of modern biology, as Finsen alleges (for previous citations from Porphyry and Plutarch indicate otherwise), she is nonetheless correct to emphasize that it is enhanced by a notion of species membership as occurring when a multitude of organisms who are genealogically related resemble each other in certain ways but differ in others. If the partially conventional boundaries between species are to be used as a basis for differences in treatment, then they must be correlated with morally significant differences: "But if we need to check whether the species boundary correlates appropriately with the morally significant boundary, we might as well just dispense with the species boundary and use the real, morally significant boundary in the first place. . . . Where boundaries are arbitrary, then, we ought to look at the characteristics of individuals themselves to decide how to treat them."[36]

In a recent book Rosemary Rodd amplifies the views on species held by Finsen, Clark, and Rachels. Rodd thinks that species loyalty counts for *something*, however, or else we would not, in extreme circumstances, prefer to sacrifice an animal instead of a normal human being. To admit this degree of loyalty, however, is not to deny the negative obligation we have, for example, to refrain from killing animals if vegetable food is available. Furthermore, Rodd, like the three thinkers whose views she amplifies, is not convinced that the reciprocity criterion helps us much to justify speciesism, even if it is helpful in some contexts. In addition to the marginal cases, which are not capable of forming contractual relations, there are domestic animals that, although not participants in an explicit contract, nonetheless function in many ways as members of human society. Further, there are some human beings to whom we obviously owe decent treatment even though they have not contracted with us, nor are they in a position to contract with us, as in remote South American Indian tribes.[37]

In effect, Rodd defends an attenuated conception of the relevance of species membership for moral questions by showing that many of the human achievements used to support anthropocentrism are of recent origin. The gap between the abilities of a band of chimpanzees and those of a group of Paleolithic human beings is smaller than that between a band of chimpanzees and space-age human beings. The gap between human beings and animals is not so small, however, on Rodd's reasoning, that we should routinely refer to animals as persons, as some animal rightists wish to do (sponges are not persons, even if higher animals are). Nor should we refrain from referring to marginal cases as persons, in that they belong to human families and possess human parents. Even given these qualifications, however, the relationship between human beings and animals, especially between marginal cases and animals, is close enough to justify the AMC.[38]

It should not be assumed that continued opposition to the AMC is due to its counterintuitive character if the relationship between theory and practice in ethics is as dialectical as it is in science. Moral theories can take command of our intuitions and practices and revise the experiential bases on which these intuitions and practices rest. For example, the theory that only those who can fulfill duties can also have rights was partly to blame for the previously held belief that the mentally retarded do not deserve decent treatment. Or again, the theory that slaves can fulfill duties but do not deserve decent treatment greatly changed many people's intuitions. (At certain points in the past, animals, too, were held responsible for their actions without being the bearers of rights.)[39] What most people now find to be counterintuitive is the Kantian view that only rational and linguistic beings fall into the scope of moral concern, for most believe that infants, the mentally retarded, the insane, the senile, the autistic, the comatose, and animals *are* within the scope of moral concern.[40] Moreover, most people have intuitions that the capacity for suffering is a sufficient condition for being morally considerable, even if it does not usually occur to them that their everyday (speciesist) practices contradict these intuitions.[41] It is the following peculiarity that the AMC is partially meant to remedy: common sense balks at the efforts of some scientists to deny consciousness to animals, but it does not balk at some scientists' rejection of moral concern for animals. The latter condition's mutability is evident when one considers that until recently it was commonsensical to tolerate painful biomedical research not only on animals but also on prisoners, indigents, primitive people, and the retarded.[42]

As I have shown, to tie moral beneficiary status to moral agency leads to disastrous consequences for marginal cases and animals. Regarding moral agency itself, it is worth noting that dogs and some other animals can be obedient, protective, and solicitous, which is more than can be said about the severely retarded.[43] Hence, once it becomes apparent that the domain of moral beneficiaries is much larger than that of moral agents, it is understandable, if not justifiable, that some would try to simplify matters by tying moral beneficiary status to species membership. As I have argued throughout this book, however, this procedure does not work. The following quotation from Thoreau indicates the optimism regarding moral progress implicit in the AMC:

> Is it not a reproach that man is a carnivorous animal? True, he can and does live, in a great measure, by preying on other animals; but this is a miserable way,—as any one who will go to snaring rabbits, or slaughtering lambs, may learn,—and he will be regarded as a benefactor of his race who shall teach man to confine himself to a more innocent and wholesome diet. Whatever my own practice may be, I have no doubt that it is part of the destiny of the human race, in its gradual improvement, to leave off eating animals, as surely as the savage tribes left off eating each other when they came into contact with the more civilized. If one listens to the faintest but constant suggestions of his genius, which are certainly true, he sees not to what extremes, or even insanity, it may lead him; and yet that way as he grows more resolute and faithful, his road lies. The faintest assured objection which one healthy man feels will at length prevail over the arguments and customs of mankind.[44]

Afterword

I have two goals in mind in this afterword: to summarize the results of this book and to explicate my own view of the AMC, which relies heavily on a view of temporal relations as asymmetrical.

In the preface (Lawrence Becker), chapter 1 (Tom Regan), and chapter 3 (R. G. Frey), I offered formal versions of the AMC that I then analyzed and criticized throughout this book, along with other less formal versions of the argument. Both Peter Singer and Regan defend the AMC. The former's version depends on a distinction between mentally undeveloped human beings and animals, on the one hand, and mentally developed human beings and animals, on the other. Because even the mentally undeveloped are sentient, they are morally considerable and deserve equal consideration by moral agents. Nonetheless, Singer thinks that the mentally undeveloped lie within the sweep of the replaceability argument because they do not have a right to life. Mentally developed human beings and animals (e.g., chimpanzees and pigs) do have a right to life because they are persons; that is, they are self-conscious beings with an awareness of their past and an anticipation of their future. To kill them is to rob them of their future. Because they have a right to life, they do not lie within the sweep of the replaceability argument, but this does not mean that their right to life is absolute, for if the consequences are weighty enough, even mentally developed beings can be sacrificed. The key point is that mentally undeveloped beings—whether human beings or animals—deserve equal consideration, and mentally developed beings—whether human beings or animals—also deserve equal consideration. Singer thinks that, as a consequence of the AMC, our views of both animals and the marginal cases of humanity need to change.

That is, they need to be brought together in a way that calls for both a loftier view of animals and a reconsideration of the view of human life as sacred. (1) The lives of both mentally undeveloped animals and marginal cases may be taken if there are weighty reasons for doing so; (2) the lives of both mentally developed human beings and animals (that is, persons) may also be taken if the reasons are weightier still. Perhaps the most problematic part of Singer's version of the AMC is that, in conjunction with the replaceability argument and as a consequence of (1), some marginal human beings are indeed marginal and replaceable. Later in this afterword I will speak against Singer's replaceability argument.

In contrast to Singer, Regan does not think that our view of marginal cases (excepting the irreversibly comatose) needs to be changed. In fact, his version of the AMC hinges on the traditional (although not ancient) respect given to marginal cases, which I think speaks in favor of Regan's view. According to the AMC, however, our view of animals needs significant modification. The AMC convincingly shows, he thinks, that the moral status of severely retarded human beings is not superior to that of animals such as dogs and cows. One of the strongest moral intuitions is that killing and eating severely retarded human beings is a moral outrage. But why? Regan convincingly argues that only the severely retarded's possession of basic rights can account for our moral outrage. These basic rights are much stronger than Singer's (nonbasic) rights because both animals and marginal cases are subjects of a life, largely because they are sentient. In this regard Regan's version of the AMC is preferable to Singer's. Although stated with less than optimal clarity, Regan's view seems to be that because animals and marginal cases are subjects of a life (i.e., they have an experiential welfare), they have inherent value as individuals and are not merely receptacles for the intrinsic values of their particular pleasures and pains. This inherent value grounds basic rights; in short, it makes marginal cases and hence animals ends in themselves rather than mere utilities. We have direct duties to marginal cases and hence to animals as a consequence of the inherent value they possess equally.

Regan's transcendental argument is an attempt to account for one of our strongest moral convictions in a way that utilitarianism, contractualism, and so on cannot: that marginal cases should not be treated in grossly immoral ways. If we assume, as Regan does, that marginal cases should not be treated in grossly immoral ways, then this must be based on the claim that they are subjects of a life who have basic rights. He does not violate another firmly held conviction, however: that normal human beings are of greater value than animals. To *have* a life, it is not enough to merely *be* alive. Sentiency seems to be a necessary condition for having a life, but mentally undeveloped beings (to use Singer's language) that are alive do not necessarily lead a life, in Regan's sense, in that the latter phenomenon requires certain sophisticated intrinsic values in addition to the inherent value of an individual. Animals (chimpanzees might be an exception) do not seem to have these sophisticated intrinsic values.

In many ways the differences between Singer and Regan mirror the classic differences between utilitarianism and deontology in general. Nowhere is this more apparent than in Singer's replaceability argument. A telling point in Regan's favor is that he, along with Evelyn Pluhar, criticizes this argument because of one of its counterintuitive implications: if morally undeveloped animals are replaceable, so are human beings with comparable characteristics in like circumstances. According to Singer, painlessly killing mentally undeveloped animals and replacing them with conspecifics involves no wrongdoing, but neither would raising mental deficients who were then killed painlessly and replaced with conspecifics, their flesh stocked for food or experimentation purposes. The problem here is not with the AMC but with Singer's attempt to link it to the replaceability argument. Hence, if we shudder at the prospect of canning "moron meat," we would do well to withdraw consent to the replaceability argument; the AMC in itself carries no implication that marginal cases be mistreated. Once again, it is Singer and not Regan who thinks that our attitudes toward mentally defective human beings need reconsideration, to the point where Singer allows the claim that marginal cases might be killed for food—if we should develop the taste for them—or for experimental purposes if the marginal cases are raised and killed humanely and are replaced. But it is unlikely that Singer would (like reciprocity theorists) explain his own personal continuing attachment to mental defectives in terms of an uncorrected speciesism: he is opposed to speciesism.

One consequence of all this is that those who, like myself, are interested in Regan-like defenses of the AMC cannot rest content with the weak version of the argument where, on the *assumption* that marginal cases have rights, we can then argue that animals, too, have rights. That is, there is a need to defend a strong version of the AMC, wherein it is shown *why* marginal cases have rights. Regan does this.

If marginal cases do not have rights, then one of our strongest moral intuitions is mistaken, and no one has yet delivered a convincing argument that this is so.

Still, although Regan's transcendental argument is intended to account for the intuition that one should not mistreat marginal cases in grossly immoral ways, or as means only rather than as ends in themselves, there is nothing sacrosanct about this intuition. That is, perhaps there could be a convincing argument that this intuition is mistaken. Singer does not supply one, nor do the opponents to the AMC. In Singer's attempt to speak against this intuition in his replaceability argument, he distorts the lives of marginal cases and animals by atomizing their experiences such that if the moment of their deaths is painless, then supposedly nothing is lost. But something *is* lost: their memories, desires, future pleasures, and lines of causal inheritance and expectation. They lose not only their biological lives but also their biographical ones. It is both their sentiency and the historical continuity of their lives that supports the intuition that one should not mistreat marginal cases and animals in grossly immoral ways.

H. J. McCloskey, Jan Narveson, John Rawls, and Richard Watson base their opposition to the AMC on some version of the thesis that to have rights, a being must be capable of reciprocal relations with free, rational beings. McCloskey, Narveson, and Watson treat the AMC explicitly, whereas Rawls does so only implicitly, but all four have generated responses from defenders of the AMC, such as Joel Feinberg, Dale Jamieson, Rachels, Pluhar, and Regan. The reciprocity objection admits of different forms: some contractualist, some based on rational egoism, and some deriving from the American pragmatist idea that animals do not have rights because they cannot regulate their attitudes by the institutional norms of rights. There is at least a family resemblance among all these views. All the reciprocity theorists indicate that rights cannot be grounded apart from agreements made by rational agents.

In a way the weak version of the AMC is compatible with the reciprocity theorists' overall point: to claim that animals have rights only if marginal humans have them does not commit one to any natural property that grounds their rights. On the strong version of the AMC, where it is asserted that marginal cases do have rights, and hence animals as well have them, it is not so clear that we can avoid the naturalistic "fallacy." Perhaps the marginal cases, and hence animals, could be granted rights by virtue of attention being paid to them by rational agents, but this position runs into trouble. For example, it cannot explain why we think that even orphans and abandoned dogs should not be mistreated. Hence, it makes sense to think that it is the sentience of marginal cases and animals and the fact that they each have an experiential welfare (they are subjects of lives) that grounds our belief that they ought not to receive gratuitous pain. That is, to respond fully to the reciprocity theorists, some sort of critical response to G. E. Moore is needed.

Mary Midgley has done an excellent job of showing that there is no major problem in arguing from facts to values; the difficulty arises in getting both the facts and the values right. That is, *good* is problematic not because it is evaluative but because it is such a general term. I agree with Midgley that the naturalistic fallacy is a stuffed dragon and that philosophers (including, to a certain extent, Regan) should stop marching around with its head on their spears. Further, there is hyperbole in G. E. Moore's boast that he has discovered a single, simple fallacy so widespread as to vitiate almost all earlier moral reasoning. For Moore, the *cordon sanitaire* around goodness is established by its being an ultimate simple, but a far more defensible view is that *good,* like any general term, is explainable in terms of its uses and provinces. For example, when a philosopher says that something is good, we might say, "Prove it" or "Explain yourself! Why is it good?" Goodness is meant not so much to conclude discussion as to begin it. In contrast, Moore erected a quasi-logical barrier meant to save him the trouble of arguing for his view of goodness.

The weblike nature of language and of conceptual connectedness makes Moore's view of logical and metaphysical atomism quite unattractive, for it is integrally connected to a Humean, empiricist metaphysics wherein all beings in the universe, considered in themselves, appear entirely loose and independent of each other. But what about the view that the infliction of gratuitous pain on an *individual* is a bad thing, as is torturing an individual being, starving it, or humiliating it? Notice that individual facts are opposed not so much to value as to unsubstantiated opinion or conjecture. It makes perfect sense to say that there are facts—even well-established ones—regarding evaluative matters. To say that inflicting gratuitous pain is wrong is not to say something that is infallible or complete, but to deny this claim is at the very least to indicate in a rather bold way where the next conversation has to begin. Goodness is a determinable that can be instantiated in many ways, but it is exceedingly difficult to imagine how it can be associated with the view that it is morally permissible to inflict avoidable pain; in addition, it is exceedingly difficult to imagine that one could get into trouble by associating it with pleasure that is conducive to the long-term well-being of one capable of such pleasure. Perhaps there are certain mysteries about goodness treated by Plato, but they do not concern its general logical status and they cannot be solved by trying to use the term without natural specifications.

Perhaps the AMC's most significant critic is R. G. Frey, who rightly pushes the defender of the AMC to think through some of the implications of the possession of sentiency but who is inconsistent regarding whether possession of sentiency is all that important in the first place. At one point he wonders why the infliction of gratuitous suffering is wrong; at another point he defends the moral truism that suffering is suffering and hence is evil. Concerning the latter tendency in Frey, it is crucial to notice that the sort of sentiency he has in mind is not merely reaction to stimuli, or even reaction to sensory stimuli, but rather the ability to feel pain. That is, the AMC builds on the fact that a central nervous system makes possible pain states that are morally relevant if anything is morally relevant. In this regard the utilitarian Frey is not only like his fellow utilitarian Singer but also like Regan. On the other hand, whereas Regan invokes the AMC and the sentience of human beings and animals to move from the rights of marginal human beings to the rights of animals, Frey moves from the present permissibility of certain painful experiments on animals to the permissibility of certain painful experiments on marginal human beings.

Clark, Becker, and Roger Paden all explore the possibility that the legitimacy of partial affections in human beings has implications for the AMC. Only Clark among these three defends the AMC. Becker tries to move from the claim that in extremis we can legitimately show preference for those close to us, including those in our own species, a claim that defenders of the AMC would grant, to the bothersome claim that in normal circumstances we can still show such a preference, even to the point where we can kill and eat animals, a claim that defenders of the AMC would not grant. Paden also opposes the AMC, basing his position on his distinction between the actually existing moral community and the theoretical, ideal community. The latter should not be forced on us by defenders of the AMC, he thinks. The problem with too much concern for actually existing moral communities, however (and this problem affects Clark as well in an odd way because of his concentration on pets and British beasts), is that it may result in a reification of certain traditional prejudices, as in classism, racism, sexism, and speciesism, as well as certain forms of patriotism.

There is much to be learned, however, from Clark's defense of the AMC and from his opposition to Frey. It is true that if I can save only my child or my neighbor, but not both, I should save my child. Nevertheless, this hierarchy of judgment or partiality of affection does not license tyranny such that I may in normal circumstances kill my neighbor so as to benefit my child. Clark is also instructive regarding why intellectual superiority does not license tyranny in that, on this reasoning, beings intellectually superior to us (God, the angels, the Nazis by self-proclamation) could then eat or painfully experiment on us as well as marginal cases and animals.

Frey's influence, however, has not stopped because of Clark's and other critics' opposition. Even some animal rightists agree with Frey on some key points. Steve Sapontzis greatly reduces the number of human beings who are marginal cases and then claims that species affinity can be used to protect the rest. That is, Sapontzis is in some ways like Frey and especially like the reciprocity theorists. Sapontzis derives a strange conclusion from the insights of reciprocity theorists, however: because reciprocity theory does not really deal with animals, it poses no obstacles to animal rights. Mary Anne Warren is also a bit like Frey and especially like the reciprocity theorists in seeing the capacity for autonomy as crucial in determining what sort of moral patient a being can be: infants are partially autonomous, and marginal cases who are properly cared for are also more likely to be partially autonomous. Warren is correct to suggest that if we accept the AMC, it is nonetheless important to note that once the minimal rights that the argument affords to marginal cases and animals are acknowledged (e.g., the right not to receive gratuitous suffering or the right to life), it is still permissible to invoke additional protections regarding marginal cases. That is, partial affections are legitimate in morality as long as they are ancillary to, rather than replacements for, impartial ascription of basic rights.

There are inadequacies associated with the Wittgensteinian nominalism of L. Duane Willard and Cora Diamond, most notably that such a position begs the question as to *why* it is legitimate to declare that marginal cases deserve moral respect but not animals, and there are problems associated with the tendentiousness in Michael Fox and Ruth Cigman, for these authors bend over backward to protect all marginal cases yet run away as quickly as possible from the effort to protect animals. Philip Devine's natural law position is problematic not because it is a natural law position but because it assumes both a normic sense of *human* regardless of any characteristics of the particular human in question and a normic sense of *animal* independent of any characteristics of the particular animal in question. In contrast to Willard and Diamond, Paul Muscari and Vinit Haksar appear to be not nominalists but essentialists in their positing, for moral if not metaphysical purposes, of a deep noumenal self in human beings. A judicious position should avoid both nominalism and essentialism.

Michael Leahy and Peter Carruthers have these and other thinkers' mistakes from which to learn, but they advance the debate regarding the AMC surprisingly little. Leahy exhibits all the strengths (e.g., an easy account of how we can justify punishment of those who have egregiously broken the implicit contract in society) *and* weaknesses of contractualist doctrine. An example of the latter is his inability to account for anything but the most indirect duties to marginal cases and animals. He thus rejects the AMC largely on the a priori basis that animals by definition are not rational contractors.

Carruthers's case is much more complicated. He legitimately requests that defenders of the AMC move beyond Rawlsian reflective equilibrium, but, his claim to the contrary notwithstanding, defenders of the AMC do not thereby run the risk of becoming moral essentialists or foundationalists in the pejorative senses of these terms. There is always some sort of hypothetical dimension to our theorizing, including our moral theorizing. For example, what are the consequences if we make rationality, sophisticated language use, or ability to enter contracts the criterion for moral beneficiary status? What are the consequences if we make sentiency the criterion? Any hypothesized criterion is open to this question. It is not hard to detect a defect in Carruthers's own resolution of these issues: on the one hand, he makes the level of intelligence necessary to enter into contracts the criterion for moral beneficiary status; on the other, he slips retarded human beings but not animals into the category of moral beneficiary status through the back door. But it is not as clear as Carruthers thinks that abuse of marginal cases is more likely than abuse of animals to lead down a slippery slope to abuse of normal adult human beings.

What is most bothersome about Carruthers's approach is his revival of the Cartesian view of animals as either incapable of pain or at least incapable of pain consciously perceived. Pluhar does an excellent job of dismantling this counterintuitive view, which she accomplishes with the aid of an inductive argument from analogy to other minds from one's own case. Beings that are neurologically similar to us and that respond to stimuli in complex, creative ways that are similar to our responses are probably conscious, just as we are. The argument from analogy has grown stronger since the time of Descartes in that it has been supplemented by centuries of observation (albeit observation often done at great cost to individual animals) that reveals detailed similarities between human and animal vertebrate systems. Many animals have the same pain mechanisms that we do, and their behaviors are consistent with this fact. We fly in the face of the theory of evolution if we assume that consciousness is uniquely human. If Carruthers had his way, scientists might well return to the Cartesian practice of nailing research animals to the wall without the benefit of anesthesia. If this accusation seems hyperbolic, it should be remembered that philosophers bear a good deal of the responsibility for the history of animal experimentation since the seventeenth century, and Carruthers seems not at all bothered by this fact.

Peter Harrison's approach has implications for the AMC because Harrison assumes that an animal is like an infant: they are each bundles of discrete sensations incapable of remembering. (In a peculiar way, Singer and other opponents to Regan's view of animals as subjects of lives, or to Rachels's view of animals possessing biographical lives, are in agreement with Harrison when they atomize the experiences of marginal cases or animals.) Significant pain, on this view, requires a continuity of consciousness not possessed by animals, infants, or some mentally impaired human beings. Harrison's view is more Cartesian than he likes to admit; it is *metaphysically* Cartesian because he thinks of mind and body as hermetically sealed compartments: for him, physiology and appropriate behavior (e.g., twitching) need not have anything to do with suffering. Carruthers's view is much like Harrison's, even if his terminology is somewhat different. Carruthers makes his point by saying that there are pain experiences in animals, but there is no feeling component linked to them. Pluhar understandably thinks that there is a contradiction here. How is "painlike" behavior in animals to be understood if not in terms of feelings that animals have? Edward Johnson is like Pluhar in being skeptical as to whether Carruthers can adequately respond to this question. According to Johnson, Carruthers comes dangerously close to reducing consciousness to self-consciousness. Such a reduction has consequences that are disastrous in the light of the AMC.

One way to counteract Harrison-Carruthers Cartesianism is to argue, as does Sarah Stebbins, that animals possess complex mental states. One must be careful, however, that emphasis of these complex mental states does not result in a new sort of "intelligenceism" (Colin McGinn's worry) or a new sort of immaterial appendix meant to separate absolutely human beings from animals (Nicholas Everitt's worry).

I have also examined the claim that opposition both to rights for the great apes and to the AMC is often based, explicitly or implicitly, on the belief that animals are our "slaves." That is, defense of rights for the great apes and defense of the AMC are integrally connected to the effort to oppose the view of animals as slaves or increments of capital. The liberal political efforts to get acknowledgment of the rights of the great apes and to ameliorate animal slavery face opposition from various "conservatives" who would like to hold onto traditional anthropocentric ways, on the one hand, and from leftists who are skeptical of the supposedly abstract nature of animal rights, on the other. I have examined several of these conservatives throughout the book. (It should be noted, however, that our heritage in ancient and medieval culture is not quite as anthropocentric as some think. If anything, it is theocentric.)

Ted Benton, however, is a leftist who in a recent book criticizes animal rights from a different political direction. Benton has a difficulty with Regan's use of the AMC. There is a huge gap between the level of abstraction at which AMC is pitched and the practical contexts in which it has to be applied. Oddly enough, Benton the leftist sounds like Clark the conservative. The latter favors not so much extending liberal rights to animals as expanding our conception of a household (with its pets) so as to include animals within one's polis; if it is possible, we should try to include all one's nation's animals (all British beasts, for Clark) or, if the Hellenistic Greeks are correct that the universe is one household, all animals. Both Benton and Clark think that some versions of the AMC prevent any sensitivity to particularity and diversity.

There are several things that can be said on behalf of the impartialist version of the AMC. First, if we give up on or deemphasize abstract reason, as Benton and Clark do, then we will have a difficult time criticizing the household or polis where marginal cases or animals are abused, experimented on, or eaten. Second, Regan in particular is willing to make distinctions when they make a moral difference, contra Benton. Consider his distinction between the "central" marginal cases and the most marginal of marginal cases, the latter failing not only the rationality/autonomy criterion but also the subject of a life criterion. Furthermore, Regan does notice the obvious difference between a child, who is potentially rational, and a severely psychologically disabled human being, who is not even potentially rational. Once these distinctions are noticed, one can imagine how Regan would respond to the charge that moral responsibility is some sort of abstract, magical, separate faculty. In fact, moral responsibility arises along the continuum of rationality occupied by some animals, some marginal cases, and all normal adults in their various degrees of mental competence.

If Benton is saying that if mentally enfeebled human beings were rational, they would want to be treated fairly, he is correct. But the same sort of conditional claim could be made on behalf of animals. It is not clear why Benton thinks that appeal to counterfactuals works for marginal cases (e.g., the claims these individuals would make if they were able to make moral claims on their own behalf) but not in the case of animals. An imaginative leap is required in either case. At base Benton appears to be a Marxist who is skeptical of the notion of individualist views of rights for human beings, whether normal or marginal. It follows a fortiori that he is skeptical of extending those rights to individual animals. Benton is to be thanked for alerting us to the fact that the AMC is part of a larger liberal political agenda concerning the rights of individuals who have a welfare that is amenable to being harmed. It is precisely this concern for individuals that is of primary concern to Rachels, contra Robert Nozick. Benton and Nozick are to be criticized in terms of the animal rightist trope that it is individual cows or chimpanzees who suffer or lose their lives, not a Platonic Cowhood or chimpness.

Nozick's supposedly parsimonious description of animals, following Skinner, commits the apathetic fallacy, which is every bit as dangerous as the more commonly known pathetic one. As a methodological claim there is nothing objectionable in saying that scientists should detach themselves from the animals they study, but serious moral harm to animals will likely follow if such a procedure results in the ontological claim that the animals studied therefore have no value or a value different in kind from that possessed by human beings with similar morally relevant characteristics. Nozick, like Leslie Pickering Francis and Richard Norman, commits this error when he tries to gain moral respect for marginal cases, but not animals, solely by means of their association with normal human beings. Positing moral respect by association, like guilt by association, indicates a failure to think through the crucial issues surrounding the AMC. Nozick admits as much when he throws up his hands regarding the "puzzle" of how to avoid speciesism.

Rachels successfully responds to Nozick using a distinction between being alive in a biological sense and having a life in a biographical sense. The former is valuable, but only as a means to the latter. The sanctity of life, Rachels insightfully argues, consists in the degree to which a being—human or animal—has a life. Rachels calls the AMC "moral individualism," a designation that indicates how we can avoid Nozick's "puzzle." Although Nozick is a mild speciesist, in that he does not think that trivial human pleasures outweigh intense animal pains, he is nonetheless an unqualified speciesist, because he thinks that species membership alone, regardless of a consideration of individual characteristics, is crucial in morality.

Susan Finsen and Rosemary Rodd both support Rachels and the AMC by analyzing the concept of "species." Because the concept is at least partially conventional, it does not lend itself, as it once did, to an exact coincidence with morally significant boundaries. Hence, when dealing with moral questions, it is best to move directly to these morally significant boundaries and only later pay attention to how these boundaries overlap species boundaries. In any event, there is a certain sloppiness in assuming that species boundaries coincide with, say, the class of beings with whom we can enter contracts. Not only the marginal cases but also members of remote South American Indian tribes are not in a position to contract with us, yet these beings obviously deserve decent treatment. Further, the sorts of achievement often cited to distinguish human beings from animals are not only not within the grasp of many human beings; they are often only recently within the grasp of normal human beings themselves.

Rachels's defense of the AMC is much like Regan's, even if the latter's distinctions among being alive, having a life, and leading a life do not exactly match Rachels's own distinction between being alive and having a life. The only human beings who lack the necessary and sufficient conditions of having a life—sentiency and having an experiential welfare that can go well or ill for the being in question—are the irreversibly comatose. Rachels is intent on arguing that for those human beings and animals whose lives are miserable and likely to remain so, euthanasia should be morally permitted. In this instance, however, the being killed is killed for his or her own benefit and with his or her permission (perhaps through a proxy). That is, marginal cases and animals should not have suffering or death inflicted on them for our benefit if the life harmed or lost is theirs.

The previous summary of the book's contents should indicate where my own view lies. In the remainder of this afterword, however, I will argue for the AMC specifically on the basis of time as asymmetrical, a basis that enables me to show some defects in Singer's version of the AMC, linked as it is to the replaceability argument, as well as in Frey's peculiar use of the AMC, where he permits experiments on marginal cases that we at present permit only on animals. I will criticize Harrison and Carruthers, too.

As utilitarians recognize, there are two ways of increasing the amount of pleasure in the world: one is to increase the pleasure of those who now exist, and the other is to increase the number of those who lead pleasant lives (the prior existence view and the total view, respectively). The replaceability argument obviously depends on the total view, for the replacement marginal cases or animals do not yet exist. The problem with the total view is that it is, as Singer admits, indifferent to whether the total amount of pleasure is adjusted by increasing the pleasure of existing beings or by increasing the number of beings who experience pleasure. A view of time as asymmetrical becomes crucial here. The past as the sum of accomplished facts is definite, even if our knowledge of it is somewhat unclear. What is done is done; more precisely, what has thus far been actualized cannot change its status as actualized. The future, however, is the region not of actuality but of possibility or, at best, of probability. Strictly speaking, there are no such things as future moral beneficiaries, only possible or probable ones. If we are given the choice between the prior existence view and the total view, we have to choose the former, because the latter has no actual future beings to which it can point as being moral beneficiaries. Once again, future entities are only possible or probable, not actual.

Singer's response in *Practical Ethics*[1] is to suggest that if we adopt the prior existence view, we will not be able to claim that it is bad, say, knowingly to bring into the world a child who will be miserable due to a defect detected during pregnancy. As he correctly notes, this is highly counterintuitive. But the devices open to the defender of the prior existence view are more numerous than Singer indicates. Three points should be emphasized: (1) The parent(s) of the fetus *already* exist as moral agents/beneficiaries, and hence their present dread at the thought of bringing a miserable child into the world is a morally relevant fact, so that they might legitimately decide to abort the fetus. (2) If the fetus is in the early stages of pregnancy—before the development of a central nervous system—it is not yet a morally considerable being, as Singer would otherwise admit. (3) After the development of a central nervous system, the fetus becomes a moral beneficiary who might then be amenable to considerations similar to those involved in decisions regarding euthanasia, considerations that I have already treated. In short, a defender of the prior existence view—and hence an opponent to the replaceability argument—can deal adequately with Singer's charge that one cannot, on the prior existence view, handle well a case where one is faced with the possibility of bringing a miserable being into the world.

Further, the replaceability argument stands or falls independently of the AMC. This is a crucial point, for Singer's linking of the two makes it easy for some to assume that they have criticized the AMC when they have only (and perhaps legitimately) criticized the replaceability argument. Furthermore, Singer moves too quickly from the admission that nonrational yet sentient animals and human beings deserve moral consideration to the claim that the consideration they deserve is amenable to tradeoffs—indeed, to replacement. This offers little consolation to individual animals or marginal cases whose present desire to continue living is shut off and whose present pleasures are terminated. That is, Singer's replaceability argument is at odds with his view that there is, other things being equal, something wrong about premature death. From a practical point of view, moreover, the adjective in the phrase *painless killing* (a phrase integral to the replaceability argument) is suspect, for the phrase refers to such practices as stunning or bludgeoning presently existing cows at the slaughterhouse, procedures that often cause intense pain, albeit momentarily.

I want to put my overall point here in the strongest possible terms: the fear expressed by critics of the AMC that the argument can be used to justify horrific things is a legitimate fear with respect to Singer's version, linked as it is to the replaceability argument, and to Frey's weak version, where we might be able to do to marginal cases what we now do to animals. In contrast, Regan's and Rachels's strong versions of the AMC should not elicit any fearful reactions. These latter thinkers (especially Rachels) have it right, I think: if we euthanize an animal or a marginal case, *it has to be for the benefit of the individual in question.*

At times Singer is in favor of euthanasia for the benefit of an individual animal or marginal case, but at other times he is in favor of euthanasia for the aggregative, utilitarian concerns found in the total view version of utilitarianism. (I am not necessarily criticizing utilitarianism per se; my target is only the total view variety.) Consider the case not of an unfortunate infant whose life is not worth living but rather of a hemophiliac infant whose life's prospects are significantly less than those of a normal child but sufficient to make the life worth living. This life has a value that should be defended, and defended rather strenuously, on the grounds provided by either virtue ethics, natural law theory, deontology or rights theory, or prior existence utilitarianism. But Singer would be willing to have the hemophiliac killed "painlessly" and replaced with another child if the parents were still able to produce a healthy replacement.

Both the replaceability argument and potentiality arguments run the risk of ignoring or deemphasizing the present state of the being in question, a neglect that often leads defenders of these arguments to speak too confidently about the outcome to future contingencies. Perhaps fetuses and infants will become rational adults; perhaps they will not. The question is, What are the characteristics of the fetus, marginal case, animal, or hemophiliac at its present stage of development? That is, it is a mistake to deny an animal, but not an infant, a right to life merely because the animal does not have the potential to become rational; the animal is already the sort of being that tries to avoid dangerous phenomena that might harm or kill it, and hence the animal no less than the marginal case ought not to be harmed or killed gratuitously. This conclusion applies to the hemophiliac that Singer would be willing to replace.

None of this should be interpreted to mean that time's arrow is irrelevant. For example, an irreversibly comatose person is a serious candidate for euthanasia in a way that a temporarily comatose one is not. If we stipulate that *the present* can refer to a period longer than a few moments (as in "the present stage of one's life"), then it is fair to say that the temporarily comatose person is at present the sort of being who values its life, whereas the permanently comatose person is not. In some sense animals, like the temporarily comatose person, are continuous selves that have present expectations regarding the future and a present desire to keep on living.

Nor am I trying to reduce animal consciousness, or the consciousness of marginal cases, to an atomic "now" that is only externally related to the past and future. Rather, my (process) view is that the present stage of animal or marginally human consciousness is internally and significantly related to the past, as when a dog or a retarded human being cowers from a person who kicked him yesterday. Nonetheless, these beings (like normal, rational human beings) are not internally related to the future. Hence, the present stage of self (which in some way incorporates the past stages) cannot be bartered away, as Singer tries to do. Previous stages in life (whether the life of a normal human being, a marginal case, or an animal) affect the present stage, but future stages do not affect the present stage. Expectation, fear, and hope are all present phenomena.

Two extreme views are to be avoided regarding the relationship between the self and temporal relations, and both of these views are symmetrical. The first is the Humean or Buddhist view treated in the previous paragraph, where the present stage of consciousness is an atomic now cut off from the future and the past. Yet it is this disastrous view, which runs afoul of all but the weakest version of scientific causation, that Harrison and Carruthers defend in the effort to deny significant pain to animals. The other is the view that the present stage of consciousness is internally related to the past and the future. This view is usually associated with a troublesome (even for certain theists) belief in divine omniscience, in that if God knows the outcome to all future contingencies, then they are not really contingencies, for one's future will already be actualized in the divine mind. Singer, the agnostic, in a peculiar way buys into this view when he treats the total view version of utilitarianism, a version where present sentient states are seen as valuable only to the extent that they outweigh future sentient states (even of another being) that are foreseen or planned by the total view utilitarian, who would need to be omniscient to do a good job.

The asymmetrical view I am defending sees the present state of consciousness as internally and significantly related to the past but externally related to the future. On this asymmetrical view, the present experiences and lives of marginal cases and animals are valuable if they seem to have the potential for rich experiences and lives in the future, but they are also valuable even if they do not seem to have such potential. We can inflict pain or death on them, but only if we can honestly say that we do so for the good of the individual in question.[2]

Notes

Introduction

1. Lawrence Becker, "The Priority of Human Interests," in *Ethics and Animals,* ed. H. Miller and W. Williams (Clifton, N.J.: Humana, 1983), 226–27.

2. See my *Philosophy of Vegetarianism* (Amherst: University of Massachusetts Press, 1984) and *Hartshorne and the Metaphysics of Animal Rights* (Albany: State University of New York Press, 1988).

3. See the recent edition of J. Bouffartigue and M. Patillon, *Porphyre de l'abstinence,* 3 vols. (Paris, 1977), with French and Greek on facing pages. Also, the Thomas Taylor translation is still available: Porphyry, *On Abstinence from Animal Food* (London: Centaur, 1965). The quotation from Porphyry is taken from this translation. Finally, see my "Vegetarianism and the Argument from Marginal Cases in Porphyry," *Journal of the History of Ideas* 45 (1984): 141–43.

Chapter 1: The Singer-Regan Debate

1. Peter Singer, *Animal Liberation* (New York: Avon, 1990 [1975]), 14–15.

2. Ibid., 16.

3. Ibid., 18–19.

4. Ibid., 20.

5. Ibid., 237; also see 21.

6. See Richard Wasserstrom, "Rights, Human Rights and Racial Discrimination," in *Human Rights,* ed. A. I. Melden (Belmont, Calif.: Wadsworth, 1970), 106.

7. Singer, *Animal Liberation,* 238–39.

8. Ibid., 240–41. Regarding John Rawls, see *A Theory of Justice* (Cambridge, Mass.: Harvard University Press, 1971), 17, 504–5, 572.

9. Peter Singer, "Not for Humans Only," in *Ethics and Problems of the 21st Century,* ed. K. Goodpaster and K. Sayre (Notre Dame, Ind.: University of Notre Dame Press, 1979), 197.

10. Peter Singer, *Practical Ethics* (Cambridge: Cambridge University Press, 1979), 65–66.

11. Ibid., 66–67.

12. Ibid., 67.

13. Ibid., 68, 70, 97.

14. Ibid., 103–4.

15. Ibid., 104–5.

16. Ibid., 118; also see Peter Singer, "The Fable of the Fox and the Unliberated Animals," *Ethics* 88 (1978): 120–21, 123.

17. Singer, "Not for Humans Only," 197.

18. Peter Singer, "Utilitarianism and Vegetarianism," *Philosophy and Public Affairs* 9 (1980): 328–29; also see 331–33.

19. Peter Singer, "Animals and the Value of Life," in *Matters of Life and Death,* ed. Tom Regan (Philadelphia: Temple University Press, 1980), 234; also see 220.

20. Ibid., 239–40.

21. Ibid., 244; also see 254.

22. See Peter Singer, "Prologue," in *In Defense of Animals,* ed. Peter Singer (Oxford: Basil Blackwell, 1985), 8–9; idem, "Animal Liberation or Animal Rights?" *Monist* 70 (1987): 3–5.

23. John Benson, "Duty and the Beast," *Philosophy* 53 (1978): 535.

24. Ibid., 536–37; also see my "On Why Patriotism Is Not a Virtue," *The International Journal of Applied Philosophy* 7 (1992): 1–4.

25. Meredith Williams, "Rights, Interests, and Moral Equality," *Environmental Ethics* 2 (1980): 159–61.

26. Thomas Young, "The Morality of Killing Animals," *Ethics and Animals* 5 (1984): 88–90.

27. Ibid., 90, 98–99, 101; also see Thomas Young, "Rational Preference Utilitarianism: Can It Justify Dissimilar Treatment of Animals and Marginal Humans?" *Philosophy in Context* 18 (1988): 19–20, 24.

28. Tom Regan, "The Moral Basis of Vegetarianism," *Canadian Journal of Philosophy* 5 (1975): 191, 193.

29. Tom Regan, "Introduction," in *Animal Rights and Human Obligations,* ed. T. Regan and P. Singer (Englewood-Cliffs, N.J.: Prentice-Hall, 1976), 16–17.

30. For an example of the former alternative see Tom Regan, "Fox's Critique of Animal Liberation," *Ethics* 88 (1978): 129–30.

31. Tom Regan, "Exploring the Idea of Animal Rights," in *Animals' Rights,* ed. D. Paterson and R. Ryder (London: Centaur, 1979), 80–81.

32. Tom Regan, "An Examination and Defense of One Argument Concerning Animal Rights," *Inquiry* 22 (1979): 189–91.

33. Ibid., 193.

34. Ibid., 196.

35. Ibid., 197–98.
36. Ibid., 204.
37. Ibid.
38. Ibid., 206.
39. Ibid., 207–9.
40. Ibid., 210–11.
41. Ibid., 212–17.
42. Tom Regan, "Utilitarianism, Vegetarianism, and Animal Rights," *Philosophy and Public Affairs* 9 (1980): 313–15.
43. Ibid., 317; also see 315–16.
44. Ibid., 318; also see 319.
45. Ibid., 320–21.
46. Ibid., 322–24.
47. Quoted in Tom Regan, "Utilitarianism and Vegetarianism, Again," *Ethics and Animals* 2 (1981): 16.
48. Ibid., 2, 16–17.
49. Tom Regan, *The Case for Animal Rights* (Berkeley: University of California Press, 1983), 42–44, 46, 152–53.
50. Ibid., 153–54.
51. Ibid., 155–56, 186–88.
52. Ibid., 188–90, 193–94.
53. Ibid., 236.
54. Ibid., 235, 237.
55. Ibid., 240–41; also see 239.
56. Ibid., 242, 245–46.
57. Ibid., 243–44.
58. Ibid., 247.
59. Ibid., 248–49.
60. Ibid., 352.
61. Ibid., 284–85, 350–51, 366.
62. Tom Regan, "The Case for Animal Rights," in *In Defense of Animals*, ed. P. Singer, 16–17.
63. Ibid., 22; also see 23.
64. See Henry Cohen, "Review of Tom Regan," *Ethics and Animals* 3 (1982): 127–29; also see idem, "Review of Tom Regan," *Ethics and Animals* 5 (1984): 13.
65. Evelyn Pluhar, "On Replaceability," *Ethics and Animals* 3 (1982): 97–98, 100–101.

Chapter 2: Reciprocity

1. See Beth Singer, "Having Rights," *Philosophy and Social Criticism* 11 (1986): 391–412.

2. Tibor Machan, "Do Animals Have Rights?" *Public Affairs Quarterly* 5 (1991): 170; also see Robin Attfield, *The Ethics of Environmental Concern* (Athens: University of Georgia Press, 1983), 142–43, who mentions the AMC.

3. See H. J. McCloskey, "The Moral Case for Experimentation on Animals," *Monist* 70 (1987): 69–73; also see idem, "Moral Rights and Animals," *Inquiry* 22 (1979): 23–54.

4. See Tom Regan, "McCloskey on Why Animals Cannot Have Rights," *Philosophical Quarterly* 26 (1976): 251–52.

5. Ibid., 253–54.

6. Ibid., 255–57.

7. See Robert Elliot, "Autonomy, Self-Determination and Rights," *Monist* 70 (1987): 84–85.

8. Joel Feinberg, "Can Animals Have Rights?" in *Animal Rights and Human Obligations,* ed. T. Regan and P. Singer (Englewood Cliffs, N.J.: Prentice-Hall, 1976), 194–95.

9. Joel Feinberg, "Human Duties and Animal Rights," in *On the Fifth Day: Animal Rights and Human Ethics,* ed. R. Morris (Washington, D.C.: Acropolis, 1978), 53.

10. Michael Wreen, "In Defense of Speciesism," *Ethics and Animals* 5 (1984): 47.

11. Ibid., 48–49, 51–54.

12. Evelyn Pluhar, "Speciesism Not Justified," *Ethics and Animals* 5 (1984): 122–25.

13. Ibid., 125–29.

14. James White, "Review of Alastair Gunn," *Ethics and Animals* 5 (1984): 15.

15. Jan Narveson, "On a Case for Animal Rights," *Monist* 70 (1987): 46.

16. Jan Narveson, "Animal Rights," *Canadian Journal of Philosophy* 7 (1977): 177–78; also see idem, "Animal Rights Revisited," in *Ethics and Animals,* ed. H. Miller and W. Williams (Clifton, N.J.: Humana, 1983), 58–59.

17. Jan Narveson, "On a Case for Animal Rights," 42; see also 35.

18. Ibid., 43, 46–47. Also see Aubrey Townsend, "Radical Vegetarians," *Australasian Journal of Philosophy* 57 (1979): 85–93, who, like Narveson, thinks that sympathy, not rights, is the key regarding how to deal with infants and the severely retarded.

19. Tom Regan, "Narveson on Egoism and the Rights of Animals," *Canadian Journal of Philosophy* 7 (1977): 182; also see 180–81.

20. Ibid., 183.

21. Ibid., 186.

22. Tom Regan, *The Case for Animal Rights,* 156–62.

23. See George Cave, "Review of Dale Jamieson," *Ethics and Animals* 2 (1981): 61–63; idem, "Review of R. I. Sikora," *Ethics and Animals* 3 (1982): 32; idem, "Review of Thomasine Kushner," *Ethics and Animals* 4 (1983): 10.

24. Dale Jamieson, "Rational Egoism and Animal Rights," *Environmental Ethics* 3 (1981): 168–71.
25. Lawrence Haworth, "Rights, Wrongs, and Animals," *Ethics* 88 (1978): 105.
26. John Rawls, *A Theory of Justice* (Cambridge, Mass.: Harvard University Press, 1971), 17.
27. Ibid., 504–5.
28. Ibid., 506.
29. Ibid., 507.
30. Ibid., 508–9.
31. Ibid., 510–11.
32. Ibid., 512.
33. Ibid., 114–15.
34. Ibid., 115–17.
35. John Rawls, "The Sense of Justice," *Philosophical Review* 72 (1963): 284.
36. Tom Regan, "Duties to Animals: Rawls' Dilemma," *Ethics and Animals* 2 (1981): 76–82. Also see idem, *The Case for Animal Rights,* 163–74.
37. Once again, see *A Theory of Justice,* 512.
38. See Alan Fuchs, "Duties to Animals: Rawls' Alleged Dilemma," *Ethics and Animals* 2 (1981): 83–87.
39. See Donald VanDeVeer, "Of Beasts, Persons, and the Original Position," *Monist* 62 (1979): 368–77.
40. Ibid., 372–73.
41. Tom Huffman, "Animals, Mental Defectives, and the Social Contract," *Between the Species* 9 (1993): 22.
42. Ibid., 26.
43. See Lilly-Marlene Russow, "Animals in the Original Position," *Between the Species* 8 (1992): 224–29, 232–33.
44. Steve Sapontzis, "On the Utility of Contracts," *Between the Species* 8 (1992): 229–32.
45. See Michael Pritchard and Wade Robison, "Justice and the Treatment of Animals: A Critique of Rawls," *Environmental Ethics* 3 (1981): 55–61; Robert Elliot, "Rawlsian Justice and non-Human Animals," *Journal of Applied Philosophy* 1 (1984): 95–106.
46. John Rawls, *Political Liberalism* (New York: Columbia University Press, 1993), 20–21.
47. Ibid., 21, 272.
48. Ibid., 244–45.
49. Ibid., 245–46.
50. Of the enormous literature on animal rights and environmental ethics that has appeared since the publication of *A Theory of Justice* (including the work of Regan and others), Rawls cites only one study to prop up his anthro-

pocentric view: Keith Thomas, *Man and the Natural World* (New York: Pantheon, 1983).

51. The traditional Christian view of animals is more complicated than Rawls indicates, in that it includes both an anthropocentric element and a stewardship element. Or better, Christians are supposed to be theocentric rather than anthropocentric. See my *St. John of the Cross* (Albany: State University of New York Press, 1992), chap. 4. Further, there is a problem with Rawls's analogy in *Political Liberalism* (246) between opposition to the gratuitous suffering and death inflicted on animals and opposition to abortion, both of which, he thinks, can be parts of a comprehensive religious view but not parts of what would be agreed to as basic elements of justice in the original position. The problem hinges on the nonsentient status of the fetus in the early stages of pregnancy, such that a fetus in the first trimester could hardly be harmed, and the sentient status of animals with functioning central nervous systems. See, e.g., my "Asymmetrical Relations, Identity, and Abortion," *Journal of Applied Philosophy* 9 (1992): 161–70. Finally, regarding an interesting view of marginal cases and animals from a Christian perspective in terms of agapic capacity, see Stephen Layman, *The Shape of the Good* (Notre Dame, Ind.: University of Notre Dame Press, 1994), 188–201.

52. It is troublesome that in *Political Liberalism* Rawls lumps together animals and the rest of nature without even a hint that there might be a difference in moral status between coyotes or pigs, on the one hand, and ferns or rocks, on the other.

53. Donald VanDeVeer, "Interspecific Justice," *Inquiry* 22 (1979): 71, 75; also see idem, "Of Beasts, Persons, and the Original Position," *Monist* 62 (1979): 372–74, 376.

54. Donald VanDeVeer, "Animal Suffering," *Canadian Journal of Philosophy* 10 (1980): 465.

55. Ibid., 470; also see 471.

56. See Donald VanDeVeer, "Interspecific Justice and Animal Slaughter," in *Ethics and Animals,* ed. H. Miller and W. Williams, 153.

57. Annette Baier, "Knowing Our Place in the Animal World," in *Ethics and Animals,* ed. H. Miller and W. Williams, 74.

58. Ibid., 75.

59. Ibid., 76.

60. See Kai Nielson, "Persons, Morals and the Animal Kingdom," *Man and World* 11 (1978): 233.

61. Jan Narveson, "Animal Rights," 164.

62. James Rachels, "Do Animals Have a Right to Liberty?" in *Animal Rights and Human Obligations,* ed. T. Regan and P. Singer, 222–23.

63. See Richard Watson, "Self-Consciousness and the Rights of Nonhuman Animals and Nature," *Environmental Ethics* 1 (1979): 99; also see Watson's article with the same title in *The Animal Rights/Environmental Ethics De-*

bate, ed. E. Hargrove (Albany: State University of New York Press, 1992), 19–20.

64. Peter Miller, "Do Animals Have Interests Worthy of Our Moral Interest?," *Environmental Ethics* 5 (1983): 331.

65. Lawrence Johnson, *A Morally Deep World* (Cambridge: Cambridge University Press, 1991), 53.

66. See Mary Midgley, "The Absence of a Gap between Facts and Values," *Aristotelian Society: Supplementary Volume* 54 (1980): 207–23.

67. See Mary Midgley, *Animals and Why They Matter* (Athens: University of Georgia Press, 1983), 60, 84, 104, where she seems to support the AMC, and 98–111, where she argues for the moral importance of species; also see 78. Finally, see A. I. Meldin, *Rights in Moral Lives* (Berkeley: University of California Press, 1988), 66–67.

68. Tom Regan, *The Case for Animal Rights,* 169–70.

Chapter 3: Frey's Challenge

1. R. G. Frey, "Interests and Animal Rights," *Philosophical Quarterly* 27 (1977): 256–59.

2. R. G. Frey, *Interests and Rights* (Oxford: Clarendon, 1980), 28–29; also see 22. Finally, see idem, "Animal Rights," *Analysis* 37 (1977): 186–89, an article incorporated into *Interests and Rights.*

3. Frey, *Interests and Rights,* 30–33. Also see Dale Jamieson and Tom Regan, "Animal Rights: A Reply to Frey," *Analysis* 38 (1978): 35.

4. Ibid., 33–34. Also see Mary Anne Warren, "Do Potential People Have Moral Rights?" *Canadian Journal of Philosophy* 7 (1977): 284.

5. Frey, *Interests and Rights,* 34–36, 51, 58–59; also see Karl Popper, *In Search of a Better World* (London: Routledge, 1992), 6.

6. R. G. Frey, *Rights, Killing, and Suffering* (Oxford: Basil Blackwell, 1983), 108–9.

7. Ibid., 109–10.

8. Ibid., 111.

9. Ibid., 114.

10. Ibid., 114–15.

11. Ibid., 115.

12. Ibid., 115–16.

13. R. G. Frey, "Autonomy and the Value of Animal Life," *Monist* 70 (1987): 50–51.

14. Ibid., 58–59.

15. Ibid., 59–61.

16. R. G. Frey, "The Significance of Agency and Marginal Cases," *Philosophica* 39 (1987): 39–43.

17. Ibid., 43.

18. Ibid., 45.

19. Tom Regan, "Frey on Interests and Animal Rights," *The Philosophical Quarterly* 27 (1977): 335–37.

20. Holmes Rolston, *Environmental Ethics* (Philadelphia: Temple University Press, 1988), 75.

21. Ibid.

22. Ibid., 75–76.

23. Ibid., 76–79.

24. Gerald Paske, "Why Animals Have No Right to Life: A Response to Regan," *Australasian Journal of Philosophy* 66 (1988): 510–11.

25. Stephen R. L. Clark, *The Moral Status of Animals* (Oxford: Clarendon, 1977), 87.

26. Ibid., 89.

27. Ibid., 90–94, 106.

28. Ibid., 108.

29. Ibid., 109, 182; also see Stephen R. L. Clark, "Animal Wrongs," *Analysis* 38 (1978): 148–49.

30. Stephen R. L. Clark, *From Athens to Jerusalem* (Oxford: Clarendon, 1984), 165.

31. Stephen R. L. Clark, "The City of the Wise," *Apeiron* 20 (1987): 65, 67.

32. Stephen R. L. Clark, "Humans, Animals, and 'Animal Behavior,'" in *Ethics and Animals*, ed. H. Miller and W. Williams (Clifton, N.J.: Humana, 1983), 180.

33. Stephen R. L. Clark, "Utility, Rights and the Domestic Virtues," *Between the Species* 4 (1988): 239, 243.

34. Stephen R. L. Clark, "Is Humanity a Natural Kind?" in *What Is an Animal?* ed. T. Ingold (London: Unwin and Hyman, 1988), 17–24.

35. Ibid., 26.

36. Ibid., 27.

37. Ibid., 28.

38. Ibid., 31.

39. Ibid.

40. Ibid., 32.

41. Ibid.

42. Clark, "Animal Wrongs," 148–49.

43. Stephen R. L. Clark, "How to Calculate the Greater Good," in *Animals' Rights*, ed. D. Paterson and R. Ryder (London: Centaur, 1979), 98.

44. Clark, "Utility, Rights and the Domestic Virtues," 238, 241.

45. Becker, "The Priority of Human Interests," 225–35.

46. Ibid., 235–38.

47. Roger Paden, "Deconstructing Speciesism," *International Journal of Applied Philosophy* 7 (1992): 56–63.

48. See Keith Tester, *Animals and Society* (London: Routledge, 1991), 12, 159, 194.

49. Dale Jamieson, "Review of Stephen R. L. Clark," *Nous* 15 (1981): 232.

50. Ibid., 233.

51. Steve Sapontzis, "Must We Value Life to Have a Right to It?" *Ethics and Animals* 3 (1982): 4–5.

52. Steve Sapontzis, *Morals, Reason, and Animals* (Philadelphia: Temple University Press, 1987), xii–xiii.

53. Steve Sapontzis, "Are Animals Moral Beings?" *American Philosophical Quarterly* 17 (1980): 45.

54. Ibid., 47.

55. See Stephen R. L. Clark, *The Nature of the Beast* (Oxford: Oxford University Press, 1982).

56. Sapontzis, *Morals, Reason, and Animals,* 141.

57. Ibid., 141–42.

58. Ibid., 142.

59. Ibid., 144, 281.

60. Mary Anne Warren, "The Rights of the Nonhuman World," in *The Animal Rights/Environmental Ethics Debate,* ed. E. Hargrove (Albany: State University of New York Press, 1992), 197.

61. Ibid., 198.

Chapter 4: The Criticisms of Leahy and Carruthers

1. L. Duane Willard, "About Animals 'Having' Rights," *Journal of Value Inquiry* 16 (1982): 177–78.

2. Ibid., 185.

3. Ibid., 183–85.

4. See Michael A. Fox, "'Animal Liberation': A Critique," *Ethics* 88 (1978): 108; also see idem, *The Case for Animal Experimentation* (Berkeley: University of California Press, 1986), 59–60.

5. Fox, *The Case for Animal Experimentation,* 60–61.

6. Ibid., 62; also see 63. It should be noted that Fox later changes many of the views defended in *The Case for Animal Experimentation;* see his "Animal Experimentation: A Philosopher's Changing Views," *Between the Species* 3 (1987): 55–60, 75, 80. It should also be noted that Michael A. Fox is not Michael W. Fox from the Humane Society of the United States, who has written positively on animal rights issues.

7. Ruth Cigman, "Death, Misfortune, and Species Inequality," *Philosophy and Public Affairs* 10 (1981): 61.

8. Philip Devine, "The Moral Basis of Vegetarianism," *Philosophy* 53 (1978): 495–96.

9. Ibid., 497–98.
10. Ibid., 498–501.
11. Philip Devine, *The Ethics of Homicide* (Notre Dame, Ind.: University of Notre Dame Press, 1990), 48.
12. Ibid., 48–49.
13. Ibid., 177–79.
14. Cora Diamond, "Eating Meat and Eating People," *Philosophy* 53 (1978): 467–68.
15. Ibid., 469.
16. Paul Muscari, "Is Man the Paragon of Animals?" *Journal of Value Inquiry* 20 (1986): 303–8.
17. See Vinit Haksar, *Equality, Liberty, and Perfectionism* (Oxford: Oxford University Press, 1979).
18. Michael Leahy, *Against Liberation* (London: Routledge, 1991), 18; also see 19, 22.
19. Ibid., 180. Also 24–25, 74, 178–79.
20. Ibid., 184–85, 201–3.
21. Ibid., 204.
22. Ibid., 205.
23. Ibid., 206–7.
24. Ibid., 220.
25. Peter Carruthers, *The Animals Issue* (Cambridge: Cambridge University Press, 1992), xi, xii, 6–9.
26. Ibid., 16–22.
27. Ibid., 27; also see 22–26.
28. Ibid., 27, 53–55, 64–65.
29. Ibid., 66; also see 67–73.
30. Ibid., 78, 83–84, 89, 101, 106.
31. Ibid., 108–11.
32. Ibid., 111–12.
33. Ibid., 115; also 113–14, 116.
34. Ibid., 121; also see 118–20.
35. Ibid., 154.
36. Ibid., 133, 135, 151, 158.
37. Ibid., 167; also see 162–65, 167–68.
38. Ibid., 192; also see 187, 189.
39. Ibid., 193.
40. Ibid., 192.
41. Ibid., 196; also see 194–95.
42. Sarah Stebbins, "Anthropomorphism," *Philosophical Studies* 69 (1993): 113. Also see Donald Griffin, *Animal Thinking* (Cambridge: Harvard University Press, 1990); Roger Crisp, "Evolution and Psychological Unity," in *In-*

terpretation and Explanation in the Study of Animal Behavior, vol. 1, ed. M. Bekoff and D. Jamieson (Boulder, Colo.: Westview, 1990).

43. Stebbins, "Anthropomorphism," 114–15.

44. See Richard Sorabji, *Animal Minds and Human Morals* (Ithaca, N.Y.: Cornell University Press, 1993), 211.

45. See Colin McGinn, *Moral Literacy* (London: Duckworth, 1992), 24–25.

46. See William Davis, "Man-Eating Aliens," *Journal of Value Inquiry* 10 (1976): 182.

47. Nicholas Everitt, "What's Wrong with Murder? Some Thoughts on Human and Animal Killing," *International Journal of Applied Philosophy* 7 (1992): 49; also see 47–48.

48. Ibid., 51; also see 50.

49. Ibid., 53; also see 52, 54.

50. Edward Johnson, "Life, Death, and Animals," in *Ethics and Animals,* ed. H. Miller and W. Williams (Clifton, N.J.: Humana, 1983), 131.

51. See James Nelson, "Review of Steve Sapontzis," *Ethics and Animals* 3 (1982): 121.

52. See my *Hartshorne and the Metaphysics of Animal Rights* (Albany: State University of New York, 1988) regarding three different sorts of sentiency.

53. Nielson, "Persons, Morals and the Animal Kingdom," 232–33.

54. R. Routley and V. Routley, "Against the Inevitability of Human Chauvinism," in *Ethics and the Problems of the 21st Century,* ed. K. Goodpaster and K. Sayre (Notre Dame, Ind.: University of Notre Dame Press, 1979), 41.

55. Richard Ryder, "Speciesism," in *Animal Experimentation: The Moral Issues,* ed. R. Baird and S. Rosenbaum (Buffalo: Prometheus, 1991), 38.

56. R. I. Sikora, "Morality and Animals," *Ethics and Animals* 2 (1981): 47; also see 48.

57. Evelyn Pluhar, "Arguing Away Suffering: The Neo-Cartesian Revival," *Between the Species* 9 (1993): 27.

58. Ibid., 28.

59. See Peter Harrison, "Theodicy and Animal Pain," *Philosophy* 64 (1989), esp. 82, n. 8. It is not my purpose to deal with the complex theological issues in Harrison's article. Also see Pluhar, "Arguing Away Suffering," 29–31, 35.

60. Pluhar, "Arguing Away Suffering," 35.

61. Ibid., 36.

62. See Edward Johnson, "Carruthers on Consciousness and Moral Status," *Between the Species* 7 (1991): 191. Pluhar and Johnson rely not on Carruthers's book but on an earlier article of his, "Brute Experience," *Journal of Philosophy* 86 (1989).

63. Pluhar, "Arguing Away Suffering," 39.

Chapter 5: The Great Ape Project and Slavery

1. Christoph Anstotz, "Profoundly Intellectually Disabled Humans and the Great Apes: A Comparison," in *The Great Ape Project,* ed. P. Cavalieri and P. Singer (New York: St. Martin's, 1993), 165; also see 158–64.

2. Ibid., 166, 168.

3. H. Lyn White Miles, "Language and the Orang-utan," in *The Great Ape Project,* ed. P. Cavalieri and P. Singer, 46; also see 49, 54.

4. See Francine Patterson and Wendy Gordon, "The Case for Personhood of Gorillas," in *The Great Ape Project,* ed. P. Cavalieri and P. Singer, 60–61, 66.

5. See Jared Diamond, "The Third Chimpanzee," in *The Great Ape Project,* ed. P. Cavalieri and P. Singer, 88.

6. Stephen R. L. Clark, "Apes and the Idea of Kindred," in *The Great Ape Project,* ed. P. Cavalieri and P. Singer, 122; also see 119–21.

7. Ibid., 123–24.

8. See Adriaan Kortlandt, "Spirits Dressed in Furs?" in *The Great Ape Project,* ed. P. Cavalieri and P. Singer, 142.

9. See Colin McGinn, "Apes, Humans, Aliens, Vampires and Robots," in *The Great Ape Project,* ed. P. Cavalieri and P. Singer, 148–49.

10. See Heta Hayry and Matti Hayry, "Who's Like Us?" in *The Great Ape Project,* ed. P. Cavalieri and P. Singer, 180. Also see, in the same volume, Ingmar Persson, "A Basis for (Interspecies) Equality," 191.

11. Tom Regan, "Ill-gotten Gains," in *The Great Ape Project,* ed. P. Cavalieri and P. Singer, 203.

12. Bernard Rollin, "The Ascent of Apes—Broadening the Moral Community," in *The Great Ape Project,* ed. P. Cavalieri and P. Singer, 209; also see 207.

13. Ibid., 215.

14. See Harlan Miller, "The Wahokies," in *The Great Ape Project,* ed. P. Cavalieri and P. Singer, 236.

15. See Robert Mitchell, "Humans, Nonhumans, and Personhood," in *The Great Ape Project,* ed. P. Cavalieri and P. Singer, 244–45.

16. Also Gary Francione, "Personhood, Property and Legal Competence," in *The Great Ape Project,* ed. P. Cavalieri and P. Singer, 248–49.

17. See Paola Cavalieri and Peter Singer, "The Great Ape Project—and Beyond," in *The Great Ape Project,* ed. P. Cavalieri and P. Singer, 304–5.

18. Ibid., 307; also see 306.

19. Ibid., 308–11.

20. See George Cave, "Rational Egoism, Animal Rights, and the Academic Connection," *Between the Species* 1 (1985): 22, 27.

21. See James Nelson, "Rights, Killing and Suffering," *Between the Species* 2 (1986): 76, 80; also see idem, "Animals, Handicapped Children, and the

Tragedy of Handicapped Cases," *Journal of Medical Ethics* 14 (1988): 191–93.

22. James Nelson, "Xenograft and Partial Affections," *Between the Species* 2 (1986): 118, 123.

23. See William Aiken, "A Commentary on Nelson's 'Xenograft and Partial Affections,'" *Between the Species* 2 (1986): 127.

24. See criticisms of Nelson by Connie Kagan, "Response to Nelson's 'Xenograft and Partial Affections,'" *Between the Species* 2 (1986): 128; Steve Sapontzis, "Concerning Therapeutic (for Humans) Research with Animals," *Between the Species* 2 (1986): 131.

25. See Mary Anne Warren, "Difficulties with the Strong Animal Rights Position," *Between the Species* 2 (1986): 170.

26. See Donna Richards, "Response to Nelson," *Between the Species* 3 (1987): 18.

27. Evelyn Pluhar, "Speciesism: A Form of Bigotry or a Justified View?" *Between the Species* 4 (1988): 88.

28. Ibid., 89.

29. Ibid., 93.

30. See Steve Sapontzis, "Speciesism," *Between the Species* 4 (1988): 97–98; also see idem, "Aping Persons—Pro and Con," in *The Great Ape Project*, ed. P. Cavalieri and P. Singer.

31. Evelyn Pluhar, "On the Relevance of Marginal Humans: A Reply to Sapontzis," *Between the Species* 4 (1988): 100.

32. R. G. Frey, "Moral Standing, the Value of Lives, and Speciesism," *Between the Species* 4 (1988): 195–98.

33. See Peter Singer, "Comment," *Between the Species* 4 (1988): 202–3.

34. Charles Fink, "The Moderate View on Animal Ethics," *Between the Species* 7 (1991): 197.

35. See Gary Comstock, "The Moral Irrelevance of Autonomy," *Between the Species* 8 (1992): 25.

36. On Locke see Kathy Squadrito, "Descartes and Locke on Speciesism and the Value of Life," *Between the Species* 8 (1992): 146.

37. Lilly-Marlene Russow, "Animals in the Original Position," *Between the Species* 8 (1992): 228.

38. See Steve Sapontzis, "On the Utility of Contracts," *Between the Species* 8 (1992): 232.

39. Quoted in Tom Huffman, "Animals, Mental Defectives, and the Social Contract," *Between the Species* 9 (1993): 22.

40. Ibid.

41. Ibid., 25; also see Gary Francione, "Animals, Property and Legal Welfarism," *Rutgers Law Review* 46 (1994): 721–70.

42. Regarding the ancient world, see my *Philosophy of Vegetarianism* (Amherst: University of Massachusetts Press, 1984); regarding Judaism and Chris-

tianity, see the first chapter of my *Hartshorne and the Metaphysics of Animal Rights* (Albany: State University of New York Press, 1988), as well as Stephen R. L. Clark, *How to Think about the Earth* (London: Mobray, 1993).

43. Ted Benton, *Natural Relations* (New York: Verso, 1993), 91.

44. Ibid., 91–92.

45. Ibid., 92.

46. Ibid., 94.

47. Ibid., 164, 198.

Chapter 6: The Nozick-Rachels Debate

1. Robert Nozick, *Anarchy, State, and Utopia* (N.Y.: Basic, 1974), 39.

2. See Robert Nozick, "About Mammals and People," *New York Times Book Review,* Nov. 27, 1983, p. 11.

3. Ibid.

4. Ibid., 29.

5. Ibid.

6. See Leslie Pickering Francis and Richard Norman, "Some Animals Are More Equal Than Others," *Philosophy* 53 (1978): 508–9.

7. Ibid., 210–11.

8. Ibid., 211–13.

9. Ibid., 214–15.

10. James Rachels, *The End of Life: Euthanasia and Morality* (Oxford: Oxford University Press, 1986), 3.

11. Ibid., 5.

12. Ibid., 14; also see 12–14.

13. Ibid., 33; also 22–25.

14. Ibid., 35–36.

15. Ibid., 58; also see 57, 59.

16. Ibid., 72–73.

17. Ibid., 74.

18. Ibid., 74–75.

19. Ibid., 76.

20. Ibid., 77.

21. James Rachels, *Created from Animals: The Moral Implications of Darwinism* (Oxford: Oxford University Press, 1990), 173; also see 131, 136–37, 141, 174.

22. Ibid., 175.

23. Ibid., 186; also see 182–83.

24. Ibid., 187.

25. Ibid., 188–89.

26. Ibid., 192; also see 190–91.

27. Ibid., 193–94.

28. Ibid., 194; also see 195.
29. Ibid., 196–97.
30. Ibid., 198–99; also see 208.
31. Ibid., 209.
32. Ibid., 222.
33. Ibid.
34. See James Rachels, "Do Animals Have a Right to Liberty?" in *Animal Rights and Human Obligations,* ed. T. Regan and P. Singer (Englewood Cliffs, N.J.: Prentice-Hall, 1976), 222–23.
35. Susan Finsen, "On Moderation," in *Interpretation and Explanation in the Study of Behavior,* ed. M. Bekoff and D. Jamieson (Boulder, Colo.: Westview, 1990), 411; also see 410.
36. Ibid., 413; also see 412.
37. See Rosemary Rodd, *Biology, Ethics, and Animals* (Oxford: Clarendon, 1990), 179–80.
38. Ibid., 251–52, 254–55.
39. See Bernard Rollin, "Beasts and Men: The Scope of Moral Concern," *Modern Schoolman* 55 (1978): 243.
40. See Bernard Rollin, *Animal Rights and Human Morality* (Buffalo, N.Y.: Prometheus, 1981), 27–28.
41. See Bernard Rollin, "The Legal and Moral Bases of Animal Rights," in *Ethics and Animals,* ed. H. Miller and W. Williams (Clifton, N.J.: Humana, 1983), 110.
42. See Bernard Rollin, *The Unheeded Cry: Animal Consciousness, Animal Pain, and Science* (Oxford: Oxford University Press, 1990), 165–66.
43. See Edwin Hettinger, "The Reasonable Use of Animals in Biomedical Research," in *Animal Experimentation: The Moral Issues,* ed. R. Baird and S. Rosenbaum (Buffalo: Prometheus, 1991), 117.
44. Henry David Thoreau, *Walden,* ed. J. Shanley (Princeton, N.J.: Princeton University Press, 1971), 215–16, from the chapter titled "Higher Laws."

Afterword

1. Peter Singer, *Practical Ethics* (Cambridge: Cambridge University Press, 1979), 86–88, 102–5, 132–36.
2. It might be wondered why plants are not also included in the view of time as asymmetrical. Once again, I refer the reader to my *Hartshorne and the Metaphysics of Animal Rights* (Albany: State University of New York Press, 1988), chaps. 3–5. Briefly put, plants are metaphysical "democracies" in that botanists explain their growth at the cellular level. Whatever "sentiency" cells have, assuming this word is appropriate in this context, is of such a primitive sort that they cannot really have a life in the relevent sense where there are memories of the past and expectations regarding the future. Ani-

mals, in contrast, are metaphysical monarchies where the whole individual is sentient: it can feel, remember, and look toward at least the immediate future. Finally, it should be emphasized that Singer alternately makes two opposite mistakes. At times he adopts total view utilitarianism, and at other times he adopts the Humean view where animal and human "identity" is little more than a stringing together of atomic experiences. It is this latter view that provides him the opportunity to defend the replaceability argument. That is, Singer alternately radically connects and radically disconnects reality (again, much like Hume).

Bibliography

Aiken, William. "A Commentary on Nelson's Xenograft and Partial Affections." *Between the Species* 2 (1986).

Anstotz, Christoph. "Profoundly Intellectually Disabled Humans and the Great Apes: A Comparison." In *The Great Ape Project,* ed. P. Cavalieri and P. Singer. New York: St. Martin's, 1993.

Attfield, Robin. *The Ethics of Environmental Concern.* Athens: University of Georgia Press, 1983.

Baier, Annette. "Knowing Our Place in the Animal World." In *Ethics and Animals,* ed. H. Miller and W. Williams. Clifton, N.J.: Humana, 1983.

Becker, Lawrence. "The Priority of Human Interests." In *Ethics and Animals,* ed. H. Miller and W. Williams. Clifton, N.J.: Humana, 1983.

Benson, John. "Duty and the Beast." *Philosophy* 53 (1978).

Benton, Ted. *Natural Relations.* New York: Verso, 1993.

Carruthers, Peter. *The Animals Issue.* Cambridge: Cambridge University Press, 1992.

———. "Brute Experience." *Journal of Philosophy* 86 (1989).

Cavalieri, Paola, and Peter Singer. "The Great Ape Project—and Beyond." In *The Great Ape Project,* ed. P. Cavalieri and P. Singer. New York: St. Martin's, 1993.

Cave, George. "Rational Egoism, Animal Rights, and the Academic Connection." *Between the Species* 1 (1985).

———. "Review of Dale Jamieson." *Ethics and Animals* 2 (1981).

———. "Review of R. I. Sikora." *Ethics and Animals* 3 (1982).

———. "Review of Thomasine Kushner." *Ethics and Animals* 4 (1983).

Cigman, Ruth. "Death, Misfortune, and Species Inequality." *Philosophy and Public Affairs* 10 (1981).

Clark, Stephen R. L. "Animal Wrongs." *Analysis* 38 (1978).

———. "Apes and the Idea of Kindred." In *The Great Ape Project,* ed. P. Cavalieri and P. Singer. New York: St. Martin's, 1993.

———. "The City of the Wise." *Apeiron* 20 (1987).
———. *From Athens to Jerusalem.* Oxford: Clarendon, 1984.
———. "How to Calculate the Greater Good." In *Animals' Rights,* ed. D. Paterson and R. Ryder. London: Centaur, 1979.
———. *How to Think about the Earth.* London: Mobray, 1993.
———. "Humans, Animals, and 'Animal Behavior.'" In *Ethics and Animals,* ed. H. Miller and W. Williams. Clifton, N.J.: Humana, 1983.
———. "Is Humanity a Natural Kind?" In *What Is an Animal?* ed. T. Ingold. London: Unwin and Hyman, 1988.
———. *The Moral Status of Animals.* Oxford: Clarendon, 1977.
———. *The Nature of the Beast.* Oxford: Oxford University Press, 1982.
———. "Utility, Rights and the Domestic Virtues." *Between the Species* 4 (1988).
Cohen, Henry. "Review of Tom Regan." *Ethics and Animals* 3 (1982).
———. "Review of Tom Regan." *Ethics and Animals* 5 (1984).
Comstock, Gary. "The Moral Irrelevance of Autonomy." *Between the Species* 8 (1992).
Davis, William. "Man-Eating Aliens." *Journal of Value Inquiry* 10 (1976).
Devine, Philip. *The Ethics of Homicide.* Notre Dame, Ind.: University of Notre Dame Press, 1990.
———. "The Moral Basis of Vegetarianism." *Philosophy* 53 (1978).
Diamond, Cora. "Eating Meat and Eating People." *Philosophy* 53 (1978).
Diamond, Jared. "The Third Chimpanzee." In *The Great Ape Project,* ed. P. Cavalieri and P. Singer. New York: St. Martin's, 1993.
Dombrowski, Daniel. *Hartshorne and the Metaphysics of Animal Rights.* Albany: State University of New York Press, 1988.
———. *The Philosophy of Vegetarianism.* Amherst: University of Massachusetts Press, 1984.
———. "Vegetarianism and the Argument from Marginal Cases in Porphyry." *Journal of the History of Ideas* 45 (1984).
Elliot, Robert. "Autonomy, Self-Determination and Rights." *Monist* 70 (1987).
———. "Rawlsian Justice and non-Human Animals." *Journal of Applied Philosophy* 1 (1984).
Everitt, Nicholas. "What's Wrong with Murder: Some Thoughts on Human and Animal Killing." *International Journal of Applied Philosophy* 7 (1992).
Feinberg, Joel. "Can Animals Have Rights?" In *Animal Rights and Human Obligations,* ed. T. Regan and P. Singer. Englewood Cliffs, N.J.: Prentice-Hall, 1976.
———. "Human Duties and Animal Rights." In *On the Fifth Day: Animal Rights and Human Ethics,* ed. R. Morris. Washington, D.C.: Acropolis, 1978.

Fink, Charles. "The Moderate View on Animal Ethics." *Between the Species* 7 (1991).

Finsen, Susan. "On Moderation." In *Interpretation and Explanation in the Study of Behavior,* ed. M. Bekoff and D. Jamieson. Boulder, Colo.: Westview, 1990.

Fox, Michael A. "Animal Experimentation: A Philosopher's Changing Views." *Between the Species* 3 (1987).

———. "'Animal Liberation': A Critique." *Ethics* 88 (1978).

———. *The Case for Animal Experimentation.* Berkeley: University of California Press, 1986.

Francione, Gary. "Animals, Property and Legal Welfarism." *Rutgers Law Review* 46 (1994).

———. "Personhood, Property and Legal Competence." In *The Great Ape Project,* ed. P. Cavalieri and P. Singer. New York: St. Martin's, 1993.

Francis, Leslie Pickering, and Ricard Norman. "Some Animals Are More Equal Than Others." *Philosophy* 53 (1978).

Frey, R. G. "Animal Rights." *Analysis* 37 (1977).

———. "Autonomy and the Value of Animal Life." *Monist* 70 (1987).

———. "Interests and Animal Rights." *The Philosophical Quarterly* 27 (1977).

———. *Interests and Rights.* Oxford: Clarendon, 1980.

———. "Moral Standing, the Value of Lives, and Speciesism." *Between the Species* 4 (1988).

———. *Rights, Killing, and Suffering.* Oxford: Blackwell, 1983.

———. "The Significance of Agency and Marginal Cases." *Philosophica* 39 (1987).

Fuchs, Alan. "Duties to Animals: Rawls' Alleged Dilemma." *Ethics and Animals* 2 (1981).

Haksar, Vinit. *Equality, Liberty, and Perfectionism.* Oxford: Oxford University Press, 1979.

Harrison, Peter. "Theodicy and Animal Pain." *Philosophy* 64 (1989).

Hartshorne, Charles. "Foundations for a Humane Ethics: What Human Beings Have in Common with Other Higher Animals." In *On the Fifth Day: Animal Rights and Human Ethics,* ed R. Morris. Washington, D.C.: Acropolis, 1978.

———. "The Rights of the Subhuman World." *Environmental Ethics* 1 (1979).

Haworth, Lawrence. "Rights, Wrongs, and Animals." *Ethics* 88 (1978).

Hayry, Heta, and Matti Hayry. "Who's Like Us?" In *The Great Ape Project,* ed. P. Cavalieri and P. Singer. New York: St. Martin's, 1993.

Hettinger, Edwin. "The Reasonable Use of Animals in Biomedical Research." In *Animal Experimentation: The Moral Issues,* ed. R. Baird and S. Rosenbaum. Buffalo: Prometheus, 1991.

Huffman, Tom. "Animals, Mental Defectives, and the Social Contract." *Between the Species* 9 (1993).

Jamieson, Dale. "Rational Egoism and Animal Rights." *Environmental Ethics* 3 (1981).

———. "Review of Stephen R. L. Clark." *Nous* 15 (1981).

Jamieson, Dale, and Tom Regan. "Animal Rights: A Reply to Frey." *Analysis* 38 (1978).

Johnson, Edward. "Carruthers on Consciousness and Moral Status." *Between the Species* 7 (1991).

———. "Life, Death, and Animals." In *Ethics and Animals*, ed. H. Miller and W. Williams. Clifton, N.J.: Humana, 1983.

Johnson, Lawrence. *A Morally Deep World.* Cambridge: Cambridge University Press, 1991.

Kagan, Connie. "Response to Nelson's 'Xenograft and Partial Affections.'" *Between the Species* 2 (1986).

Kortlandt, Adriaan. "Spirits Dressed in Furs?" In *The Great Ape Project*, ed. P. Cavalieri and P. Singer. New York: St. Martin's, 1993.

Layman, Stephen. *The Shape of the Good.* Notre Dame, Ind.: University of Notre Dame Press, 1994.

Leahy, Michael. *Against Liberation.* London: Routledge, 1991.

Machan, Tibor. "Do Animals Have Rights?" *Public Affairs Quarterly* 5 (1991).

McCloskey, H. J. "The Moral Case for Experimentation on Animals." *Monist* 70 (1987).

———. "Moral Rights and Animals." *Inquiry* 22 (1979).

McGinn, Colin. "Apes, Humans, Aliens, Vampires and Robots." In *The Great Ape Project*, ed. P. Cavalieri and P. Singer. New York: St. Martin's, 1993.

———. *Moral Literacy.* London: Duckworth, 1992.

Meldin, A. I. *Rights in Moral Lives.* Berkeley: University of California Press, 1988.

Midgley, Mary. "The Absence of a Gap between Facts and Values." *Aristotelian Society: Supplementary Volume* 54 (1980).

———. *Animals and Why They Matter.* Athens: University of Georgia Press, 1983.

Miles, H. Lyn White. "Language and the Orang-utan." In *The Great Ape Project*, ed. P. Cavalieri and P. Singer. New York: St. Martin's, 1993.

Miller, Harlan. "The Wahokies." In *The Great Ape Project*, ed. P. Cavalieri and P. Singer. New York: St. Martin's, 1993.

Miller, Peter. "Do Animals Have Interests Worthy of Our Moral Interest?" *Environmental Ethics* 5 (1983).

Mitchell, Robert. "Humans, Nonhumans, and Personhood." In *The Great Ape Project*, ed. P. Cavalieri and P. Singer. New York: St. Martin's, 1993.

Muscari, Paul. "Is Man the Paragon of Animals?" *Journal of Value Inquiry* 20 (1986).

Narveson, Jan. "Animal Rights." *Canadian Journal of Philosophy* 7 (1977).

———. "Animal Rights Revisited." In *Ethics and Animals,* ed. H. Miller and W. Williams. Clifton, N.J.: Humana, 1983.

———. "On a Case for Animal Rights." *Monist* 70 (1987).

Nelson, James. "Animals, Handicapped Children, and the Tragedy of Handicapped Cases." *Journal of Medical Ethics* 14 (1988).

———. "Review of Steve Sapontzis." *Ethics and Animals* 3 (1982).

———. "Rights, Killing and Suffering." *Between the Species* 2 (1986).

———. "Xenograft and Partial Affections." *Between the Species* 2 (1986).

Nielson, Kai. "Persons, Morals and the Animal Kingdom." *Man and World* 11 (1978).

Nozick, Robert. "About Mammals and People." *The New York Times Book Review,* Nov. 27, 1983.

———. *Anarchy, State, and Utopia.* New York: Basic, 1974.

Paden, Roger. "Deconstructing Speciesism." *International Journal of Applied Philosophy* 7 (1992).

Paske, Gerald. "Why Animals Have No Right to Life: A Response to Regan." *Australasian Journal of Philosophy* 66 (1988).

Patterson, Francine, and Wendy Gordon. "The Case for Personhood of Gorillas." In *The Great Ape Project,* ed. P. Cavalieri and P. Singer. New York: St. Martin's, 1993.

Pluhar, Evelyn. "Arguing Away Suffering: The Neo-Cartesian Revival." *Between the Species* 9 (1993).

———. *Beyond Prejudice: The Moral Significance of Human and Nonhuman Animals.* Durham, N.C.: Duke University Press, 1995.

———. "On the Relevance of Marginal Humans: A Reply to Sapontzis." *Between the Species* 4 (1988).

———. "On Replaceability." *Ethics and Animals* 3 (1982).

———. "Speciesism: A Form of Bigotry or a Justified View?" *Between the Species* 4 (1988).

———. "Speciesism Not Justified." *Ethics and Animals* 5 (1984).

Porphyry. *On Abstinence from Animal Food.* Trans. T. Taylor. London: Centaur, 1965.

Pritchard, Michael, and Wade Robison. "Justice and the Treatment of Animals: A Critique of Rawls." *Environmental Ethics* 3 (1981).

Rachels, James. *Created from Animals: The Moral Implications of Darwinism.* Oxford: Oxford University Press, 1990.

———. "Do Animals Have a Right to Liberty?" In *Animal Rights and Human Obligations,* ed. T. Regan and P. Singer. Englewood Cliffs, N.J.: Prentice-Hall, 1976.

———. *The End of Life: Euthanasia and Morality.* Oxford: Oxford University Press, 1986.

Rawls, John. *Political Liberalism.* New York: Columbia University Press, 1993.

———. "The Sense of Justice." *Philosophical Review* 72 (1963).

———. *A Theory of Justice.* Cambridge, Mass.: Harvard University Press, 1971.

Regan, Tom. *The Case for Animal Rights.* Berkeley: University of California Press, 1983.

———. "The Case for Animal Rights." In *In Defense of Animals,* ed. P. Singer. Oxford: Blackwell, 1985.

———. "Duties to Animals: Rawls' Dilemma." *Ethics and Animals* 2 (1981).

———. "An Examination and Defense of One Argument concerning Animal Rights." *Inquiry* 22 (1979).

———. "Exploring the Idea of Animal Rights." In *Animals' Rights,* ed. D. Paterson and R. Ryder. London: Centaur, 1979.

———. "Frey on Interests and Animal Rights." *Philosophical Quarterly* 27 (1977).

———. "Fox's Critique of Animal Liberation." *Ethics* 88 (1978).

———. "Ill-gotten Gains." In *The Great Ape Project,* ed. P. Cavalieri and P. Singer. New York: St. Martin's, 1993.

———. "Introduction." In *Animal Rights and Human Obligations,* ed. T. Regan and P. Singer. Englewood Cliffs, N.J.: Prentice-Hall, 1976.

———. "McCloskey on Why Animals Cannot Have Rights." *Philosophical Quarterly* 26 (1976).

———. "The Moral Basis of Vegetarianism." *Canadian Journal of Philosophy* 5 (1975).

———. "Narveson on Egoism and the Rights of Animals." *Canadian Journal of Philosophy* 7 (1977).

———. "Utilitarianism and Vegetarianism, Again." *Ethics and Animals* 2 (1981).

———. "Utilitarianism, Vegetarianism, and Animal Rights." *Philosophy and Public Affairs* 9 (1980).

Richards, Donna. "Response to Nelson." *Between the Species* 3 (1987).

Rodd, Rosemary. *Biology, Ethics, and Animals.* Oxford: Clarendon, 1990.

Rollin, Bernard. *Animal Rights and Human Morality.* Buffalo, N.Y.: Prometheus, 1981.

———. "The Ascent of Apes—Broadening the Moral Community." In *The Great Ape Project,* ed. P. Cavalieri and P. Singer. New York: St. Martin's, 1993.

———. "Beasts and Men: The Scope of Moral Concern." *Modern Schoolman* 55 (1978).

———. "The Legal and Moral Bases of Animal Rights." In *Ethics and Animals,* ed. H. Miller and W. Williams. Clifton, N.J.: Humana, 1983.

———. *The Unheeded Cry: Animal Consciousness, Animal Pain, and Science.* Oxford: Oxford University Press, 1990.

Rolston, Holmes. *Environmental Ethics.* Philadelphia: Temple University Press, 1988.

Routley, R., and V. Routley. "Against the Inevitability of Human Chauvinism." In *Ethics and the Problems of the 21st Century,* ed. K. Goodpaster and K. Sayre. Notre Dame, Ind.: University of Notre Dame Press, 1979.

Russow, Lilly-Marlene. "Animals in the Original Position." *Between the Species* 8 (1992).

Ryder, Richard. "Speciesism." In *Animal Experimentation: The Moral Issues,* ed. R. Baird and S. Rosenbaum. Buffalo, N.Y.: Prometheus, 1991.

Sapontzis, Steve. "Aping Persons—Pro and Con." In *The Great Ape Project,* ed. P. Cavalieri and P. Singer. New York: St. Martin's, 1993.

———. "Are Animals Moral Beings?" *American Philosophical Quarterly* 17 (1980).

———. "Concerning Therapeutic (for Humans) Research with Animals." *Between the Species* 2 (1986).

———. *Morals, Reason, and Animals.* Philadelphia: Temple University Press, 1987.

———. "Must We Value Life to Have a Right to It?" *Ethics and Animals* 3 (1982).

———. "On the Utility of Contracts." *Between the Species* 8 (1992).

———. "Speciesism." *Between the Species* 4 (1988).

Sikora, R. I. "Morality and Animals." *Ethics and Animals* 2 (1981).

Singer, Beth. "Having Rights." *Philosophy and Social Criticism* 11 (1986).

Singer, Peter. *Animal Liberation.* New York: Avon, 1990 (1975).

———. "Animal Liberation or Animal Rights?" *Monist* 70 (1987).

———. "Animals and the Value of Life." In *Matters of Life and Death,* ed. T. Regan. Philadelphia: Temple University Press, 1980.

———. "Comment." *Between the Species* 4 (1988).

———. "The Fable of the Fox and the Unliberated Animals." *Ethics* 88 (1978).

———. "Not for Humans Only." In *Ethics and Problems of the 21st Century,* ed. K. Goodpaster and K. Sayre. Notre Dame, Ind.: University of Notre Dame Press, 1979.

———. *Practical Ethics.* Cambridge: Cambridge University Press, 1979.

———. "Prologue." In *In Defense of Animals,* ed. P. Singer. Oxford: Blackwell, 1985.

Sorabji, Richard. *Animal Minds and Human Morals.* Ithaca, N.Y.: Cornell University Press, 1993.

Sprigge, T. L. S. "Metaphysics, Physicalism, and Animal Rights." *Inquiry* 22 (1979).

Squadrito, Kathy. "Descartes and Locke on Speciesism and the Value of Life." *Between the Species* 8 (1992).

Stebbins, Sarah. "Anthropomorphism." *Philosophical Studies* 69 (1993).

Tester, Keith. *Animals and Society.* London: Routledge, 1991.

Thomas, Keith. *Man and the Natural World.* New York: Pantheon, 1983.

Thoreau, Henry David. *Walden.* Ed. J. Shanley. Princeton, N.J.: Princeton University Press, 1971.

Tooley, Michael. *Abortion and Infanticide.* Oxford: Oxford University Press, 1983.

Townsend, Aubrey. "Radical Vegetarians." *Australasian Journal of Philosophy* 57 (1979).

VanDeVeer, Donald. "Animal Suffering." *Canadian Journal of Philosophy* 10 (1980).

———. "Interspecific Justice." *Inquiry* 22 (1979).

———. "Interspecific Justice and Animal Slaughter." In *Ethics and Animals,* ed. H. Miller and W. Williams. Clifton, N.J.: Humana, 1983.

———. "Of Beasts, Persons, and the Original Position." *Monist* 62 (1979).

Warren, Mary Anne. "Difficulties with the Strong Animal Rights Position." *Between the Species* 2 (1986).

———. "Do Potential People Have Moral Rights?" *Canadian Journal of Philosophy* 7 (1977).

———. "The Rights of the Nonhuman World." In *The Animal Rights/Environmental Ethics Debate,* ed. E. Hargrove. Albany: State University of New York Press, 1992.

Wasserstrom, Richard. "Rights, Human Rights and Racial Discrimination." In *Human Rights,* ed. A. I. Melden. Belmont, Calif.: Wadsworth, 1970.

Watson, Richard. "Self-Consciousness and the Rights of Nonhuman Animals and Nature." In *The Animal Rights/Environmental Ethics Debate,* ed. E. Hargrove. Albany: State University of New York Press, 1992.

White, James. "Review of Alastair Gunn." *Ethics and Animals* 5 (1984).

Willard, L. Duane. "About Animals 'Having' Rights." *Journal of Value Inquiry* 16 (1982).

Williams, Meredith. "Rights, Interests, and Moral Equality." *Environmental Ethics* 2 (1980).

Wreen, Michael. "In Defense of Speciesism." *Ethics and Animals* 5 (1984).

Young, Thomas. "The Morality of Killing Animals." *Ethics and Animals* 5 (1984).

———. "Rational Preference Utilitarianism: Can It Justify Dissimilar Treatment of Animals and Marginal Humans?" *Philosophy in Context* 18 (1988).

Index of Names

Daniel A. Dombrowski is a professor of philosophy at Seattle University. He is the author of nine books, the latest of which are *Analytic Theism, Hartshorne and the Concept of God,* and *Kazantzakis and God,* both published by the State University of New York Press.